PLOTS AND CHARACTERS
IN THE FICTION OF
HENRY JAMES

PLOTS AND CHARACTERS
IN THE FICTION OF
HENRY JAMES .

Robert L. Gale

With a Foreword by

Oscar Cargill

First published 1965 as an Archon Book by The Shoe String
Press, Inc., Hamden Ct. This MIT Press edition published
by arrangement with The Shoe String Press, Inc.

First MIT Press paperback edition, October 1972

Printed and bound in The United States of America

Library of Congress Cataloging in Publication Data

Gale, Robert L.
       Plots and characters in the fiction of Henry James.

       1. James, Henry, 1843–1916—Plots. 2. James, Henry, 1843–1916—
Characters. I. Title.
[PS2124.G32   1972]   813'.4   72–6897
ISBN 0–262–57031–9 (pbk.)

To Gale, Mary Anne "Maureen" (nee Dowd)

TABLE OF CONTENTS

FOREWORD

No scholar or critic who has worked on Henry James in the last decade but owes something to Robert L. Gale. His widely scattered papers on the imagery of the novelist, culminating in his book *The Caught Image*, his excursions into such things as James's knowledge of chess, James's relationship to the American sculptor Thomas Crawford, his acquaintance with Wagnerian opera, or even Professor Gale's table of the estimated wordage in each piece of James's fiction, have been useful to the reader and the researcher. But perhaps Professor Gale has eclipsed his previous services with this book. One no longer need trust one's faulty memory in regard to story outlines or the location in any one tale of an obscure character — or of a famous one. (I remember the editor of a widely used encyclopedia calling me on the phone some years back to ask where Millicent Henning is found!) Moreover this book obviates the necessity of committing quite needlessly fictional substance that no one ought to commit to the mind: I think of the details of such novels of little merit as *Confidence* and *The Outcry*, such tales as "A Problem" and "The Solution." I have worked on Henry James in a desultory way for nearly forty years and have compassed the whole *corpus* of his work several times, but I should hate to have to testify without warning as to the details of these fictions. Can the reader identify and locate off-hand Lady Valda Gwyther, Miss Brownrigg (I believe her name was changed), and Richard Clare? Probably Robert Gale and Leon Edel can, but I should like to try them out some time. I shall rely much on this book in the future, for I know my limitations and I value my time.

Yet let me issue a word of caution, which is also Mr. Gale's word. While most intelligent readers would digest a list of Jamesian fictions so that there would be a general resemblance in the results, there might also be broad disagreement over the reading of any one tale. Thus if the issue is of vital importance, no digest, no plot outline will serve the reader, and he will have to have recourse to the tale itself. In the main, Mr. Gale's plots should serve as an associational trigger to bring back the richer details of a story the reader has read before. They are no life-savers for the lazy. They do not forfend reading the original.

This book reinforces again one's impression of the wonderful richness of James's fiction. How little repetition, all things considered, there is of narrative situations, of devices, of denouements. How little repetition in character portrayal. Where Henry James repeats, society and nature repeat more effusively. Even the unnamed narrator "I" is not repeated in one sense — he is far from always Henry James, and when he is, he is not Henry James in precisely the same mood. Properly, because he cannot always be identified, he is not in Mr. Gale's list of characters.

An extraordinarily useful tool, this book, like other tools, has a cutting edge; hence it is not for children but for the initiated who can skilfully employ it. They will be aware of the prodigious labor that has gone into it, for only patience and much work could have created such a labor-saving, sentient device.

Oscar Cargill

New York University
October, 1964.

But he, attended by these shining names,
Comes (best of all) himself — our welcome James.
— Robert Louis Stevenson [1]

"He is interested in indexes," said Henry James
with profound stupefaction.
— Constance Fenimore Woolson [2]

[1] "Henry James," in Works of *Robert Louis Stevenson*, 24 vols. (New York: Charles Scribner's Sons, 1900), XVI, 124.

[2] Quoted in Leon Edel, *Henry James: The Middle Years: 1882-1895* (Philadelphia and New York: J. B. Lippincott Company, 1962), p. 369.

PREFACE

The reader of this handbook will, I hope, find it useful in many ways. He may wish to have some understanding of the plot of a certain Jamesian novel or short story before reading it, or he may wish to review the plot of a fictional work after — perhaps long after — he has read it. If he is more of a specialist, he may wish to review the plots of several works to compare James's treatment of certain subjects and themes early in his career and later, or perhaps to compare James's treatment of some element with that of another writer, American, British, or Continental. It may be that he will wish to refresh his memory of a certain name or the function of a certain character among James's dramatis personae. If he remembers the work in which the name figures, he can easily find the name in the alphabetized list of characters after the plot-summary of the given work. If he remembers the character but not the work, he can find what he needs in the alphabetized list of all named persons in James's fiction; the entry there will also enable him to recollect where the character may be found in James. If he wants to review James's activity during a certain phase of his career, he may well begin by consulting the chronology of James or the chronological list of his fictional production.

The diligent reader of James's plots summarized here will be struck by the brilliance of Richard P. Blackmur's division of James's themes into three big groups: "the international theme, the theme of the artist in conflict with society, and the theme of the pilgrim in search of society."[1] He will also admire Osborn Andreas for aptly categorizing James's topics into "emotional cannibalism" and consideration; love, the past, art, and personal identity; the sheltered life and false values; and the international theme and "fables for critics."[2] But he will finally agree that no groupings can fully 'embrace James's thematic variety. What of James's treatment of misunderstanding, masochistic renunciation, friendship, marriage, sickness, science, publicity, money, joy, ghosts, alternate identities, and death? Some of these topics may be subsumed under Blackmur's or Andreas's categories, but others may not. The reader will find help here if he desires to study these and other elements in James. However, it should be noted at the outset that summaries of plots are not at all the same as recapitulations of themes, and also that it is difficult to say for certain what really happens in some of James's stories.

James chose the names of his characters with care and ingenuity. First names vary widely, and few last names are repeated. Sometimes his names come from relatives and friends (William, Minny, Coquelin, Wells); often from his knowledge of literature (Dormer [Trollope's *Ayala's Angel*], Laura Guest [Eliot's *Mill on the Floss*], Merle [Musset's "Histoire d'un Merle Blanc"], Pynsent [Thackeray's *Pendennis*]), history and famous people (Amerigo, Christopher Newman), and even place-names (Antrim [Ireland], Aspern [Austria], Grantham, Rye, Sutton, Ventnor [England]). But more important than sources of names are their amazing functions in James. By means of pleasant-sounding names (Marie de Vionnet, Laura Wing, Felix Young) James often appeals to us to be predisposed in favor of their bearers, while unpleasant names (Fanny Assingham, George Flack, Jim Pocock) occasionally warn us away. Persons socially inferior in his view James demeans with short, often harsh names (Bray, Gotch, Gulp, Lutch, Mudge, Peck). Comically alliterative names usually belong to comic characters in James (Benjamin Babcock, Louis Leverett, Willie Woodley). Some alliteratively named persons

---

[1] Richard P. Blackmur, "Henry James," in *Literary History of the United States,* ed. Robert E. Spiller *et al.,* rev. ed. (New York: The Macmillan Company, 1953), p. 1042.

[2] Osborn Andreas, *Henry James and the Expanding Horizon: A Study of the Meaning and Basic Themes of James's Fiction* (Seattle: University of Washington Press, 1948), p. xiii.

may be more charming but are still superficial (Mortimer Marshal, Tom Tristram, Susan Shepherd Stringham). Often names are foreshadowing devices (Mrs. Alsager, Alfred Bonnycastle, Lord Mellifont, Ulick Moreen). Often names in James are latently ironical (Louisa Brash, Lord Deepmere, Grant-Jackson, Mrs. Hope, Major Monarch). Some names remain puzzling, like the characters of those wearing them (Christina Light, Gabriel Nash, Gilbert Osmond, Adam Verver). Much can be learned about James through a study of the names of his characters.

It is hoped that this work will prove useful and stimulating to persons involved in many scholarly plots and possessing an endless variety of names.

———

It is a pleasure to acknowledge most gratefully the prompt and professional assistance given to me by librarians of the Library of the University of Pittsburgh, the Carnegie Public Library in Pittsburgh, the Library of the University of Pennsylvania in Philadelphia, and Butler Library of Columbia University in New York. Finally, I am deeply grateful to the Division of the Humanities research fund, the University of Pittsburgh, for a grant-in-aid enabling me to bring this work more quickly to completion.

———

Please note: Dates in parentheses are dates of first book publication; if no date is given in parentheses, the date given is that of first magazine and/or first book publication. Titles in italics are of works more than 50,000 words in length; titles in quotation marks are of works under 50,000 words in length. Deceased characters are named and identified only if, in my opinion, they have a direct bearing on the plot.

Robert L. Gale

University of Pittsburgh
Pittsburgh, Pennsylvania

CHRONOLOGY

1840   Marriage of Henry James and Mary Robertson Welsh, James's parents.
1842   William James, James's brother, born.
1843   Henry James born April 15 at 2 Washington Place, New York City.
1843-1844   Lives in Paris and Windsor.
1845   Garth Wilkinson James, James's brother, born.
1846   Robertson James, James's brother, born.
1848   Alice James, James's sister, born.
1845-1855   Lives in New York City and Albany.
1855-1860   Cosmopolitan and varied schooling in Geneva, London, Paris, Boulogne, Newport, Bonn; studies art and literature.
1861   Injures back in Newport.
1862-1863   Studies law at Harvard.
1864-1869   Lives in Boston and Cambridge; does apprenticeship writing.
1869-1870   Travels alone to England, Switzerland, Italy, France.
1870-1872   Does more apprenticeship writing, in Cambridge.
1872-1874   Travels again in Europe, then returns to Cambridge.
1874-1875   Writes in Cambridge and New York City.
1875   Publishes *A Passionate Pilgrim and Other Tales* (first book of fiction) and *Transatlantic Sketches* (first of many travel books).
1875-1876   Lives in Paris with the literati there and then establishes permanent residence in London.
1877   Revisits Paris and Rome, thus starting his practice of frequent Continental vacations.

1878	Publishes *French Poets and Novelists* (first of many critical books).
1879-1881	Intensely productive.
1882	Returns twice to America; mother dies January, father dies December.
1883	Returns to London; publishes 14-volume collected edition of fiction; Garth Wilkinson James dies.
1884-1886	Intensely productive, ending with critical and popular failure of *The Bostonians* and *The Princess Casamassima.*
1888	Depressed over lack of popularity.
1890	Failure of *The Tragic Muse* makes James decide to write plays and short fiction.
1892	Alice James dies.
1890-1895	Writes plays, culminating in stage failure of *Guy Domville* 1895.
1896	Moves to Lamb House, Rye; begins to dictate writings at this time.
1897-1904	Writes short stories, short novels, novels, and other works in a sustained period of phenomenal creativity.
1904-1905	Returns to America, observing and lecturing in New England, New York City, Florida, and California.
1906-1907	Begins revising his fiction and writing critical prefaces.
1907	*The Novels and Tales of Henry James* (The New York Edition) begins to appear (26 volumes, 1907-1917).
1908	Resumes writing plays, with little financial success.
1909	Sick.
1910	Robertson James dies; James, sick himself, returns to America with sick William James, who dies in August.
1911	Returns to England; health improves.
1912	Seriously sick again.
1913	Publishes *A Small Boy and Others* (first of three autobiographical volumes).
1914	Deeply disturbed by the beginning of World War I.
1915	Becomes a naturalized British subject.
1916	Dies February 28 in London.

CHRONOLOGICAL LIST OF JAMES'S FICTION [1]

1864
"A Tragedy of Error" (1962)

1865
"The Story of a Year" (1947)

1866
"A Landscape Painter" (1885)
"A Day of Days" (1885)

1867
"My Friend Bingham" (1950)
"Poor Richard" (1885)

1868
"The Story of a Masterpiece" (1950)
"The Romance of Certain Old Clothes" (1875)
"A Most Extraordinary Case" (1885)
"A Problem" (1950)
"De Grey, A Romance" (1919)
"Osborne's Revenge" (1950)

1869
"A Light Man" (1885)
"Gabrielle de Bergerac" (1918)

1870
"Travelling Companions" (1919)

1871
"A Passionate Pilgrim" (1875)

"At Isella" (1919)
Watch and Ward (1878)
"Master Eustace" (1885)

1872
"Guest's Confession" (1919)

1873
"The Madonna of the Future" (1875)
"The Sweetheart of M. Briseux" (1919)

1874
"The Last of the Valerii" (1875)
"Madame de Mauves" (1875)
"Adina" (1919)
"Professor Fargo" (1919)
"Eugene Pickering" (1875)

1875
Roderick Hudson
"Benvolio" (1879)

1876
The American, 1876-1877 (1877)
"Crawford's Consistency" (1950)
"The Ghostly Rental" (1949)

1877
"Four Meetings" (1879)

[1] Grateful acknowledgement is hereby made to Leon Edel and Dan H. Laurence, compilers of *A Bibliography of Henry James* (London: Rupert Hart-Davis, 1957).

1878
"Rose-Agathe"
  (as "Theodolinde") (1885)
"Daisy Miller"
The Europeans
"Longstaff's Marriage" (1879)
"An International Episode,"
  1878-1879 (1879)

1879
"The Pension Beaurepas"
  (1881)
"The Diary of a Man of Fifty"
Confidence, 1879-1880 (1879)
"A Bundle of Letters" (1880)

1880
Washington Square
The Portrait of a Lady, 1880-
  1881 (1881)

1882
"The Point of View" (1883)
"The Siege of London" (1883)

1883
"The Impressions of a Cousin"
  (1884)

1884
"Lady Barbarina" (as "Lady
  Barberina")
"Pandora" (1885)
"The Author of Beltraffio"
  (1885)
"Georgina's Reasons" (1885)
"A New England Winter"
"The Path of Duty" (1885)

1885
The Bostonians, 1885-1886
  (1886)

The Princess Casamassima,
  1885-1886 (1886)

1887
"Mrs. Temperly" (as "Cousin
  Maria") (1889)

1888
"Louisa Pallant"
The Reverberator
"The Aspern Papers"
"The Liar" (1889)
"The Modern Warning"
"A London Life" (1889)
"The Lesson of the Master"
  (1892)
"The Patagonia" (1889)

1889
The Tragic Muse, 1889-1890
  (1890)
"The Solution," 1889-1890
  (1892)

1891
"The Pupil" (1892)
"Brooksmith" (1892)
"The Marriages" (1892)
"The Chaperon" (1893)
"Sir Edmund Orme" (1892)

1892
"Nona Vincent" (1893)
"The Private Life" (1893)
"Lord Beaupre" (as "Lord
  Beauprey") (1893)
"The Real Thing" (1893)
"The Visits" (as "The Visit")
  (1893)
"Sir Dominick Ferrand" (as
  "Jersey Villas") (1893)

"Collaboration" (1893)
"Greville Fane" (1893)
"The Wheel of Time," 1892-
   1893 (1893)
"Owen Wingrave" (1893)

1893
"The Middle Years" (1895)

1894
"The Death of the Lion" (1895)
"The Coxon Fund" (1895)

1895
"The Next Time" (1896)
"The Altar of the Dead"

1896
"The Figure in the Carpet"
"Glasses"
The Spoils of Poynton (as *The
   Old Things*) (1897)
"The Friends of the Friends" (as
   "The Way It Came")
The Other House

1897
What Maisie Knew

1898
"John Delavoy" (1900)
"The Turn of the Screw"
The Awkward Age, 1898-1899
   (1899)
"The Given Case" (1900)
"Covering End"
"In the Cage"

1899
"Europe" (as " 'Europe' ")
   (1900)

"The Great Condition" (1900)
"Paste" (1900)
"The Real Right Thing" (1900)

1900
"The Great Good Place"
"Maud-Evelyn"
"Miss Gunton of Poughkeepsie"
"The Special Type" (1903)
"The Tone of Time" (1903)
"Broken Wings" (1903)
"The Two Faces" (as "The
   Faces") (1903)
"The Abasement of the North-
   mores"
"The Third Person"
"The Tree of Knowledge"

1901
Mrs. Medwin" (1903)
"The Beldonald Holbein"
   (1903)
The Sacred Fount

1902
"The Story in It" (1903)
"Flickerbridge" (1903)
The Wings of the Dove

1903
The Ambassadors
"The Beast in the Jungle"
"The Birthplace"
"The Papers"

1904
"Fordham Castle" (1909)
The Golden Bowl

1908
"Julia Bride" (1909)

"The Married Son "
"The Jolly Corner" (1909)

1910
"A Round of Visits"

1909
"The Velvet Glove" (1910)
"Mora Montravers" (1910)
"Crapy Cornelia" (1910)
"The Bench of Desolation,"
    1909-1910 (1910)

1911
The Outcry

1917
The Ivory Tower
The Sense of the Past

PLOTS

"The Abasement of the Northmores," 1900.

Though he is in poor health and his wife urges him to stay home, Warren Hope tells her that he should really go to Lord John Northmore's funeral at the grave. Mrs. Hope says that Northmore used Warren's brilliance and stepped on him to get ahead. But Warren goes anyway, catches a chill, and quickly dies of pneumonia. Mrs. Hope is in anguish to think that Warren left nothing publishable to justify her high opinion of him. She soon feels worse when Lady Northmore writes to report a projected edition of Northmore's letters and to ask Mrs. Hope for any addressed to Warren. Though tempted to burn the many she finds, Mrs. Hope honorably sends a bundle of them on but not the love letters which Northmore wrote her before she accepted Warren. She now plans to publish Warren's undoubtedly numerous letters, but when she asks around in an effort to assemble them, she learns that none were saved. Northmore's letters are published: the reviews on first reading seem favorable, but the letters themselves, Mrs. Hope judges, are inane. When re-read, the reviews seem to contain veiled criticism. She fancies that her husband saved his letters from Northmore for a mere joke. Momentarily she is tempted to publish Northmore's love letters to her; going to the Northmores for permission, she senses their abasement, kisses Lady Northmore, and returns home. She prepares for publication her husband's lovely letters to her, has one true copy printed, makes provision in her will for later publication, and then hopes for death.

Warren Hope, Mrs. Warren Hope, Johnson, Lord John Northmore, Lady Northmore, Thompson.

"Adina," 1874.

The narrator is with his friend Sam Scrope when on the campagna outside Rome Scrope tricks a simple Italian named Angelo Beati out of a priceless intaglio of Tiberius Caesar. Angelo later seeks out Scrope, fails to obtain proper payment for his gem, and therefore vows revenge. Even so, the narrator is unable to persuade Scrope to be generous. Then one night Adina Waddington, Scrope's fiancee, refuses to continue their engagement; the next morning she elopes with Angelo and marries him. Failing to get her back, Scrope desperately hurls the accursed topaz into the Tiber.

Angelo Beati, Castillani, Doria, Esther, Padre Girolamo, Ninetta, Sam Scrope, Adina Waddington, Mrs. Waddington.

"The Altar of the Dead," 1895.

Aging George Stransom loved Mary Antrim, but she died; so he has gradually built a religion of the dead, with a spiritual altar. He chances to read in the newspaper of the death of Acton Hague, an estranged friend who once did him a great wrong. One gloomy London day Stransom walks to a Catholic chapel and obtains permission to light candles for all his dead — except Hague. Later he strikes up an acquaintance with a mournful woman whom he has seen at his chapel. When permitted to call upon her, he finds a picture of Hague, who, she says, wronged her cruelly. She can forgive him, however, although Stransom cannot. Thus Hague alienates them to a degree. A year or so passes, and Stransom is now dying. When he goes back to his altar, the spirit of Mary Antrim seems to shine from a central candle and infuse him with a sense of forgiveness. He turns, dying, and sees the other woman, who explains that she has come for his sake. The one more candle which is needed Stransom regards as Hague's, but the woman regards it as his.

Mary Antrim, Paul Creston, Mrs. Paul (Kate) Creston,
Mrs. Paul Creston, Acton Hague, George Stransom.

The Ambassadors, 1903.

In Chester on his way to Paris to rescue Chad, his widowed
fiancee Mrs. Newsome's son, from some woman, and to return
with him to America, Lambert Strether first meets Maria Gostrey
and then his old friend Waymarsh. After sampling the theater
in London, Strether goes on to Paris, soon meeting Chad and
noting great improvement in him. Chad's fellow-American friend
Little Bilham reassuringly tells Strether that any attachment
with a woman which Chad has is virtuous. Next, at sculptor
Gloriani's garden party in Paris Strether meets beautiful
Madame Marie de Vionnet, estranged from her husband, and
her daughter Jeanne. Strether is uncertain whether the object
of Chad's virtuous affection is mother or daughter; meanwhile,
he continues to relish lovely Paris and to delay attempting to
rescue Chad. In reply to irate Mrs. Newsome's cable, he writes
a letter and then tears it up, cabling the next day his intention
to stay another month. Now more ambassadors come: Mrs.
Newsome's daughter Sarah, her common husband Jim Pocock,
and his gentle sister Mamie, who according to family plans is
to marry Chad when he returns to his senses and to the un-
specified family business. Now it is revealed that Jeanne de
Vionnet is getting married to a Frenchman whom Chad helped
Madame de Vionnet select. Strether, feeling that life in Paris
has improved Chad and should therefore continue to hold him,
suggests unsuccessfully to Little Bilham that he marry Mamie.
Meanwhile Waymarsh, although he is picking up with Mrs.
Pocock, puritannically urges Strether to quit his association
with Chad's friends and to persuade the young man to return
home to his duties. Sarah Pocock is viciously critical of
Madame de Vionnet and denies seeing any improvement in
her brother Chad. One day sacrificial and somewhat lonely
Strether takes a train from Paris into rural France and wanders
with muted pleasure into a pastoral picture whose beauty is
suddenly shaken by the sight of week-ending Chad and Madame
de Vionnet in a boat. After an embarrassed conversation,
Strether leaves the couple. Later he sees Madame de Vionnet
and promises to do what he can to help her, then sees Chad

and in the strongest terms urges him never to abandon Marie, and finally says goodbye to responsive Maria Gostrey, who has been watching from the sidelines the development of his vision.

Baptiste, Miss Barrace, John Little Bilham, Francois, Gloriani, Mme. Gloriani, Maria Gostrey, M. de Montbron, Munster, Mrs. Munster, Abel Newsome, Mrs. Abel Newsome, Chadwick Newsome, Lewis Lambert Strether, Mrs. Lewis Lambert Strether, Strether, Jim Pocock, Mrs. Jim (Sarah Newsome) Pocock, Mamie Pocock, Jeanne de Vionnet, Mme. Marie de Vionnet, Compte de Vionnet, Waymarsh, Mrs. Waymarsh.

The American, 1876-1877.

Christopher Newman, Civil War veteran and rich retired businessman, meets widowed young Claire de Cintre in Paris, through matchmaker Lizzie Tristram, his friend Tom's wife. Claire's widowed mother Madame de Bellegarde, backed by her stiff son Marquis Urbain de Bellegarde, agrees to let Newman court Claire. However, a short while after she has accepted the American, her mother and her brother dishonorably order her to reject him. Valentin, Urbain's much younger brother, has been supporting Newman's rights and is now thoroughly ashamed of his family. Through Newman, Valentin has met Noemie Nioche, an art copyist and later an obviously disreputable young adventuress. Fatally wounded by Stanislas Kapp in a duel over Mlle. Nioche, Valentin tells the American that Mrs. Bread, a servant of the Bellegarde family, has a secret which he may be able to use to exert pressure on the family. Mrs. Bread gives Newman evidence that Madame de Bellegarde murdered her husband; but when Newman threatens mother and son with exposure, hoping thereby to win Claire after all, the Bellegarde pair resolutely defy him, evidentally relying on his good will not to go through with his unsavory plan. Newman has unsuccessfully appealed to docile Claire, who enters a Carmelite nunnery; so he pensions Mrs. Bread and then, not nobly but in disgust at everything, burns the evidence.

Rev. Mr. Benjamin Babcock, Blanche de Bellegarde,

Marquis Henri-Urbain de Bellegarde, Mme. Henri-Urbain
(Emmeline) de Bellegarde, Marquis Urbain de Bellegarde,
Mme. Urbain de Bellegarde, Valentin de Bellegarde, Princess
Borealska, Mrs. Catherine Bread, Claire de Bellegarde de
Cintre, Dandelard, Mme. Dandelard, Lord Deepmere, Dora
Finch, M. de Grosjoyeux, C. P. Hatch, Stanislas Kapp,
Ledoux, Duchesse de Lusignan, Christopher Newman,
Noemie Nioche, Nioche, Mme. d'Outreville, General Packard,
Mme. Robineau, Count de la Rochefidele, Countess de la
Rochefidele, Lord Saint Dunstans, Tom Tristram, Mrs. Tom
(Lizzie) Tristram, Kitty Upjohn.

"The Aspern Papers," 1888.

The narrator, an American editor, has come to Venice to
try to get the papers of dead Jeffrey Aspern, renowned American
poet of the early nineteenth century. With the encouragement
of Mrs. Prest, the narrator succeeds in renting some rooms,
at a high price, in the palace of Juliana Bordereau, Aspern's
aged former mistress who presumably controls the papers.
Next appears the old woman's niece Tina Bordereau, whom
the narrator soon shocks by confidentially telling of his hopes
regarding the papers. After the narrator takes Tina to the
Piazzetta, at her aunt's callous suggestion, the young woman
begins to confide in him and promises to aid him. Old Juliana
shows him a portrait of Aspern and, implying that she knows
his game, says that she would sell the picture for a thousand
pounds. Juliana becomes sick and is examined by doctors. The
narrator succumbs to the temptation of entering her room and
rifling her desk for the papers; she catches him, he is horribly
ashamed, and she collapses in nearby Tina's arms. Returning to Venice after an absence of many days, he learns that
Juliana is dead. Tina gives him the portrait with which Juliana
taunted him but explains that she is under orders to burn
the papers to prevent their falling into any stranger's hands.
She would give them to a member of the family. The narrator
does not propose marriage, rushes out in confusion, mulls
over his alternatives, and then returns the following morning
to the villa only to be told by Tina that she burned the papers
one by one.

Contessa Altemura, Jeffrey Aspern, Cavaliere Bombici, John

Cumnor, Churton, Mrs. Churton, Juliana Bordereau, Tina Bordereau, Goldie, Mrs. Goldie, Olimpia, Pasquale, Mrs. Prest, Pochintesta, Mrs. Stock-Stock.

"At Isella," 1871.

Walking from Switzerland to the Italian border town of Isella, the narrator there meets and aids a beautiful lady who is escaping her husband by carriage across the border to join her lover. The narrator watches the inn host lie to the enraged pursuing husband.

Madeleine Brohan, Mrs. B—, Miss B—, Ernesto, Giuseppino.

"The Author of Beltraffio," 1884.

The narrator greatly admires British novelist Mark Ambient, the author of *Beltraffio*, and through a friend is able at last to visit him at his country home in Surrey. There he also meets the author's cold, attractive wife Beatrice, his sickly son Dolcino, and his odd sister Gwendolyn Ambient. Mrs. Ambient dislikes her husband's writing and feels that it might have an evil influence upon her son later. Through Miss Ambient the narrator learns that the novelist is worried about Dolcino's suddenly worsening health and that the mother, who usually disagrees, is therefore unconcerned. A physician is summoned nonetheless, suspects diphtheria, but is then rudely dismissed by Mrs. Ambient. The boy dies, his medicine withheld by his mother so that he would not recover to be corrupted by his father's works. Soon the mother dies; Ambient's latest book, which his wife read in proofs during Dolcino's illness, finally appears.

Dolcino Ambient, Gwendolyn Ambient, Mark Ambient, Mrs. Mark (Beatrice) Ambient, Dr. Mackintosh.

The Awkward Age, 1898-1899.

Years ago Longdon loved Lady Julia, but she married another and had a daughter, now Mrs. Brookenham, center of an effete social circle in London and mother of wastrel Harold and charming but awkward Nanda. Now Vanderbank, whom

Longdon meets at a Brookenham party, admires Mrs. Brook
and especially her daughter. Mrs. Brook next greets her husband's cousin Duchess Jane, who wants her sheltered daughter
Aggie to come out socially and marry well. The two women
callously discuss prospects for their daughters: Jane says that
rich Mitchett will not do for Aggie but might for Nanda, in
whom, however, Van might be interested. Longdon is upset
by hearing Mrs. Brook gossip perplexingly with Mitchy about
the propriety of letting Nanda stay with supposedly loose
Tishy Grendon, sister of Carrie Donner, allegedly too intimate
with Cashmore, whose wife Fanny is the sister of Lord Petherton,
who reputedly sponges off Mitchy. Longdon is moved by
Nanda's resemblance to her dead grandmother Julia, the woman
he loved. Mrs. Brook hopes to capitalize on his devotion to
the girl now. A couple of months later Nanda is at the country
estate of Mitchy, whom Longdon urges her to marry, so that
she can avoid loneliness like his. But Jane tells Longdon that
she now hopes Mitchy will wed her Aggie, though — she adds
— Mrs. Brook would oppose the idea so that Van, whom she
likes, would hang around Nanda in uncertainty. When pressed,
Van admits to Longdon his love for Nanda; so Longdon
promises a dowry. Distressed Van gradually reveals this
promise to Mrs. Brook, who contends that she is backing
more stable Mitchy for Nanda; then Mrs. Brook cruelly tells
it all to Mitchy when he enters. He sees that Van wants him
to marry Aggie and clear out. Later Van goes to Longdon's
estate in Suffolk and finds Nanda and others visiting there.
The girl is critical of her conscienceless family; she urges
Mitchy to marry fine Aggie. Mitchy and Van discuss Longdon's
offer to enrich Nanda. At a party later at Tishy's — after
Mitchy and Aggie have married — Mrs. Brook's anger at the
presumable loss of Mitchy to Nanda is revealed, and with it
the thought that Van may have grown reserved toward Nanda
because of all the meddling gossip, which also shocks unnerved
Longdon, with whom Nanda has been staying for some months
now. Minor hilarity is caused by Lord Petherton's chasing
Aggie for a questionable book which Nanda confesses borrow-
ing and reading. Later the group around Mrs. Brook seems
to be breaking up. Cashmore visits Nanda, now a tea-giver
herself, while Van through dislike of the others hesitates to call.
Mrs. Brook thinks that Longdon will surely reward Nanda

for her manifold embarrassments. Mitchy returns and hints at his marital miseries. At Mrs. Brook's request, he tells Longdon that Nanda is selflessly unhappy, adding that he wishes to augment any sum Longdon may give her. Then at tea Nanda begs Van to be nice to her brilliant mother; when Mitchy appears, she urges him to be so as well, adding attempted reassurances concerning now worrisome Aggie. During conversation shortly thereafter with Longdon, she denies her love for Van but then cries. Longdon appears to wish that Van had accepted his offer of money with Nanda's hand but says that Van might well have married Aggie, thus leaving Mitchy for Nanda, who, however, rejects this version but admits to worry concerning Mitchy. Nanda will soon go with Longdon to his estate.

Aggie, Bagger, Mrs. Bagger, Dr. Beltram, Edward Brookenham, Mrs. Edward Brookenham, Harold Brookenham, Nanda Brookenham, Lady Fanny Cashmore, Lord Cashmore, Sarah Curd, Sir Digby Dence, Beach Donner, Mrs. Beach (Carrie) Donner, Garlick, Gelsomine, Harry Grendon, Mrs. Harry (Tishy) Grendon, Duchess Jane, Lady Julia, Longdon, Algie Manger, Booby Manger, Manger, Mrs. Manger, Miss Merriman, Mitchett, Lord Petherton, Mary Pinthorpe, Randage, Baron Schack (or Schmack), Tatton, Nancy Toovey, Gustavus Vanderbank, Mary Vanderbank, Miles Vanderbank.

"The Beast in the Jungle," 1903.

John Marcher meets May Bartram at an English country estate party at Wetherend. She reminds him that when they first met, in Sorrento ten years before, he told her that something most unusual was to happen to him. He now explains that it has not yet occurred, adding that it was not love because the touch of love which he once knew did not fulfill the conditions. She promises to watch and wait with him for the beast in the jungle of his life. When her aunt dies, May is able to establish herself in London in fair comfort. Year after year passes, and Marcher visits her primly; one day, smiling at his incredulity, she implies that she has identified the beast but will never tell. They continue to associate somewhat familiarly. She grows weak and then weaker; there are hints that she will die. Fearing that nothing is to happen to him, Marcher feels sold. One April she is very sick, and he feels that this is unfair to him. Is this the beast? He asks her if she knows what is in store for him. She does, and when he cannot guess its nature, she says that that failure is his answer. She becomes sicker, and he more lonely. When he visits again, she insists that he has experienced the beast but that it is better that he does not know it, better for him not to suffer. When he wonders if the knowledge of it is what is killing her, she replies that she would live on for him if she could. When she dies at last, he is only another mourner. Her grave tells him nothing, and he travels to distant lands. Finding no answer there, he returns after considerable time. Much later, one autumn day in her cemetery again, he is moved by the grief-ravaged face of an unknown mourner at a fresh grave. This, then, was the beast — to be the one man in all the world who never felt grief for another, the one man to whom nothing ever happened. May loved him for himself, for the good she might do him, whereas he associated with her only so that she might help him identify his beast. He might have saved her from death by genuinely unselfish love. Too late he meets the spring of the beast, and falls face down upon May's grave.

May Bartram, Boyer, Mrs. Boyer, John Marcher, Pemble, Mrs. Pemble.

"The Beldonald Holbein," 1901.

Mrs. Munden tells the painter-narrator that Lady Nina Beldonald, her brother's agelessly beautiful widow, wants her portrait painted. Lady Beldonald has as a foil for her hard beauty the loyally ugly Miss Dadd, who comes to the studio once but soon thereafter dies. Lady Beldonald replaces her with an ugly widowed cousin from America, Louisa Brash. At a reception given by the narrator, a French colleague Paul Outreau declares that Mrs. Brash is a perfect Holbein. Feeling that her position as reigning attraction is in jeopardy, Lady Beldonald refuses to permit Mrs. Brash to go to Paris to be painted, quits sitting for the narrator, and becomes so annoyed at Mrs. Brash's sudden fame among the artists — the narrator and others paint her — that she sends the poor woman back to an obscure American city. There her face is not appreciated,

and she soon dies. Lady Beldonald quickly hires a new foil,
this time a pretty, brainless, blank-faced woman.

   Lady Nina Beldonald, Mrs. Louisa Brash, Miss Dadd,
   Mrs. Munden, Paul Outreau.

"The Bench of Desolation," 1909-1910.
   Long ago Herbert Dodd was told by his fiancee Kate
Cookham that if he did not marry her she would sue him. In
revulsion, he paid her off at terrible cost to himself. By the
end of ten years, he had mortgaged and lost his second-hand
book-business, married Nan Drury (whose father went bankrupt because of a dishonest partner), and had two daughters
by her. Under the pressure of time and poverty all are now
dead but Herbert, who is a clerk in the gas company; and
here he sits on a desolate bench by the sea in southern England.
Kate returns to him, no longer seemingly vicious but now a
real lady, and offers him all his accumulated money, which,
she explains, she demanded only to force him into marriage
(since she always loved only him) and which she then carefully invested for him. To discuss matters, she has him to
tea at her hotel, snubbing a suitor to impress Herbert. The
next Sunday they meet at the seaside bench; she puts her arm
around him, and he, ever passive, lets her, knowing now that
they will share the fateful bench of desolation.

   Kate Cookham, Charley Coote, Dean, Herbert Dodd, Nan
   Drury Dodd, Drury, Bill Frankle, David Geddes, Captain
   Roper.

"Benvolio," 1875.
   Part of the time Benvolio, a split personality, loves Scholastica
and enjoys conversing with her father, a blind philosopher.
But he also cares for the worldly Countess, who at one point
forces Scholastica to become the governess in a traveling family.
Later Benvolio denounces the haughty Countess and returns to
the garden of Scholastica, but the philosopher is dead and the
girl is gone. Benvolio is fretful until he goes after Scholastica
and brings her back.

   Benvolio, Scholastica.

"The Birthplace," 1903.

Morris Gedge, not to mention his wife Isabel, is thrilled to be rescued from a dreary librarianship when Grant-Jackson, remembering the Gedges for their kindness once to his sick son, offers Gedge the position of caretaker at The Birthplace of the renowned (but unnamed) English poet. Arriving at the shrine, Gedge is indoctrinated by Miss Putchin, who is now retiring from the position as guide there. Taking over, Gedge soon begins to grumble at the excessive commercializing of The Birthplace and at the crassness of the stupid tourists who visit it. He comes to hate himself for lying about details concerning the place instead of being permitted to lecture on what is important, namely the works of the poet born there. His worried wife fears that he will be reported to and discharged by Grant-Jackson, spokesman for the committee behind The Birthplace. B. D. Hayes and his pretty wife, American visitors, draw from Gedge late in the summer a confession that the whole program is a fraud since little is actually known about the poet. But when critical Grant-Jackson descends upon him in the autumn, Gedge is so thoroughly frightened that he soon develops into a conscienceless barker at The Show. The Hayeses return, listen to his new spiel, and — when Grant-Jackson comes back again — agree with Mrs. Gedge that he will probably be released for now going too far in the other direction. But no, Gedge emerges triumphant from his interview with Grant-Jackson: he has been given a raise, since gate receipts are now at a new high.

Morris Gedge, Mrs. Morris (Isabel) Gedge, Grant-Jackson, B. D. Hayes, Mrs. B. D. Hayes, Miss Putchin.

The Bostonians, 1885-1886.

Basil Ransom, a Civil War veteran and a lawyer from Mississippi, takes a trip to Boston from his present location in New York to visit his cousins widowed Mrs. Adelina Luna and her sister radical Miss Olive Chancellor. Olive takes him to a feminist movement meeting, introducing him to militant Mrs. Farrinder, impractical old Miss Birdseye, sensible Dr. Mary J. Prance, and others. He also sees a thrilling, beautiful speaker named Verena Tarrant, daughter of phoney animalmagnetist Dr. Selah Tarrant and his feminist wife. Olive is annoyed at Basil's interest in Verena, whom she invites to stay in her home and study with her. Basil is attracted to Verena's beauty but not to her talk, dislikes Olive more and more, and begins seeing Mrs. Luna again. Wherever Olive goes, she is jealous of those whom Verena impresses and she is possessive toward the girl. Verena prefers Olive to Matthias Pardon, who would exploit her, and to Henry Burrage, a Harvard law school student whose mother from New York dominates his tea party. Olive buys off Dr. Tarrant, after which Verena moves in with her. Meanwhile Basil, who has been doing badly in law practice in New York, returns to Boston to see avid Mrs. Luna again. He and Verena have a most pleasant walk through the grounds at Harvard and visit its Civil War memorial. He later hears Verena speak at Mrs. Burrage's home in New York; and Olive, also there and discomfited by his sudden presence, soon begins to suspect Verena of drifting from her to him. After a supposed understanding, the two women plan to remain in New York a while, Olive now hoping that Verena will play up to Henry Burrage only long enough to humiliate and discourage Basil. But Verena is so attracted to Basil, who is now thoroughly contemptuous of her lecturing, that she returns to Boston. Late in the summer at Marmion, while dying Miss Birdseye is attended by Dr. Mary Prance, Basil proposes to Verena, who resists — and asks Olive's aid — but does love him now. The two go boating; Olive is distraught but the next day is pleased to tell Basil that Verena is gone. After ten weeks, Basil learns that she is to lecture at the Boston Music Hall, goes there, and confronts her with a choice. Verena leaves Olive, the other feminists, and lecturing for them, and accepts an uncertain role as Basil's wife.

Miss Birdseye, Henry Burrage, Jr., Mrs. Henry Burrage, Sr., Miss Catching, Olive Chancellor, Mrs. Croucher, Amariah Farrinder, Mrs. Amariah Farrinder, Filer, Ada T. P. Foat, Gracie, Abraham Greenstreet, Mrs. Abraham Greenstreet, Mrs. Adelina Luna, Newton Luna, Mirandola, Eliza P. Moseley, Matthias Pardon, Dr. Mary J. Prance, Basil Ransom, Miss Winkworth, Dr. Selah Tarrant, Mrs. Selah Tarrant, Verena Tarrant.

"Broken Wings," 1900.

After a long separation, Stuart Straith and Mrs. Harvey see one another at a big house party but do not meet. The same evening Mrs. Harvey confesses to a friend that her profession of writing pays badly, and that long ago she would have married Straith but for his ambition as a painter. A short while later, Mrs. Harvey chances to meet Straith at a new play, for which he tells her he designed some of the costumes for a fee. She says that she would like to write an article on him for her art column. When she visits him at his studio, she says that she needs his pity; he replies that her prospects were such that she never needed him in any way. She recognizes that he does not see that she loved him and would have married him. He later visits her and reports that no one has bought his paintings for years. Their pride gone, they embrace, vow to abandon unrewarding society, and work together for art.

Lady Claude, Mrs. Harvey, Stuart Straith.

"Brooksmith," 1891.

The narrator is saddened by the death of his charming London friend Oliver Offord, whose salon, almost presided over and certainly much appreciated by his impeccable servant Brooksmith, was justly revered by all. But Offord's death is more tragic for Brooksmith, who can find no other employment which challenges his unique virtues of culture and loyalty. After some years, he and the narrator lose touch with one another.

Brooksmith, Mrs. Brooksmith, Lady Kenyon, Oliver Offord.

"A Bundle of Letters," 1879.

To her mother in Maine, Miranda Hope writes of her impressions in Paris. She is living in the pension of Madame de Maisonrouge and is learning French. Meanwhile Violet Ray, a somewhat more fashionable New York girl, writes from the same pension of the provinciality of Miss Hope. And at the same time Louis Leverett writes home from Paris to a Boston friend about the conceited New Yorker and the angular New Englander, and also about a pictorial English girl named

Evelyn Vane. When Miss Hope writes home again, she praises Leverett, comments on the aloofness of pretty Miss Ray, notes the timidity of Miss Vane and the brilliance of a certain German and also the fluency of Madame de Maisonrouge's cousin Leon Verdier. Miss Vane next writes of certain family plans, then describes Miss Ray as nice, Miss Hope as vulgar, Leverett as too aesthetic, Verdier as low, and the German as boring. Verdier writes a friend of what fun it is to observe a delicate English girl, one pretty American, and another forward one. Then the German, Dr. Rudolph Staub, writes a colleague in condemnation of all decadent Americans, Englishmen, and Frenchmen; he closes by predicting German supremacy. Finally Miss Hope blithely sends home another letter explaining that she is leaving France to go on to another equally interesting European country.

Clara Bernard, Lady Battledown, Clementine, Desmond, Mrs. Desmond, Lady Augusta Fleming, Prosper Gobain, Dr. Julius Hirsch, Mrs. Abraham Hope, Miranda Hope, Johnson, Louis Leverett, Mme. de Maisonrouge, William Platt, Violet Ray, Ray, Mrs. Ray, Agnes Rich, Dr. Rudolph Staub, Harvard Tremont, Miss Turnover, Adelaide Vane, Evelyn Vane, Fred Vane, Georgina Vane, Gus Vane, Harold Vane, Mary Vane, Vane, Mrs. Vane, Leon Verdier.

"The Chaperon," 1891.

At the death of her father, Rose Tramore braves the opposition of all members of his family — including her grandmother and an aunt — and even her own brother Eric and sister Edith, and decides to go to her mother, who years ago left her husband to run away with a lover who unfortunately died too abruptly to marry her. When Bertram Jay, a captain of the Royal Engineers who has proposed unsuccessfully to Rose, also takes sides against her, she leaves him even more definitely and in great disappointment. Lady Maresfield seeks to promote her son Guy Mangler's interest in Rose, but the determined girl refuses an invitation from the woman since it does not include her mother Mrs. Tramore. And so mother and daughter are ostracized through the London winter. Late the following summer they go to Switzerland and then on to Italy, where they bump into vacationing Jay, whom they permit to travel quietly with them a while so long as he does not presume to judge. Now Rose begins to emerge as her mother's chaperon. In Venice on their way to Constantinople, Lady Maresfield and many members of her big family, including a married daughter named Charlotte Vaughan-Vesey, fear that Jay may win Rose before Guy can try again; so they invite the Tramores to luncheon. Sensing that Rose and her mother may become a social drawing card, Mrs. Vaughan-Vesey begins to support them both in society. Soon Mrs. Tramore, no longer a pariah, goes out alone even — so much that Rose and Jay feel rather neglected.

Mrs. Bray, Mrs. Donovan, Mrs. Hack, Captain Bertram Jay, Bessie Mangler, Fanny Mangler, Guy Mangler, Maggie Mangler, Lady Maresfield, Mrs. Charles Tramore, Edith Tramore, Eric Tramore, Julia Tramore, Rose Tramore, Mrs. Tramore, Bob Vaughan-Vesey, Mrs. Bob (Charlotte Mangler) Vaughan-Vesey, Lord Whiteroy.

"Collaboration," 1892.

At the American narrator's Parisian salon, poet Felix Vendemer meets composer Herman Heidenmauer, who is arguing about English poetry with another guest. When Heidenmauer, a German, and Vendemer, a Frenchman, decide to collaborate on an opera, Vendemer's fiancee Paule de Brindes and her mother spurn him, since they cannot forget that Paule's father was killed by the Germans in 1870 at Sedan.

Albert Bonus, Mme. Marie de Brindes, Paule de Brindes, Miss Brownrigg, Herman Heidenmauer, Felix Vendemer.

Confidence, 1879-1880.

While sketching in Siena, Bernard Longueville meets Angela Vivian and her mother. Soon he is called to Baden-Baden by his rich friend Gordon Wright to meet and pass judgment on a girl. He meets Blanche Evers (whom he wrongly guesses Wright loves), her follower Augustus Lovelock, and the Vivians. Angela seems cynical, but it is she whom Wright rather uncertainly loves. Wright then goes to England, leaving the three spying on her. When Wright returns, Longueville irritatedly tells him that he thinks Angela would marry Wright for his money. Two years later he hears that Wright has married Blanche. Traveling through New York, Longueville observes Blanche's flirtatious manner with Lovelock, newly arrived. Then at the beach in northern France, Longueville sees Angela and her mother again, feels that he wronged the girl, and suddenly realizes that he loves her deeply. In Paris they come to an understanding. Angela, resentful that Wright should ask Longueville to pass judgment on her at Baden-Baden, deliberately acted badly, she now says. The Wrights, with Lovelock, come over to Paris. Wright is puzzled to learn of Longueville's impending marriage to Angela, who confuses Longueville by telling him that she refused Wright when he proposed following Longueville's denunciation of her and withheld this information from Longueville hoping to cause him remorse so that strong love might follow. She adds that in her opinion Wright hoped for the second refusal from her. When Wright says that Blanche wants Lovelock and asks Angela to wait until he is free, she startlingly agrees to give him another chance and to make him happy, and orders Longueville to London, where he sees an annoyed Lovelock. Angela next persuades Wright that he loves his wife. The Wrights send a letter from Egypt which arrives during the Parisian honeymoon of Longueville and Angela.

Blanche Evers, Ella Maclane, Maclane, Mrs. Maclane, Bernard Longueville, Captain Augustus Lovelock, Angela Vivian, Mrs. Vivian, Gordon Wright.

"Covering End," 1898.

To Captain Clement Yule's heavily mortgaged estate of Covering End, Prodmore the mortgage-holder comes with his daughter Cora, whom he strongly urges to try to captivate Captain Yule. When Yule enters, he is taunted by Prodmore for lacking the means of reclaiming his ancestral home. An attractive, rich, young American widow, Mrs. Gracedew, has been visiting the estate as a tourist and briefly talking with Chivers, Yule's kind old servant. She now encourages Yule to accept any terms to keep the lovely old home, even if it means marrying Cora and giving up politics. But when Cora explains that she dislikes her father's idea because she would prefer to marry Hall Pegg, a rich Londoner's son, Mrs.

Gracedew buys up the mortgages from Prodmore for an out-rageously high figure, thereby forcing Prodmore to support Cora's marriage to Pegg. Mrs. Gracedew has saved and will marry Yule.

Chivers, Mrs. Gracedew, Hall Pegg, Cora Prodmore, Prod-more, Captain Marmaduke Clement Yule, Dame Dorothy Yule, John Anthony Yule.

"The Coxon Fund," 1894.

The narrator visits the Mulvilles at Wimbleton and is im-pressed by the conversational powers of their slovenly house-guest Frank Saltram. When the narrator tells George Gravener about Saltram, Gravener is critical of the Mulvilles for allowing such an imposition. Saltram once fails to appear to give a lecture, and the narrator is obliged to explain to the audience, after which he meets there a pretty American named Ruth Anvoy, who is anxious to see Saltram. She is the well-to-do niece of wealthy Lord Gregory Coxon's widow, at whose country estate Gravener later meets the girl, soon becoming lingeringly engaged to her. Saltram falls out with the Mulvilles, goes to the Pudneys, argues with them, and returns to the Mulvilles. After many delays, Miss Anvoy meets Saltram and is im-pressed by his conversational brilliance. Ruth's father goes bankrupt in New York. Lady Coxon sets up a £13,000 fund to be administered by Ruth and paid to any great but im-poverished philosopher. Lady Coxon and Ruth's father then both die. Ruth, who may keep the money if she cannot find a proper recipient, is distressed that Gravener wants her not to disburse the funds to articulate Saltram, who is also alcoholic. The narrator is tempted to tell her about Saltram but resists; at the same time he senses her sadness at Gravener's material-ism. One morning estranged Mrs. Saltram conscientiously delivers a letter to the narrator which contains a denunciation of her husband by Pudney, who wants Miss Anvoy to have the truth through the respected narrator. Virtually promising Mrs. Saltram that he will not deliver the letter, the narrator locks it up unread. Gravener urges him to inform Ruth, who can then keep the money without embarrassment. When the narrator asks him if he would marry Ruth without the money, Gravener refuses to answer. The narrator tells Miss Anvoy of the letter in general, and she idealistically urges him to destroy it. He is immensely enamored of her. She is directly approached by the Pudneys but too late, for she has given the funds to Saltram, who apparently proceeds to drink himself into silence and then death. The narrator burns the letter unread in loyalty to Miss Anvoy. Neither marries. Gravener later weds a rich, dull woman and through family deaths becomes Lord Maddock.

Ruth Anvoy, Anvoy, Lord Gregory Coxon, Lady Coxon, George Gravener, Lady Maddock, Lord Maddock, Kent Mulville, Mrs. Kent (Adelaide) Mulville, Pudney, Mrs. Pudney, Frank Saltram, Mrs. Frank Saltram.

"Crapy Cornelia," 1909.

Sitting in a New York park in April, middle-aged White-Mason thinks that he will soon go and propose to flashy, rich Mrs. Worthingham. When he goes to her gaudy new house, he finds another guest there, whom he soon identifies as Cornelia Rasch, an old friend. Mrs. Worthingham later speaks slightingly of her. White-Mason resists proposing and instead goes back to the park to muse again, recalling that he knew Miss Rasch years ago here in New York and further that Mrs. Worthingham has no notion of the charm that old New York had. He visits crapy Cornelia, having asked leave earlier to do so. They quickly renew pleasant memories, and he relishes the tone of time about all her old things. When she speaks of Mrs. Worthingham, who she says loves White-Mason and has plenty of things herself, he is critical and clearly prefers, old as he now feels, to frequent Miss Rasch's comfortable old place and simply share old memories with her.

Mary Cardew, Cornelia Rasch, White-Mason, Mrs. Worthingham.

"Crawford's Consistency," 1876.

The physician-narrator learns that his friend Crawford, a studious and wealthy young man, has been renounced by his fiancee Elizabeth Ingram at the insistance of her socially ambitious parents. So he marries a vicious low-brow and parades her commonness before New York society. Miss Ingram's second engagement is wrecked when her beauty is blasted by smallpox. Crawford next loses his money in a bank failure, and he becomes a druggist. His ugly wife turns vindictive and permanently cripples him by pushing him down a flight of stairs. But Crawford never complains, reasoning that he promised her only money and now cannot provide it. His wife dies drinking.

Dr. Beadle, Crawford, Mrs. Crawford, Elizabeth Ingram, Peter Ingram, Mrs. Peter (Sabrina) Ingram, Niblett.

"Daisy Miller," 1878.

Frederick Winterbourne meets the attractive but exceedingly independent Daisy Miller at Vevey. In spite of his aunt Mrs. Costello's refusal to associate with the Millers — mother, daughter, and son — because of Daisy's brashness, Winterbourne goes by boat with the girl to the Chateau de Chillon. They agree to meet in Rome the following winter. At the Roman residence of Mrs. Walker, an American friend, Winterbourne again meets Daisy. He walks with her to meet her new Italian friend Giovanelli. Mrs. Walker drives up and objects to unmarried Daisy's walking on the streets of Rome, but Giovanelli merely laughs and Daisy is flippant. Winterbourne drives off with Mrs. Walker, who fails in her attempt to have him drop Daisy. Later, at Mrs. Walker's party, Daisy is cruelly snubbed by her hostess and then independently rejects Winterbourne's advice that she leave Giovanelli alone. Daisy's gauche mother naively reports to Winterbourne that she rather thinks her daughter must be engaged. He often sees Giovanelli and the girl together, once at midnight in the miasmal Colosseum. Mortally sick soon, Daisy sends Winterbourne word that she remembers their trip on the lake in Switzerland and that she was never engaged. Then she dies. Before her Roman grave, Giovanelli tells Winterbourne that Daisy was completely innocent. Winterbourne has a long moment of self-doubt, feeling that Daisy would have returned his love if he had offered it.

Mrs. Costello, Dr. Davis, Eugenio, Miss Featherstone, Giovanelli, Annie P. "Daisy" Miller, Ezra B. Miller, Mrs. Ezra B. Miller, Randolph Miller, Mrs. Sanders, Mrs. Walker, Frederick Forsyth Winterbourne.

"A Day of Days," 1866.

Adela Moore has come to live with her scientist brother Herbert near Slowfield. Thomas Ludlow calls at the Moore home in an unsuccessful effort to see Herbert before going over to Europe for study. He takes a wistful walk with Adela and reluctantly parts with her later the same afternoon.

Becky, Laura Benton, Thomas Ludlow, Adela Moore, Herbert Moore, Rev. Mr. Weatherby Pynsent.

"The Death of the Lion," 1894.

The narrator is sent by editor Pinhorn to interview novelist Neil Paraday, but the resulting critical essay is rejected as insufficiently personal. Just as the narrator is becoming fond enough of Paraday to regret that sudden publicity may overwhelm him, Morrow of *The Empire* magazine enters. The narrator protects the manuscript of Paraday's latest superb novel from Morrow, who nonetheless chattily writes up the author's home life. Next, Mrs. Weeks Wimbush of London begins to lionize unresisting Paraday — now painted by popular artist Rumble — and even invites him to Prestidge, her country home, to appear with such other notables as female novelist Guy Walsingham and tweedy, moustached writer Dora Forbes. Abused Paraday grows sick and dies, while Lady Augusta Minch and Lord Dorimont deny knowledge of Paraday's manuscript, which was loaned to and lost somewhere between them. The narrator presumably marries Fanny Hurter, whom he earlier persuaded not to seek Paraday's autograph; together they continue the search for the lost manuscript.

Miss Braby, Deedy, Mrs. Deedy, Lord Dorimont, Dora Forbes, Fanny Hurter, Mrs. Milsom, Lady Augusta Minch, Morrow, Neil Paraday, Pinhorn, Rumble, Guy Walsingham (Miss Collop), Weeks Wimbush, Mrs. Weeks Wimbush.

"De Grey, A Romance," 1868.

Mrs. George De Grey, a widow living near New York, is spiritually comforted by her priest Father Herbert and has as a paid companion a young orphan named Margaret Aldis. When Mrs. De Grey's son Paul returns from Europe following the death of his estranged fiancee there, he falls in love with

Miss Aldis. But Father Herbert warns her that all male De Greys have vampirized their true loves. Margaret bravely determines to love Paul anyway; drained by her, he falls sick and dies, and the girl goes mad.

> Margaret Aldis, Deborah, Blanche Ferrars, Mary Fortescue, Antonietta Gambini, George De Grey, George De Grey, George De Grey, Mrs. George De Grey, John De Grey, John De Grey, Paul De Grey, Paul De Grey, Paul De Grey, Stephen De Grey, Father Herbert, Miss L—, Lucretia Lefevre, Magdalen Scrope, Henrietta Spencer, Isabel Stirling.

"The Dairy of a Man of Fifty," 1879.

The diarist, a retired British general, writes of returning to Florence after twenty-seven years and of meeting young Edmund Stanmer while asking about Countess Salvi. The diarist loved widowed Countess Bianca Salvi, whose husband had been killed in a duel by Count Camerino; after the perplexed diarist left her, she married Camerino for security. Now her daughter, Countess Bianca Salvi-Scarabelli, widow of Count Scarabelli, is the object of the affections of Stanmer, who is thus in a position similar to that of the diarist years ago. He tries unsuccessfully to warn Stanmer about his Bianca. Three years later in London, the two men meet again, and the happy young man insists that the general was mistaken about the older countess. The diarist wonders.

> Count Camerino, Lady H—, Count Salvi, Countess Bianca Salvi, Countess Bianca Salvi-Scarabelli, Count Scarabelli, Signorina Scarabelli, Edmund Stanmer.

"Eugene Pickering," 1874.

When his father dies, sheltered young Eugene Pickering leaves America and travels to Germany, where in Homburg he meets the narrator, a former boyhood friend. Pickering falls in love with a German widow named Anastasia Blumenthal, aged thirty-eight. She leads him to a proposal only to accept and then heartlessly reject him. All this time, Pickering has been nominally engaged, through a long-standing arrangement made by his father, to Isabel Vernor, the daughter of an American businessman in the Middle East. Miss Vernor's father suddenly writes releasing Pickering from the engagement. Sad at being toyed with by Mme. Blumenthal, Pickering wanders to Smyrna, from which city he writes the narrator, still in Italy where the two parted, that he has met Miss Vernor and pronounces her charming.

Mme. Anastasia Blumenthal, Blumenthal, Niedermeyer, Adelina Patti, Eugene Pickering, Pickering, Isabel Vernor, Vernor.

"Europe," 1899.
Back from Europe, the narrator goes to a Boston suburb to visit old Mrs. Rimmle and her mature and even aging daughters, bright Becky, pretty Jane, and reserved Maria. The daughters plan for two of them to go to Europe while the third will stay home to care for the mother, widow of a well-traveled, windy American speaker. But the selfish mother gets sick whenever the plan is close to consummation. Later, however, a friendly couple, the Hathaways, take Jane over to Europe, where according to Maria she so thrives that she will not return. Becky, who now rather resembles the still-living mother, once tells the narrator that Jane will never come back to them. When he next visits Boston, old Mrs. Rimmle tells him that Jane has died in Europe (which is not the case) and that Becky — now sick and lying down somewhere — is going next. Maria says not yet. During his final visit, the narrator is told by Mrs. Rimmle that Becky has gone to Europe; evidently Maria lets her mother think so rather than tell her that Becky is dead.

Hathaway, Mrs. Hathaway, Jane Rimmle, Maria Rimmle, Rebecca "Becky" Rimmle, Rimmle, Mrs. Rimmle.

The Europeans, 1878.
Artistic Felix Young and his sister Baroness Eugenia Munster, morganatic wife of Prince Adolf of Silberstadt-Schreckenstein, have come from Germany to the Boston area, to visit their relatives the well-to-do Wentworths, who live in the country. Felix calls at their home and meets William Wentworth, the rigid half-brother of Felix's dead father; he also meets Wentworth's children — Gertrude, whom the Rev. Mr. Brand loves;

Charlotte; and young Clifford, awkward and a bit addicted to drink. Felix returns and reports to his sister Eugenia; then they both call upon the Wentworths and are hospitably welcomed, Eugenia even moving into a cottage on the Wentworth estate. Soon they are an exotic addition to the little community, which also includes Robert Acton. He is a Wentworth cousin who is attracted to Eugenia and whose gentle old mother rather likes her too. Eugenia hints that she has nearly decided to mail a document to her husband which will result in their legal separation. When Felix learns from Gertrude that she will never marry Brand, he suggests that they make a match between Brand and Charlotte. Eugenia helps Clifford become socially more mature but causes him some embarrassment too. Acton catches Eugenia in a lie and therefore, suspicious of her, refuses to propose. Charlotte urges her father to permit Gertrude and Felix to marry. Eugenia announces her departure. Acton feels rather sorry for himself for a time. At the end, Felix marries Gertrude, Brand Charlotte, Clifford Lizzie (Acton's sister), and Acton (after his mother's death) a nice young lady.

Lizzie Acton, Robert Acton, Mrs. Acton, Prince Adolf of Silberstadt-Schreckenstein, Augustine, Azarina, Rev. Mr. Brand, Broderip, Rev. Mr. Gilman, Mrs. Morgan, Baroness Eugenia Munster, Charlotte Wentworth, Clifford Wentworth, Gertrude Wentworth, William Wentworth, Mrs. Whiteside, Adolphus Young, Mrs. Adolphus Young, Felix Young.

"The Figure in the Carpet," 1896.

Critic George Corvick assigns the critic-narrator the task of reviewing a new novel by Hugh Vereker, whom the narrator is happy to meet later at a party. Vereker apologizes for his remark to a dinner companion that the narrator's review contained only routine twaddle, which remark the narrator overheard. But then Vereker seriously continues by saying that there is a "figure in the carpet" of his fictional production which no critic has discovered. The narrator conscientiously re-reads Vereker's works but cannot trace any figure. He tells Corvick, who after much study professes to have the secret, which he will confide only to his fiancee Gwendolyn Erme and only after their marriage. On their honeymoon Corvick is killed in a dogcart accident. Gwendolyn has the secret, she claims, but will not share it with the narrator. Instead, she marries an inferior critic named Drayton Deane. Vereker dies of fever in Rome, and then his widow dies. Gwendolyn dies having Deane's second child. When the narrator asks Deane about the reputed figure, that imperceptive man disclaims any knowledge of it.

George Corvick, Drayton Deane, Mrs. Drayton (Gwendolyn Erme Corvick) Deane, Mrs. Erme, Lady Jane, Miss Poyle, Hugh Vereker, Mrs. Hugh Vereker.

"Flickerbridge," 1902.

American painter Frank Granger goes to London and paints Mrs. Bracken, contracts influenza, and then receives a letter from Paris from his fiancee, a successful but pushy journalist named Addie Wenham, suggesting that he recuperate at Flickerbridge, an estate in northern England owned by her distant relative Miss Adelaide Wenham. Frank goes, partly to rest but also partly to reconsider his engagement; he is so charmed by the estate, with its last-century grace, and by shy, aging, delightful old Miss Wenham that he gradually fears that his Addie will come too and thus spoil the fragility of Flickerbridge with her breezy publicity. Frank learns that Addie is coming, to the other Miss Wenham's joy; so he leaves and even says that he is no longer engaged.

Mrs. Bracken, Mrs. Dunn, Frank Granger, Adelaide Wenham, Adelaide "Addie" Wenham, Dr. Wenham, Mrs. Wenham, Mrs. Wenham.

"Fordham Castle," 1904.

Abel F. Taker is in a Geneva pension where he is receiving mail from his wife Sue, who has sent him, a social failure at forty-five, from America, has insisted on his changing his name — to C. P. Addard — and is now making her own way socially in England under a new name. Into the pension comes a new guest, Mrs. Vanderplank. It soon appears that she is really Mrs. Magaw, whose daughter Mattie, as discontent with her name as Sue Taker was with hers, has abandoned her mother and is also making her way alone in society, like Mrs. Taker. At about the time Taker receives a letter from his wife, now in Fordham Castle, Wilts, England, Mrs. Magaw gets one from her daughter, who has just met helpful Mrs. Sherrington Reeves, who Taker knows is his wife Sue. Mattie next writes that she is engaged to Lord Dunderton and that Mrs. Reeves thinks the mother can safely reappear now. Taker miserably tells Mrs. Magaw that Lord Dunderton must be so in love that it is safe for the plain mother to be introduced but that he will never be recalled by his wife. He puts Mrs. Magaw on the train and tells her that he will become the ghost of Fordham Castle. He feels utterly alone, very sad, and even dead.

Lord Dunderton, Mattie Magaw ("Miss Vanderplank"), Mrs. Magaw ("Mrs. Vanderplank"), Magaw, Mme. Massin, Abel F. Taker ("C. P. Addard"), Mrs. Sue Taker ("Mrs. Sherrington Reeves").

"Four Meetings," 1877.

The supercilious but pleasant narrator first meets Caroline Spencer at the home of his traveling friend Latouche's mother in New England. When he talks of Europe, Miss Spencer tells him that she is saving her pay as a schoolteacher to go. Three years later the narrator meets her again, this time in Le Havre, where he has gone to meet his sister and brother-in-law. Miss Spencer is delighted by what she is seeing of France but worries the narrator by telling him that her art-student cousin has come to meet her. The narrator meets and is instantly suspicious of the cousin. At their third meeting, a few hours later, the narrator learns that Miss Spencer has given her cousin all her money, to help him and his Provencal countess wife. The narrator is in anguish but can do nothing. Five years later, calling upon the now dead Latouche's mother, back in New England, he meets Miss Spencer for the last time and sees that the "countess," in reality a shabby Parisienne, has come to live with the American cousin of her dead "husband."

Alcibiade, Latouche, Mrs. Latouche, Mixter, Caroline Spencer.

"The Friends of the Friends," 1896.

Among a dead woman's private papers is found the curious

story of her two friends, neither of whom is named. A young lady saw her absent father's spirit just before learning of his death; and a young man similarly saw his mother's spirit just before learning of her death. Years later the narrator tries unsuccessfully to introduce the man, now her fiance, and the woman, now an estranged wife. Before a meeting can occur, the woman reports the death of her husband, which makes the narrator refuse to permit her fiance to meet the widow. The narrator, whose conscience bothers her because of her presumably unfounded incipient jealousy, goes to explain to the widow, who, however, has died just the night before. The narrator reports this shocking news to her fiance, but he says that it is impossible since the widow was in his room the night before, staring silently at him. The narrator suspects another ghost and feels that her fiance is continuing to see it; this suspicion causes her to release her fiance, who jokingly admits seeing the ghost but then retracts the statement. The two never marry. Later the man dies, and the narrator theorizes that he killed himself to be with the other woman's spirit.

(No named characters.)

"Gabrielle de Bergerac," 1869.

Pierre Coquelin is the tutor of Chevalier de Bergerac, aged nine, and falls in love with the Chevalier's maiden aunt Gabrielle de Bergerac, who, however, is courted by Vicomte Gaston de Treuil. Gabrielle's brother, head of the family, favors Gaston but foolishly precipitates the elopement of Pierre and Gabrielle by accusing his sister of improper conduct with the entirely honorable but passionately devoted Pierre. During the French Revolution, the loving pair die on the scaffold with the Girondists.

Gabrielle de Bergerac, Baron de Bergerac, Baron de Bergerac, Baroness de Bergerac, Chevalier de Bergerac, Marie de Chalais, Marquis de Chalais, Pierre Coquelin, Mme. Coquelin, Marquis de Rochambeau, M. de Sorbieres, Abbe Tiblaud, Vicomte Gaston de Treuil.

"Georgina's Reasons," 1884.

In return for his promise not to reveal the fact until she

agrees, Georgina Gressie secretly marries Raymond Benyon, an American naval officer. She soon goes with her friend Mrs. Portico to Genoa, gives birth to Benyon's son there, and abandons it for a payment to an Italian woman. Dying, Mrs. Portico writes Benyon of the circumstances, but he fails in his efforts to trace the boy. In Naples some time later, Benyon, now a captain, falls in love with Kate Theory, through whose sister-in-law Agnes he learns that Georgina has committed bigamy by marrying a relative of Agnes's named William Roy. Benyon goes to Georgina in New York; she callously admits everything, defies him, and even introduces him to her other husband. Unwilling to break his solemn promise, Benyon cannot do more than wait.

Amanda, Captain Raymond Benyon, Benyon, Bessie, Draper, Mrs. Draper, Gressie, Mrs. Gressie, Harriet, Henry Platt, Mrs. Portico, Mrs. Cora Roy, William Roy, Mrs. William (Georgina Gressie Benyon) Roy, Roy, Kate Theory, Mildred Theory, Percival Theory, Mrs. Percival (Agnes Roy) Theory, Vanderdecken, Mrs. Vanderdecken.

"The Ghostly Rental," 1876.

The narrator, a young divinity student at Harvard, sees old Captain Diamond bow before a mysterious house, enter, and later emerge with money. The narrator asks a local gossip, Miss Deborah, for an explanation. She hesitantly tells him that Diamond once cursed his daughter presumably to death, because of a man who said that he was her husband. Diamond is now haunted. The narrator becomes friendly with him. Later he sees him again as he is coming from the house with his quarterly payment. Once when Diamond is sick, the narrator goes to collect and sees that the ghost is a real woman, Diamond's daughter. It is revealed that after being cursed, she went away but did not marry; she has posed as a ghost ever since, for revenge upon her father and also because she cannot hope for forgiveness. Suddenly the woman "sees" the ghost of her father and drops her light. The narrator returns to Diamond and learns that he is dead. The house burns.

Belinda, Miss Deborah, Captain Diamond, Mrs. Diamond, Miss Diamond.

"The Given Case," 1899.

Barton Reeve loves Kate Despard, wife of an absent cad
Col. Despard, and appeals to Margaret Hamer, her friend,
to explain his love to Kate. Miss Hamer promises to try.
At a country estate soon thereafter Philip Mackern, who loves
Margaret, beseeches Mrs. Despard to speak favorably of him
to the girl and to urge her to break off her too-long engagement
with absent and negligent John Grove-Stewart. Philip tells Mrs.
Despard that when a girl leads a man on she must be prepared
to do everything. Later Margaret depresses Barton by informing
him that Kate will be dutiful to her husband when he returns.
Barton tells Margaret that she would be more generous in
Kate's place. Dismissing Barton one day, Kate then urges
Philip to believe that Margaret's one chance is at once to marry
Grove-Stewart, who is returning from India. Kate is curiously
annoyed when her wandering husband comes back to her;
however, now deciding to abandon Barton, she righteously
criticizes Margaret for not being faithful to her fiance. Barton
goes back to Kate, but she tells him that her husband is now
home and that she therefore will not see Barton again though
she loves only him. Philip appeals again to Margaret, who
senses her degree of responsibility for leading him on and
decides not to act like Kate; she accepts Philip, knowing that
Grove-Stewart will never understand her conduct.

   Col. Despard, Mrs. Kate Despard, John Grove-Stewart,
   Mrs. Gorton, Margaret Hamer, Philip Mackern, Lady
   Orville, Barton Reeve, Amy Warden.

"Glasses," 1896.

In Folkestone the painter-narrator meets bespectacled old
Mrs. Meldrum, who introduces him to Flora Saunt. She needs
glasses but considers them disfiguring to her radiant beauty.
Geoffrey Dawling falls permanently in love with the narrator's
portrait of Flora and then with the original, but she has set
her sights upon rich young Lord Iffield. When the narrator
returns from America, he finds Flora's engagement to Iffield
broken and the girl in glasses. She hopes that her vision will
improve long enough for her to capture a rich Italian at least.
When the narrator returns from America after another voyage,
he sees radiant Flora, without glasses, in a London opera box,

apparently smiling at him in happy recognition; but upon going to her box, he discovers that she is totally blind. Dawling enters. She is now his wife.

Betty, Lady Considine, Lord Considine, Geoffrey Dawling, Dawling, Miss Dawling, Miss Dawling, Miss Dawling, Miss Dawling, Floyd-Taylor, Mrs. Fanny Floyd-Taylor, Lord Iffield, Mrs. Meldrum, Flora Louise Saunt, Bertie Hammond Synge, Hammond Synge, Mrs. Hammond Synge.

The Golden Bowl, 1904.

Prince Amerigo, engaged to Maggie Verver, visits their London friend Mrs. Fanny Assingham and learns that Charlotte Stant, his former inamorata, will attend his wedding. Charlotte and the Prince in a shop resist buying a golden bowl as a wedding present for Maggie, since it is probably cracked. A couple of years later, married and with a baby boy, Maggie laments that her widowed father Adam Verver, immensely rich and an avid collector, is lonely, and hoping that he will remarry, persuades him to write Charlotte an invitation to visit. She comes to Adam's British estate at Fawns and quickly drives away his harpy-guests. He decides to wed her to give his daughter the sense that he misses her less. Seemingly accepted by Maggie and the Prince, Charlotte agrees to Adam's proposal, and they marry. Soon ignored by Adam, who appears to prefer his daughter's companionship, Charlotte is thrown into the Prince's company at parties, to the terror of Fanny Assingham, who frequently communicates her fears to her husband Colonel Bob. One rainy day in London, the Prince and Charlotte, agreeing that their *sposi* care inordinately more for each other, embrace. Later they attend — without their *sposi* — a glittering party at the estate of Matcham; feeling ever more confident, they stay on to visit Gloucester, refusing distressed Fanny's invitation to return in the same train with her. Now Maggie begins to feel left out, gives a party, and at its conclusion suggests that the Prince take distant, seemingly docile Adam off on a trip — to which the Prince says that Charlotte should make such a proposal. Able to talk with Adam when he visits their sick baby, Maggie urges him to take the Prince off somewhere; but he counters with the suggestion that

both couples spend some time at Fawns. Tormented by more
doubts, Maggie is temporarily relieved by Fanny's lying denial
of any sense of suspicion. But one day Maggie wanders into
the shop where the golden bowl is, and buys it for Adam;
later the remorseful shopkeeper comes and explains its flaw,
adding details which inform Maggie that the Prince and
Charlotte went shopping together just before his marriage.
Fanny, to whom Maggie tells all this, denies Maggie's interpre-
tation of events and throws the bowl to the floor, breaking
it into three pieces. The Prince enters at this point, hears
Maggie's story of the bowl, and is left to wonder what Adam
may have learned. At Fawns later, Maggie feels a degree of
pity for her husband, who, she tells Fanny, has lied to avoid
telling Charlotte. That forceful woman demands of Maggie
whether she is silently accusing her of anything; serenely lying,
Maggie senses that thus she is closer to the Prince, who has
also lied to Charlotte. Adam tenderly tells his daughter that
he and Charlotte will move to his American City if doing so
will help Maggie. Without saying so, they inform each other of
the supremacy of their mutual regard over any other affections.
Later, at the close of a huge hot party at Fawns, Charlotte
pursues Maggie into the garden to say that she is taking Adam
away because Maggie has opposed their marriage and has
failed. Self-sacrificially, Maggie professes to admit failure. The
Prince now passively stays in London with Maggie, who at
his approaching once to embrace her tells him to wait. Adam
and Charlotte come for a farewell tea. Charlotte seems regal,
but Adam knows, and says goodbye gently; the Prince returns
and sees only Maggie.

> Prince Amerigo, Principino, Col. Robert "Bob" Assingham,
> Mrs. Robert (Fanny) Assingham, Mrs. Betterman, Blint,
> Miss Bogle, Bradshaw, Dr. Brady, Sir John Brinder,
> Calderoni, Lady Castledean, Lord Castledean, Crichton,
> Guterman-Seuss, Dotty Lutch, Kitty Lutch, Miss Maddock,
> Father Mitchell, Mrs. Noble, Don Ottavio, Rance, Mrs.
> Rance, Charlotte Stant, Adam Verver, Princess Maggie
> Verver.

"The Great Condition," 1899.
When Bertram Braddle must leave Liverpool for London

and hence seem to neglect Mrs. Damerel, one of his fellow passengers from America, his friend and another passenger Henry Chilver volunteers to stay near her rather than proceed to London at once. Henry recalls his routine vacation in America and how Mrs. Damerel, an attractive American widow on the ship returning, quickly became friendly with Bertram. Henry dutifully escorts her to London and on to Brighton as he promised, but he finds himself falling in love with her himself. Later Bertram calls on him and explains that he loves the woman but fears something strange in her background. Henry suggests that Bertram propose and hope that she will explain her whole past, but Bertram fears that she would accept but explain nothing. This is exactly what happens. Then later Bertram tells Henry that she did finally admit vaguely to something in her past but added that she would tell him nothing until after six months of marriage. This is her condition. While Bertram hedges and goes back to America to investigate Mrs. Damerel, Henry calls upon her, finds that she considers herself absolutely free, and within a week proposes. Soon they marry. Finding nothing scandalous about her, Bertram returns to England, gets her to admit privately that there was never anything even slightly improper about her past conduct; but he has promised never to tell Henry, who, she adds, never asked her about her past and considers himself rather noble for this fact.

Bertram Braddle, Henry Chilver, Mrs. Damerel.

"The Great Good Place," 1900.

Writer George Dane is so oppressed one beautiful morning, after a rainy night of unfinished work, by the sense of his multitudinous duties — writing, social obligations, a breakfast guest who soon enters, and the like — that he suddenly awakens in a totally new environment. All is peaceful. There are pleasant bells and slow footsteps all about. To a Brother seated on a bench with him, Dane tells of the young man at breakfast who volunteered to handle all his work for him while he leaned back on the sofa, indulgently and gratefully watching him. Three weeks seem to have passed at the good place with the many comrades. Dane is finding his soul again. Then he and the Brother, noticing rain outside the "hotel," discuss the inevitability of his returning. He is, however, refreshed and therefore ready. Then his servant is awakening him, and he finds that the young visitor has indeed tidied up all of his work for him.

Brown, George Dane, Lady Mullet.

"Greville Fane," 1892.

At the death of the potboiler-novelist Greville Fane, really Mrs. Stormer, the journalist-narrator recalls many things about her. Her daughter Lady Ethel Luard is a cold social-climber, and her son Leolin Stormer sponged off his hard-working mother for years while being educated and later while professing to be gaining experience for novels which he never has written. When Ethel married Sir Baldwin Luard, the mother paid for everything, only to be told that she could not live with them. Publishing the mother's literary remains, Ethel and Leolin quarrel over the proceeds. Finally Leolin marries an old woman, and he still talks about the writing he will do when he has conquered problems of form.

Greville Fane (Mrs. Stormer), Sir Baldwin Luard, Lady Ethel Stormer Luard, Leolin Stormer, Mrs. Leolin Stormer.

"Guest's Confession," 1872.

David the narrator meets Laura Guest in a church at L—, a watering spot. He goes on to meet his hypochondriac stepbrother Edgar Musgrave's train and learns that Edgar has been swindled out of $20,000 by John Guest. Edgar forces Guest's confession in writing and witnessed by the narrator, who only later comes to realize that Laura is Guest's daughter. David falls in love with the girl at about the time a silvermillionaire from the West named Crawford enters the scene and prepares to court Laura's companion Mrs. Clara Beck. Guest saddens his daughter by writing her of his financial plight. When he returns to L— and finds his enemy Musgrave's step-brother David with Laura, he orders the young man to leave. But David obtains as his legacy from the dying Musgrave the confession of Guest, with which he forces Guest to permit Laura to accept him.

Mrs. Clara Beck, Crawford, David, John Guest, Laura Guest, Hale, Edgar Musgrave, Stevens, Stoddard.

"The Impressions of a Cousin," 1883.

The narrator, a painter named Catherine Condit, visits her cousin Eunice in New York. Eunice's financial affairs are handled by a dishonest man named Caliph, whose half-brother Adrian Frank courts Eunice but in reality soon comes to love Miss Condit. A matchmaker named Mrs. Ermine wishes to see Eunice and Caliph marry. The narrator discovers that Caliph has dishonestly managed the funds of Eunice, but the infatuated girl makes her promise not to expose him. Nonetheless, Miss Condit hints to Frank that Caliph is a swindler; so Frank in his love for her makes good the losses. In anguish, Eunice sends her cousin away. Thinking that the girl is now cured, Miss Condit taunts Caliph by saying that Eunice once would have loved him. Then, however, he begins to attract the girl again; the result is that the narrator promises poor Frank that she will marry him if Eunice, rich again, weds Caliph.

Caliph, Catherine Condit, William Ermine, Mrs. William (Lizzie) Ermine, Eunice, Adrian Frank, Freddy, Harry, Latrobe, Letitia, Willie Woodley.

"An International Episode," 1878-1879.

Through the kindness of New York businessman J. L. Westgate, visitors Lord Lambeth and Percy Beaumont are entertained at Newport by Westgate's wife Kitty and her sister Bessie Alden. Lambeth is entranced by Miss Alden; but when she innocently asks Beaumont certain questions concerning his friend's rank and prospects in England, he alerts Lambeth's mother, who calls her supposedly endangered son home by a subterfuge. The following spring Kitty Westgate and her sister Bessie go to England, where through an American named Willie Woodley they meet Lambeth again. Mrs. Westgate warns Bessie that it may be thought that she is running after Lambeth, who is now attentive and says that he wants her to visit at Branches, his family's country estate. When Kitty asks whether Bessie is in love with Lambeth, the girl says that she is not; so Kitty suggests their scaring Lambeth's family by making them think that she is. The girl does not reply. Although Beaumont warns Lambeth that his family will never accept Miss Alden, Lambeth persuades his mother, the Duchess of Bayswater, and his sister, the Countess of Pimlico, to call upon her. The conversation of the four women is cool: the British ladies are apprehensive and aloof; Kitty realizes that they hope the Americans will not visit Branches; Bessie professes to think them charming if reserved. Although Lambeth tells Beaumont that he would not like to propose to Miss Alden only to be refused, that is evidently exactly what happens the day following the visit of his mother and sister. Bessie writes to decline the invitation to Branches. Lambeth is in anguish at his rejection. Kitty is annoyed when she thinks that the British ladies will wrongly fancy that they scared the Americans away. Bessie apparently resents nothing.

> Bessie Alden, Duchess of Bayswater, Duke of Bayswater, Percy Beaumont, Lady Beatrice Bellevue, Marquis of Blackborough, Mlle. Boquet, Butterworth, Mrs. Butterworth, Duke of Green-Erin, Lady Julia, Lord Lambeth, Captain Littledale, Countess of Pimlico, J. L. Westgate, Mrs. J. L. (Kitty) Westgate, Willie Woodley.

"In the Cage," 1898.

The unnamed girl who works in the post-and-telegraph cage of Cocker's store is asked by her fiance Mudge to move from her Mayfair employment to Chalk Farm and live with her mother to save money until they can marry. But she declines, since she loves to imagine details in the lives of her opulent customers. One such person is a splendid lady, who turns out to be Lady Bradeen, while another is glittering Captain Count Philip Everard. Meanwhile she also declines the invitation of her friend widowed Mrs. Jordan, a professional arranger of flowers for the parties of others, to participate in this work. One day she helps Lady Bradeen alter a telegram, to that woman's astonishment. At another time she seeks out Everard's residence and even talks and sits with him in Hyde Park, strangely crying and telling him that she will happily stay in the cage at Cocker's to be of aid to him. She goes on vacation to Bournemouth with her mother and Mudge and is perturbed by the news that he has been given the raise necessary for them to marry. She tells him that she must remain at Cocker's to aid Everard, who she says appears badly embroiled with a certain lady. One day Everard enters in search of a certain wire sent earlier that year by Lady Bradeen and dangerously intercepted. The girl quotes its message from memory; since Lady Bradeen happened to send the wrong contents, no harm was done and Everard is relieved and grateful. Later the girl meets Mrs. Jordan, who is going to marry Drake, Lady Bradeen's new butler. Through Mrs. Jordan, who has the story from Drake, the girl learns that Lady Bradeen is to marry Everard, who compromised her while Lord Bradeen was alive; Lady Bradeen once stole something to save Everard and hence has him in her power. The girl decides to marry Mudge at once and ponders the strangeness of recent events which she has participated in vicariously.

Lady Bradeen, Lord Bradeen, Mrs. Bubb, Buckton, Burfield, Buttons, Mrs. Buttons, Dr. Buzzard, Cissy, Cocker, Cooper, Miss Dolman, Drake, Captain Count Philip Everard, Fritz, Haddon, Mrs. Jordan, Ladle, Mason, Marguerite, Mary, Montenero, Mudge, Lady Agnes Orme, Lord Rye, Savoy, Simpkin, Thrupp, Lady Ventnor.

The Ivory Tower, 1917.

Rosanna Gaw visits the Newport grounds of rich, dying Frank B. Betterman, the estranged former partner of her wealthy, sick old father Abel Gaw. She talks with Davey Bradham, her friend Gussy's husband, about various matters including the expected arrival of Betterman's nephew Graham Fielder, whom Rosanna knew some years earlier in Europe. Cissy Foy, also now at Newport, is supposed to be pursuing Graham now. Horton Vint, who once proposed to Rosanna, is also there. Cissy says that Graham loves Rosanna, which fact she learned from his mother's second husband. Old Gaw grows worse when he hears of Betterman's temporary physical improvement. Cultured Graham Fielder reports to his uncle, who likes him at once and plans to leave him a fortune; later Graham sees Rosanna, who gives him a letter in an ivory tower from her grasping father, who, it is suddenly announced, has died. Cissy tells Horton that she thinks Graham and Rosanna are now engaged, adding that she would like to steal Graham away. Next Betterman dies. Graham and Horton meet, and the two discuss their past, the two rich men's deaths, and Graham's possible inheritance. Graham tells Horton that he

needs a confidential friend to take care of the many details
of his new life. He shows Horton the letter from Gaw, which
he fears to open because it might hurt his fine opinion of his
uncle Betterman, yet cannot destroy because it might contain
important information concerning Rosanna. After a couple of
weeks, Graham is thinking of his mistakes and his inability
to adjust to his new position, when Davey Bradham arrives
and evidently persuades him of his proper duty . . .

Frank B. Betterman, Davey Bradham, Mrs. Davey (Gussy)
Bradham, Crick, Graham "Gray" Fielder, Cecelia "Cissy"
Foy, Abel Gaw, Rosanna Gaw, Miss Goodenough, Dr.
Hatch, Miss Mumby, Northover, Mrs. Fielder Northover,
Dr. Root, Roulet, Miss Ruddle, Mrs. Minnie Undle, Horton
"Haughty" Vint.

"John Delavoy," 1898.
At the theater, the critic-narrator sees Miss Delavoy, who
is the sister of the recently dead novelist John Delavoy, with
Beston, powerful editor of the *Cynosure*, to which the narrator
has just sent an analytical essay on Delavoy's works. When
the two meet about it, Beston without having read it says that
he wants it redone to be more chatty; then he offers to introduce
Miss Delavoy. Beston is soon surprised when she so admires
the essay — he now calls it too frank — that she will permit
the reproduction in the magazine of her unique portrait of her
brother, which Beston now has in his offices, only if the essay
accompanies it. But Beston crassly prints only the picture,
thereby losing Miss Delavoy to the narrator.

Beston, John Delavoy, Miss Delavoy, Windon, Lord
Yarracome.

"The Jolly Corner," 1908.
After thirty-three mature years abroad, Spencer Brydon returns to New York to supervise the razing of inherited property
near his family home on a jolly downtown corner, in which
home he begins to hear ghosts from his past. He wonders
what he would have been like if he had remained in America
and developed what he feels now to be an incipient business

ability. He begins to stalk this alter ego. A charming friend, Alice Staverton, so sympathizes with him that she twice dreams — she says — of his alter ego. Brydon spends night after night in the old home. One night he looks on the fourth floor toward a far room and finds closed the door to it which he left open. He pursues the ghost no farther but goes instead to the window, even contemplating suicide by way of escape. He finally descends all but the last flight of stairs; then, lighted eerily, his ravaged alter ego stares up at him from inside the front door. Brydon faints. Later he revives with his head in the lap of Miss Staverton, who, worried about him, came in with the cleaning woman the following noon. When he describes the circumstances briefly, she says that she knows because she dreamed again in the dim dawn about the ghost, which must have sent her to Brydon. He feels different, and the two embrace.

Spencer Brydon, Mrs. Muldoon, Alice Staverton.

"Julia Bride," 1908.

Six-times-engaged, radiantly pretty Miss Julia Bride says goodbye at a museum to Basil French, in whom she is now interested, and prepares to meet her former step-father Mr. Pitman, her much-divorced mother Mrs. Connery's second husband. Julia hopes that Pitman may be willing to lie about her mother to enable her to get ahead with Basil. But Pitman instead asks her to criticize truthfully her wayward mother to widowed Mrs. David E. Drack, whom he wishes to marry but who has been hesitant because of stories concerning his divorce. Obliging Pitman but to her own detriment, Julia vilifies her mother in conversation with appreciative Mrs. Drack. Then she meets one of her former fiances, Murray Brush, whom she still loves; but all he is willing to do is exaggerate her innocence in talking to others, since he is now engaged to proper Miss Mary Lindeck.

Julia Bride, Murray Brush, Connery, Mrs. Bride Pitman Connery, Mrs. David E. Drack, Basil French, Mary Lindeck, Mrs. George Maule, Miss Maule, Miss Maule, Miss Maule, Miss Maule, Pitman.

"Lady Barbarina," 1884.

At Hyde Park, Lord Canterville rides by with two of his dozen or so children, Barbarina and Agnes. Jackson Lemon, a rich American physician, loves Lady Barb in spite of being warned by a sympathetic friend that he will be lost if he does so. Still he proposes to Barbarina, whose parents stall until their solicitor draws up a marriage contract which is exceedingly favorable to her. Six months after the wedding, they are in New York, where cold Lady Barb has her sister Agnes, aged nineteen, with her. Barb dislikes America and wants to return for a prolonged visit to London, partly to get Lady Agnes away from Herman Longstraw, a parasite from the West. When Agnes elopes, marries, and goes to California with Longstraw, Barbarina is ordered home to London for an accounting. At the end, the Lemons, with a daughter now, are permanently in England, supporting among other things Agnes and her husband, who is much in demand socially.

Lady Lucretia Beauchemin, Lord Beauchemin, Lady Canterville, Lord Philip Canterville, Mrs. Chew, Lady Agnes Clement, Dr. Sidney Feeder, Dexter Freer, Mrs. Dexter Freer, Hardman, Dr. Jackson Lemon, Mrs. Jackson (Lady Barbarina Clement) Lemon, Mrs. Mary Lemon, Miss Lemon, Herman Longstraw, Sir Henry Marmaduke, Lady Marmaduke, Trumpington, Mrs. Trumpington, Mrs. Vanderdecker.

"A Landscape Painter," 1866.

Locksley, a rich young painter jilted by Josephine Leary, goes alone to Chowderville and obtains rooms with retired sea-captain Richard Quarterman, whose daughter Miriam is a self-supporting teacher. Locksley pretends poverty, and the two fall in love. When he becomes sick, Miriam reads his diary, learns that he is rich, and plans to marry him. On their honeymoon she confesses that she read his diary and was made but the more lovable by his money.

Alfred Bannister, Miss Blankenberg, Cynthia, Dawson, Josephine Leary, Locksley, Prendergast, Miriam Quarterman, Captain Richard Quarterman.

"The Last of the Valerii," 1874.

The painter-narrator is the godfather of Martha, American wife of Count Marco Valerio of Rome. When a statue of Juno is exhumed from his villa grounds, he begins to worship it to the neglect of his wife. He goes so far as to worship the statue in a make-shift pagan temple. So Martha buries it again and thus reclaims her husband from the clutch of the past.

Count Marco Valerio, Countess Martha Valerio.

"The Lesson of the Master," 1888.

At a British country home, Paul Overt, a young novelist, meets his ideal the master novelist Henry St. George, his wife, General Fancourt, and his attractive daughter Marian. After supper St. George a little bitterly tells Paul to write and stay single, since a wife is not an inspiration but a hindrance. Back in London, Paul sees Marian again and soon falls in love with her; but when he visits St. George at his home, the master more strongly urges him to live for the muse only. So Paul goes alone to Switzerland and slowly completes a second book. Then he learns from Marian that Mrs. St. George has suddenly died. When he returns to London, he hears from General Fancourt that Marian and St. George are to be married. The two writers meet, and after Paul accuses St. George of shameful conduct, the older man says that his advice was right: he will not write again, but Paul will achieve greatness.

Lady Egbert, Marian Fancourt, General Fancourt, Lady Jane, Lord Masham, Mulliner, Paul Overt, Mrs. Overt, Henry St. George, Mrs. Henry St. George, Lady Watermouth, Lord Watermouth.

"The Liar," 1888.

Going to the Ashmore country estate to paint Sir David, the aged father of his host, Oliver Lyon observes among the guests Colonel Clement Capadose, a liar now married to Everina Brant, whom Lyon once loved and lost. During his sitting, Sir David amuses Lyon by describing Capadose's addiction to lying. The painter wonders what fine Everina's attitude is toward a prevaricating partner. He paints Amy, daughter of the Capadoses, and then a portrait of "the liar," during one

of whose sittings a girl enters the studio supposedly in search
of work as a model. The Colonel spins an incredible story
about her. After the painting of "the liar" is finished, Lyon
returns to his studio secretly at one time and chances while
unseen to witness Capadose and his wife in wrath over the
painting, which appears to reveal its subject's inner nature.
Lyon observes the Colonel when alone slash it savagely. Later
the Colonel suggests to him that the unemployed model must
have destroyed it. To the painter's anguish, Everina lies too,
saying that she adored the painting.

> Arthur Ashmore, Mrs. Arthur Ashmore, Sir David Ashmore,
> Amy Capadose, Colonel Clement Capadose, Mrs. Clement
> (Everina Brant) Capadose, Dean Capadose of Rockingham,
> General Capadose, Oliver Lyon, Harriet Pearson (Miss
> Geraldine?, Miss Grenadine?), Grand Duke of Silberstadt-
> Schreckenstein.

"A Light Man," 1869.
Worthless adventurer Maximus Austin, returned from Europe,
begins to keep a journal on his arrival in New York. A letter
from his friend Theodore Lisle soon takes him to the estate
of rich, dying Frederick Sloane at D—. Almost at once the two
men are vying for the money of Sloane, who soon begins
to prefer Max and asks him at one point to go get his old
will. Max finds his friend busily perusing it. They note that
it is made out in to Lisle. When Max tells him that Sloane
wishes to destroy it, Lisle in a fit of remorse burns it. Sloane
dies without writing a new will, and his money goes to a niece,
whom Max now determines to pursue.

> Maximus Austin, Mrs. Austin, Brooks, Dr. Jones, Theodore
> Lisle, Lisle, A.L., Miss Meredith, Mrs. Parker, Miss Parker,
> Robert, Frederick Sloane.

"A London Life," 1888.
Miss Laura Wing, a penniless American, is visiting her sister
Selina Berrington, who does not get along with her wealthy
husband Lionel in London. Laura gossips freely with Lady
Davenant, a friend of Lionel's widowed and expropriated
mother. Laura sympathizes with Lionel when he complains

that Selina is in Paris with her latest lover Captain Charley Crispin. He adds that he intends to divorce Selina and urges Laura not to speak against him. When Selina returns, Laura asks her about Crispin, requires her to swear that she was not with him, but then feels that her sister is taking a false oath; Selina, however, insists that Lionel is corrupt and therefore threatens vainly. Through Selina, Laura meets a young and boring American named Wendover; they chat, and later Lady Davenant opines that he will do as Laura's husband. One day Laura goes with Wendover to St. Paul's and then the Soane Museum, where Selina, who has reported that she is visiting a sick friend out of town, appears with bearded Crispin. When the two sisters get together again, Selina criticizes Laura for going unescorted with Wendover and calls her hypocritical, adding that since she herself is married to a cad she can roam more freely. Lady Davenant advises Laura to leave Selina and hope to marry Wendover, who is becoming more interested. One night at the opera, Selina leaves Wendover and Laura alone, hoping thus to compromise the girl; Laura frantically tries to force his hand before he can guess Selina's motive, but he remains merely gallant. Laura then becomes feverish at the home of Lady Davenant, who calls puzzled Wendover and explains the situation. Learning from Lionel that Selina is now in Brussels with Crispin, Laura spurns Wendover's belated proposals and goes to her sister; getting nowhere with her, Laura sails to visit relatives in Virginia, to which Wendover evidently will proceed.

Miss Bald (or Bold), Lord Bamborough, Ferdy Berrington, Geordie Berrington, Lionel Berrington, Mrs. Lionel (Selina Wing) Berrington, Mrs. Berrington, Booker, Collingwood, Mrs. Collingwood, Captain Charley Crispin, Lady Davenant, Miss Frothingham, Motcomb, Lady Ringrose, Babe Schooling, Fanny Schooling, Katie Schooling, Schooling, Mrs. Schooling, Miss Steet, Lady Watermouth, Wendover, Laura Wing.

"Longstaff's Marriage," 1878.
Rich Diana Belfield travels in Europe with her companion Agatha Josling. At Nice they meet sick Reginald Longstaff, who on his death-bed proposes to Diana. Her refusal wounds

his pride and thus enables him to recover. Later, sick in her
turn in Rome, Diana proposes to Longstaff. He accepts her,
and they are married. Then, although he sincerely loves her,
she deliberately dies, feeling that by so doing she can most
tenderly show her love.

Diana Belfield, Mrs. Belfield, Agatha Josling, Reginald
Longstaff.

"Lord Beaupre," 1892.

Guy Firminger tells Mrs. Ashbury and her daughter Maud
and Mrs. Gosselin and her daughter Mary that he is much
beset by husband-hunters. Later to the Gosselins he jokingly
suggests that they pretend he is engaged to Mary to stop such
pursuit of him. A couple of years later Guy has become Lord
Beaupre through the deaths of three cousins. To prevent him
from marrying either his cousin Charlotte Firminger or Maud
Ashbury, both of whom are hovering about anxiously, Mrs.
Gosselin boldly announces that he is engaged to her daughter
Mary. Miss Gosselin has long loved him but is now disgusted
by both his obtuseness and his delight in the comfort which
the ruse is providing him. Meanwhile Bolton-Brown, a rich
New York friend of her brother Hugh, loves Mary but has
been put off by her fraudulent engagement, until Hugh tells
him the truth. Mary's relations with Guy are so strained by
this time that before he can suggest that they make the engagement real she asks to break it off to marry Bolton-Brown,
whom she does wed. Her mother tells Hugh that she fears
Mary will not like America, will therefore return to England
to find Guy married to Charlotte (whom he does marry),
and will then dangerously sympathize with him. Hugh replies
to his mother that she sees too much.

Miss Maud Ashbury, Mrs. Ashbury, Lord Beaupre,
Beaupre, Bolton-Brown, Mrs. Bolton-Brown, Miss Bolton-
Brown, Miss Bolton-Brown, Charlotte Firminger, Major
Frank Firminger, Mrs. Frank Firminger, Guy Firminger
(later Lord Beaupre), Miss Firminger, Miss Firminger,
Miss Firminger, Hugh Gosselin, Mary Gosselin, Mrs. Gosse-
lin, Raddle, Raddle, Mrs. Raddle, Lady Bessie Whiteroy,
Lord Whiteroy.

"Louisa Pallant," 1888.

In Homburg the narrator runs into widowed Louisa Pallant, who once jilted him badly, and her beautiful but mercenary daughter Linda. The narrator is joined by his ingenuous nephew Archie Parker, aged twenty. When Louisa sees that Linda would seize rich Archie, she takes her away; but Linda writes Archie from Italy, and the two men follow to Baveno. In expiation for her treatment of the narrator, Louisa tells Archie such damaging things about Linda that he does not propose.

Gimingham, Henry Pallant, Mrs. Henry (Louisa) Pallant, Linda Pallant, Archie Parker, Mrs. Charlotte Parker, Miss Parker.

"Madame de Mauves," 1874.

Through a traveling American friend named Mrs. Draper, Longmore meets at Saint-Germain-en-Laye Euphemia Cleve de Mauves, young American wife of Comte Richard de Mauves, forty years of age, fat, cold, and faithless. He urges Longmore to be nice to his wife, to make her feel less serious and intro-spective. But Longmore holds back, until in Paris he sees Mauves entertaining a disreputable woman in a cafe. Then he rushes back to Saint-Germain to declare his love but again restrains himself, even though Madame de Mauves is obviously moved by his consideration and even though Mauves's sister Marie Clairin tells him that Mauves has a mistress and hopes that his wife will take a lover. Longmore wanders into the forest, enviously notices an artist and his girl-friend at an inn, and later dreams of being separated from Madame de Mauves by a stream on which Mauves is a boatman. Two years later, in America he learns from Mrs. Draper that Mauves, repenting of his follies and then unsuccessfully begging his wife's forgiveness, has committed suicide. Longmore thinks at once of returning to Europe, but he has not done so as yet.

Butterworth, Mme. Marie de Mauves Clairin, Clairin, Chalumeau, Claudine, Mrs. Cleve, Maggie Draper, Mrs. Draper, Longmore, Mme. Euphemia Cleve de Mauves, Comte Richard de Mauves, Mme. de Mauves, Webster.

"The Madonna of the Future," 1873.

In Florence the narrator H— meets the painter Theobald, who is chided for unproductivity by an American hostess Mrs. Coventry. Theobald confides in the narrator that he is slowly producing a masterpiece of a madonna. He introduces him to his model, the faded Serafina, whom the narrator abruptly pronounces old. This stuns Theobald, who becomes mortally sick. Before the painter dies, H— visits him in his ragged room and sees that the canvas for the madonna is old and blank.

Mrs. Coventry, H—, Serafina, Theobald.

"The Marriages," 1891.

Fearful that her adored father Colonel Chart, a widower, will remarry, Adela goes to his fiancee, the rich widow Mrs. Churchley, and tells her something so atrocious about her father that the marriage is postponed. Her twenty-year-old brother Godfrey Chart, who is studying for foreign service examinations, is mysteriously enfuriated with Adela, tells her that the marriage is canceled, and says that he is in desperate straits and that Mrs. Churchley was to have aided him. But he passes his examinations. Next, at the Chart family country house Adela is suddenly visited by Godfrey's secret wife, a horrible middle-aged hag, who then extorts money from Colonel Chart to stay away and not ruin Godfrey's diplomatic career. It seems that Godfrey was counting on aid from Mrs. Churchley, to whom Adela now goes and tells the truth; but that woman explains that she never believed the hideous stories, wanted Colonel Chart to send the girl away, and permanently broke with him when he defended his daughter. Now Adela must make it all up to her lonely father.

Adela Chart, Basil Chart, Beatrice Chart, Godfrey Chart, Mrs. Godfrey Chart, Muriel Chart, Colonel Chart, Mrs. Churchley, Lord Dovedale, Miss Flynn, Millward, Mrs. Millward, Lady Molesley, Nutkins.

"The Married Son," 1908 (Part VII of *The Whole Family*).

[A local editor interviews the father Cyrus Talbert about the engagement of his daughter Peggy to Harry Goward, her college friend. Harry was formerly interested in Aunt Elizabeth, who, however, was less interested in him than many imaginative family members think. One of them follows Aunt Elizabeth to New York because of her supposed elopement with the village physician.] Charles Edward Talbert, "the married son" who is contrasted with his commercially canny brother-in-law Tom Price, suggests that the problem of Peggy's undesirable engagement can be solved by his going abroad (with his wife Lorraine) and taking Peggy along. Charles Edward would prefer to study art in Europe for a year instead of continuing his employment in his father's glass factory. [However, Peggy's psychology professor Stillman Dane turns up, and wins and weds Peggy. And so four voyage to Europe instead of just three.]

Ronald Chataway, Mrs. Ronald Chataway (the only names James added).

"Master Eustace," 1871.
Spoiled and pampered Eustace Garnyer is reared by his widowed mother with the help of the narrator, a governess-companion. Eustace goes to Europe at the age of seventeen, at the urging of businessman Mr. Cope of India, who in the selfish lad's absence returns and weds the widow Mrs. Garnyer. When Eustace comes home, he raises such objections that Cope is forced to explain that he, not idolized dead Mr. Garnyer, is his father. Eustace is prevented by Cope from shooting himself, but Mrs. Garnyer dies anyway of a broken heart.

Cope, Eustace Garnyer, Henry Garnyer, Mrs. Henry Garnyer, Hauff.

"Maud-Evelyn," 1900.
Lady Emma, the narrator, recalls both Lavinia's rejection long ago of Marmaduke and also later circumstances in his life. After a trip to Switzerland, he hoped for a moderate position in his uncle's business in England; but in Switzerland he met Mr. and Mrs. Dedrick, and began to travel with them. Back in England, Marmaduke explains matters to Lady Emma and also to Lavinia. It seems that the Dedricks' daughter Maud-Evelyn died at fourteen years of age, and the parents have been going to mediums to communicate with her spirit.

They adopt Marmaduke, who gradually imagines with them a past life shared with them and especially with Maud-Evelyn. He comes to believe that the girl was much older when she died, in fact was married to him before dying. From time to time Lavinia sees him and begins to concur in his fanciful story. The Dedricks die and bequeath everything to their "son-in-law" Marmaduke; he dies three years later, tended by the curiously sympathetic Lavinia, and leaves his inherited effects to her. Soon Lady Emma is to see them.

Maud-Evelyn Dedrick, Dedrick, Mrs. Dedrick, Mrs. Jex, Lady Emma, Lavinia, Marmaduke.

"The Middle Years," 1893.

Novelist Dencombe, convalescing at Bournemouth, fingers while sitting near the water his latest book *The Middle Years* when suddenly Dr. Hugh leaves two women companions to talk with him about it. Dencombe quickly grows confused and faints. By the time he revives in his room, Dr. Hugh has recognized him and is trying to comfort him professionally. Dencombe learns that Dr. Hugh is traveling with a rich, sick countess and her companion Miss Vernham. But soon he is paying exclusive attention to Dencombe, whose works he reveres. Miss Vernham comes and brutally demands that Dencombe stop monopolizing Dr. Hugh, who she says thus stands to lose much from the countess. In a few days Dencombe has a fatal relapse, attended by Dr. Hugh, who cheerfully tells him that the countess meanwhile has died, leaving him nothing.

Dencombe, Dr. Hugh, Miss Vernham.

"Miss Gunton of Poughkeepsie," 1900.

Lady Champer is sympathetic with the Prince on learning that rich and indulged young Lily Gunton of Poughkeepsie is evidently leading this Italian scion on. Miss Gunton wants the Prince's mother to deviate from European tradition and write to invite her into the family. Lily travels from Rome to Paris to London, and, still encouraging the Prince, finally to New York. He tells Lady Champer that his mother will probably break down and write but will assuredly hate him afterward. But by the time the letter comes, Lily has decided to refuse, becoming engaged instead to Adam P. Bransby, with whose family she returned from London. The Prince learns that Lily's grandfather has just died leaving a fortune to the girl. Her expected money probably attracted him. However, he tells Lady Champer that he really loved her, his mother is disgraced socially, and Lily in all likelihood wanted mainly to humble a European family.

Adam P. Bransby, Mrs. Bransby, Miss Bransby, Miss Bransby, Brine, Mrs. Brine, Lady Champer, Donna Claudia, Lily Gunton, Gunton.

"The Modern Warning," 1888.

Mrs. Grice and her daughter Agatha greet the arrival of their son and brother Macarthy Grice at Cadenabbia, by Lake Como. He quickly takes his uncomplaining sister away from a suitor, conservative Britisher Sir Rufus Chasemore. Six years later, however, the pair has been wed two years, and Agatha's mother has been dead three. The couple comes to New York; while Agatha remains with her brother, Sir Rufus sets out alone to see America. When Agatha discovers that he is writing a book critical of the United States, she persuades him to abandon it but then, thinking that his acquiescence is too magnanimous, relents. Later, as Macarthy arrives at their home in London to visit the Chasemores, servants rush out shouting that Agatha has committed suicide. Sir Rufus blames Macarthy, whom — he argues — Agatha always feared; Macarthy in turn blames Sir Rufus and his critical British ways.

Lady Bolitho, Sir Rufus Chasemore, Mrs. Eugene, Lady Laura Fitzgibbon, Agatha Grice (Lady Chasemore), Macarthy Grice, Mrs. Grice, Mrs. Long, Mrs. Redwood, Mrs. Ripley.

"Mora Montravers," 1909.

Mora Montravers, the daughter of Jane Traffle's dead half-sister, has lived with Mrs. Traffle and her husband Sidney until now, when the young lady, aged twenty-one, leaves them to join an arty group including painter Walter Puddick, in whose studio she begins innocently to lodge. To protect the girl's reputation, prim Jane meddlingly offers Mora £450 per annum if she will marry Puddick. The two wed, and Jane must pay up; then, however, Mora promptly leaves Puddick. Traffle wistfully admires Mora and her jaunty independence. He returns home from a chance encounter with her in an art gallery to learn that Puddick, a decent enough young fellow, has just charmed Jane into honorably continuing the promised allowance, which Mora has made over to him before taking up with Sir Bruce Bagley.

Sir Bruce Bagley, Malcolm Montravers, Mrs. Malcolm Montravers, Mora Montravers, Walter Puddick, Sidney Traffle, Mrs. Sidney (Jane) Traffle.

"A Most Extraordinary Case," 1868.

Grievously sick Union Army Colonel Ferdinand Mason is taken from a New York hotel by his aunt Mrs. Maria Mason to her home up the Hudson River. He convalesces there and falls in love with her niece Caroline Hofmann, who, however, becomes engaged to Dr. Horace Knight, by chance an army acquaintance of Mason's. The news forces premature gaiety upon Mason, who, worn out by a relapse following a drive with Miss Hofmann, suddenly dies, leaving a sum of money to Dr. Knight.

William Bowles, Mrs. Bradshaw, Dr. Gregory, Caroline Hofmann, Dr. Horace Knight, Mrs. Knight, Augustus Mason, Mrs. Augustus (Maria) Mason, Colonel Ferdinand Mason, Miss Masters, Michael, Dr. Middlemas, Mrs. Middlemas, Edith Stapleton, George Stapleton, Stapleton, Thomas.

"Mrs. Medwin," 1901.

Miss Mamie Cutter argues with her sponging but attractive half-brother Scott Homer, until he tells her that he can help her in her curious job of getting fallen persons back into British society for a fee. Promising to return, he then leaves. Mrs. Medwin, a would-be socialite now out of favor, presents herself and learns from Mamie that Lady Wantridge may possibly approve of her readmittance into society. Mamie explains her embarrassment at again being bothered by her half-brother.

They leave; and Scott returns, forcing his way past the timid maid and into the drawing-room, where he proceeds to take a nap. When Mamie returns, she is aghast upon being told that Lady Wantridge has been there and has seen Scott, who correctly evaluates the formidable woman. The following morning, as Scott has predicted, Lady Wantridge comes back and refuses to sanction Mrs. Medwin's return to proper society. The lady is sympathetic, even offering to pay Mrs. Medwin's commission to Mamie, who can thus be rid of the woman. Then Scott enters and talks familiarly with both Mamie and Lady Wantridge. Mamie escorts the lady downstairs and then with a sudden inspiration hints that Scott is offensive and trails an evil past. All of this intrigues Lady Wantridge, who evidently is smitten by Scott's charms; Mamie follows up this revelation by saying that Scott will attend Lady Wantridge's party at Catchmore only if Mrs. Medwin is also invited. Shortly thereafter the lady capitulates, and Mrs. Medwin soon sends Mamie a check from Catchmore.

Lady Bellhouse, Lord Considine, Mamie Cutter, Lady Edward, Scott Homer, Mrs. Medwin, Mrs. Pouncer, Mrs. Short Stokes, Lady Wantridge.

"Mrs. Temperly," 1887.
When Raymond Bestwick asks his cousin Mrs. Maria Temperly in New York if he may marry her daughter Dora, aged seventeen, she explains that she is taking Dora with her younger sisters Effie and Tishy to Paris — to find them rich husbands, it may be deduced. Following them five years later, Bestwick finds Dora mutely loyal to her mother. Her sisters must marry well before she will be allowed to wed below their high aim. Dora is thus sacrificing herself, since Tishy remains of stunted growth. Bestwick's probation continues.

Raymond Bestwick, Mlle. Bourd, Marquise de Brives, Eleonore, Gregorini, Parminter, Mrs. Parminter, Dora Temperly, Effie Temperly, Mrs. Maria Temperly, Tishy Temperly, Susan Winkle.

"My Friend Bingham," 1867.
The narrator Charles has a rich young friend named George

Bingham. The two men go to the seaside resort town of B—.
Hunting on the beach, Bingham accidentally shoots and kills
the little son of widowed Mrs. Lucy Hicks. Charles and Bingham
do what they can for the poor woman, and Bingham stays on
in the town while Charles returns to his work in the city. Mrs.
Hicks is living with a relative named Miss Margaret Horner,
who is outraged that Mrs. Hicks should receive Bingham and
hence turns her out. So she goes back to the city with Bingham
and sets up lodgings there. After some six months, Mrs. Hicks
and Bingham marry; she becomes a devoted wife, he a somewhat complacent husband.

George Bingham, Rev. Mr. Bland, Charles, Mrs. Lucy
Hicks, Hicks, Margaret Horner.

"A New England Winter," 1884.

Florimond Daintry returns from Paris art study to spend
a few months in Boston with his widowed mother Susan
Daintry, who asks her sister-in-law Miss Lucretia Daintry to
invite Rachel Torrance up from Brooklyn in order to brighten
Florimond's winter. Lucretia laughingly refuses but then asks
her friend Pauline Mesh to invite Miss Torrance, who is related
to her husband Donald Mesh. Florimond arrives and soon
criticizes his sister Joanna Merriman for being submerged by
her six children. He visits his Aunt Lucretia, who regards him
as affected and conceited, and who urges him to call upon
Mrs. Mesh and meet her guest Miss Torrance. Aunt Lucretia
hopes that sensible Rachel will attract and then jilt him; but
when he goes to the Mesh home — as Rachel later confides to
Lucretia — he only bores the girl while he dangerously intrigues
Mrs. Mesh. Miss Torrance's removal to Lucretia's home annoys
Florimond's mother until she learns that her son is still calling
at the Mesh house, obviously to see Pauline. Mrs. Daintry is
relieved when she can lure her son Florimond away — perhaps
by fibbing about his sister Joanna — and later bid him god-
speed back to Paris.

Beatrice, Florimond Daintry, Lucretia Daintry, Mrs. Susan
Daintry, Arthur Merriman, Mrs. Arthur (Joanna Daintry)
Merriman, Donald Mesh, Mrs. Donald (Pauline) Mesh,
Rosalie, Rachel Torrance, Mrs. Torrance.

"The Next Time," 1895.

Successful Mrs. Jane Highmore asks the critic-narrator to review her latest potboiler novel favorably. She is the sister of Maud Stannace, whom the narrator once loved but who married Ray Limbert, a brilliant but unpopular novelist. Once long ago, Ray lost a position as a London correspondent because he wrote a thoughtful rather than a chatty review of the narrator's first volume of criticism. Loss of the job delayed his marriage, which, however, finally took place. Now his household includes Maud, three babies, and his mother-in-law. But Ray has achieved only perfection in his fiction, never popular success with it. One night the narrator meets him and learns that he is to edit a distinguished literary magazine which cares little for mere popularity. Soon, however, he is released because his fiction serialized in it is simply too fine for it. Next, Ray plans a novel which will be popular, but it too turns out to be financially unrewarding if artistically superb. Dying now and ordered to Egypt, Ray instead produces yet another unselling masterpiece. He had to write as he did, and so did the shallow but popular Mrs. Highmore.

> Bousefield, Dr. Cecil Highmore, Mrs. Cecil (Jane) Highmore, Ray Limbert, Mrs. Ray (Maud Stannace) Limbert, Minnie Meadows, Pat Moyle, Stannace, Stannace, Mrs. Stannace.

"Nona Vincent," 1892.

Allan Wayworth, aided and encouraged in London by wealthy Mrs. Alsager, to whom he is devoted, is able to put his play *Nona Vincent* on stage, with Violet Grey in the title role. Both women love Allan but Mrs. Alsager is married. The actress is ineffective on stage during the first performance, although the play itself is well received. Napping uneasily late the next afternoon, Allan has a dream in which Nona Vincent appears in her own nature, not that of either Violet the actress or Mrs. Alsager the inspiration, and tells him, "I live." That night Violet is perfect in her role. At supper in her absent aunt's home, she tells Allan that Mrs. Alsager visited her late that afternoon and by her example inspired the girl to play her role differently and in conformity with Allan's ideas. Mrs.

Alsager returns to Torquay to visit a sick friend; Allan marries Violet.

> Alsager, Mrs. Alsager, Beaumont, Mrs. Beaumont, Violet Grey, Loder, Mrs. Mostyn, Nona Vincent, Allan Wayworth, Wayworth, Mrs. Wayworth, Miss Wayworth, Miss Wayworth.

"Osborne's Revenge," 1868.

Presumably because of being jilted by Henrietta Congreve, Robert Graham has killed himself in St. Paul. His friend Philip Osborne determines upon revenge but learns from Major Dodd, cousin of a friend of Miss Congreve, that the girl was innocent of any flirtatious wrongdoing.

> Mrs. Carpenter, Henrietta Congreve, Mrs. Maria Dodd, Major Dodd, Robert Graham, Holland, Jane, Miss Latimer, Philip Osborne, Rev. Mr. Stone, Angelica Thompson, Mrs. Anna Wilkes, Tom Wilkes.

The Other House, 1896.

Mrs. Beever of Wilverley goes over to the nearby other house, Bounds, with her guest Jean Martle in response to a luncheon invitation; but she learns that the mistress of Bounds, Julia Bream, who has just had a baby daughter Effie, is sick and is attended by Dr. Ramage. So she sends Jean home to Wilverley, stays herself, and talks with Rose Armiger, a former school friend of Julia, who now begs her husband Tony Bream to promise never to remarry if she should die. It seems that Julia was miserably unhappy as a step-child and wants her daughter to avoid a similar fate. Rose urges Tony to promise, but on condition that Effie lives. Meanwhile Rose's fiance Denis Vidal appears, soon announcing that he must go on business to China for some years; Rose refuses to marry him yet, and they part in silence. Four years later — Julia is dead, Rose apparently is in love with Tony, Vidal is returning, and Tony cares too much for Jean to suit Mrs. Beever, since she wants Jean for her son Paul. Soon Rose is lecturing Paul on how to woo Jean. When Tony comes over to Wilverley, Jean goes back to the other house for little Effie, whose birthday it is, without the accompaniment of Paul, though Rose suggests it. Urged by Rose, Tony dutifully suggests that Jean marry Paul, but the girl pensively declines. In disappointment at her son's rejection, Mrs. Beever harshly tells Tony that he loves Jean. Rose professes loyalty to Effie and suspicion of Jean's sincerity. When Vidal enters, Rose apologizes to him in front of Tony for her shabby conduct four years earlier. Alone, Rose alerts Vidal to be wary of Jean with Effie. Jean's joy at hearing that Rose is engaged to Vidal confirms Rose's worst fear, that Jean herself loves Tony. Having disputed with Jean, Rose takes Effie back to the other house to rest. Later Dr. Ramage enters to report that Effie is drowned. After much confusion, it is revealed that Rose drowned the little girl, that Dr. Ramage will convert the murder to fatal illness, that Tony must stop feeling obliged to shield anyone, and that Vidal will claim Rose and take her away. Tony urges Jean to discard all desire for revenge upon Rose, who will be terribly punished in knowing that her act of murder only freed Tony for another. Rose enters to make final explanations to sympathetic Paul, who would aid her; but she chooses Vidal.

Rose Armiger, Paul Beever, Mrs. Paul (Kate) Beever, Paul Beever, Anthony "Tony" Bream, Mrs. Anthony (Julia Grantham) Bream, Effie Bream, Paul Bream, Mrs. Gorham, Mrs. Grantham, Manning, Marsh, Mrs. Marsh, Jean Martle, Martle, Dr. Robert Ramage, Mrs. Robert Ramage, Denis Vidal, Walker.

The Outcry, 1911.
Lord Theign has many art treasures at Dedborough Place. He also has two daughters. They are widowed Kitty Imber, deeply in debt and hoping for aid from Theign, and lovely young Lady Grace, wanted by Lord John, son of the Duchess to whom gambling Kitty owes thousands of pounds. If Theign is to rescue Kitty, he must persuade Grace to marry Lord John and promise her a sizable inheritance (the Duchess in gratitude would then cancel Kitty's debt). To do so, Theign invites rich Breckenridge Bender, an avid and aggressive art collector from America, to Dedborough to bid on his "Duchess of Waterbridge" by Sir Joshua Reynolds. Lady Sandgate, a close friend of the widower Theign, is also an object of Bender's greed, since she has a portrait by Sir Thomas Lawrence of

her great-grandmother. Meanwhile the young art critic Hugh Crimble, whom Grace prefers to Lord John, has come at her invitation to see the Dedborough collection of paintings, among which is included a supposed Moretto. Bender spurns the Moretto when offered it in place of the Reynolds which he wants, until he gets wind of Crimble's theory that it is really a rare and hitherto-unsuspected painting by Mantovano. In a family argument which now transpires, Theign is tempted to sell the painting, Grace wants him to keep it through loyalty to England, Lord John wants Grace, and Grace sides with Crimble, whom she urges to authenticate the "Mantovano." The newspapers raise an outcry against Bender, who is only pleased by the publicity. Out of favor now with her mettlesome father, Grace meets Hugh at Lady Sandgate's London home. One day he reports that art authority Pappendick denies that Mantovano is the painter of the so-called Moretto. Because of the outcry, Theign begins both to dislike the notion of selling his painting out of England and also to suspect Lord John of being mercenary. Coming to Lady Sandgate's home armed with his check-book, Bender fails to meet Theign, who has just left for Kitty's. A little later he is making out a check for Lady Sandgate's Lawrence when Theign returns with the premature but ultimately true report, that he is giving his Moretto to the National Gallery, for which the Prince himself is coming to congratulate him for his beneficent patriotism. Hugh then arrives with superior art authority Bardi's statement that the Moretto is indeed a Mantovano. All leave but Theign and Lady Sandgate; he spies Bender's check and tears it up, challenging its would-be recipient to match his generosity by giving her Lawrence to the Gallery. Her agreeing unites the two.

   Banks, Bardi, Breckenridge Bender, Hugh Crimble, Gotch, Lady Grace, Lady Kitty Imber, Lord John, Lady Lappington, Mackintosh, Mantovano, Pappendick, Penniman, Mrs. Penniman, Lady Amy Sandgate, Lord Theign, Duchess of Waterbridge.

"Owen Wingrave," 1892.
   Owen Wingrave tells his preparatory school superintendent Spencer Coyle that he does not intend to follow family wishes and train further for a military career. Coyle recalls Wingrave

family circumstances: Owen's grandfather Sir Philip Wingrave was an illustrious soldier and is now erect and tough at eighty years of age; Owen's father was killed in an Afghan raid; and Owen now has an imbecile older brother Philip and a maiden aunt Jane Wingrave, whose companion Mrs. Julian is the sister of Captain Hume-Walker, once engaged to Jane but broken with and sent to a military death in India. Coyle confers with Jane and meets Mrs. Julian's impertinent young daughter Kate, who loves Owen but doubts and taunts him. The young man reports home when ordered, but the entire family fails to press him into reconsidering his decision. A week later Coyle and his wife go to the Wingrave country estate of Paramore for dinner and an overnight stay. Coyle begins to admire oppressed and sincere Owen. Kate refuses to believe that Owen is brave enough to spend a night in a room supposedly haunted by the ghost of a Wingrave killed by a remote ancestor; insisting that he spent the previous night there, Owen does so again. At dawn he is found dead in the haunted room.

Spencer Coyle, Mrs. Spencer Coyle, Captain Hume-Walker, Mrs. Julian, Kate Julian, Lechmere, Jane Wingrave, Owen Wingrave, Owen Wingrave, Sir Philip Wingrave, Philip Wingrave, Colonel Wingrave, Wingrave.

"Pandora," 1884.

Aboard ship from Germany and Southampton to New York, Count Otto Vogelstein sees the Days, an American family, and talks to Pandora Day, the older daughter. Warned by Mrs. Dangerfield of the vulgarity of the Days and prejudiced against American girls in general by reading "Daisy Miller," Vogelstein fears that he will not like his assignment at the German legation in Washington. Eighteen months later Vogelstein again sees Miss Day, this time at a party given by the fashionable Bonnycastles which the President attends. Vogelstein watches Pandora gaily ask the President to give her friend D. F. Bellamy of Utica a foreign assignment. Through Mrs. Steuben, Pandora's social sponsor in Washington, Vogelstein renews his acquaintance with the girl at a Mount Vernon picnic. She is critical of his conduct aboard ship and in other ways cools his ardor. Later it is revealed that Bellamy is to be minister to Holland and that he and Pandora are to be married.

D. F. Bellamy, Alfred Bonnycastle, Mrs. Alfred Bonnycastle, Mrs. Dangerfield, Pandora Day, P. W. Day, Mrs. P. W. Day, Day, Miss Day, Lansing, Mrs. Runkle, Commodore Steuben, Mrs. Steuben, Count Otto Vogelstein.

"The Papers," 1903.

Howard Bight, a competent reporter, and Maud Blandy, who is less able in that line of work, talk together about normally publicity-mad Sir A. B. C. Beadel-Muffet, K. C. B., M. P., whom Howard says he has driven into disappearance and perhaps even suicide. It seems that Beadel-Muffet's fiancee Mrs. Chorner professes to loathe publicity and has been distressed by seeing his name frequently in the tabloids. Meanwhile Maud's friend Mortimer Marshal, an inept playwright, desires publicity. So, to josh him, Howard suggests that he produce some news concerning Beadel-Muffet, who a little later is announced as a suicide in Frankfort. Howard is aghast and Maud remorseful. Yet Howard continues to twit Mortimer, with whom Maud rather sympathizes. Suddenly it is announced that Beadel-Muffet is very much alive: the suicide rumor merely created more publicity. Having valuable notes from an interview with Mrs. Chorner, tactful Maud is happy that she did not write them up for publication, because it might hurt the woman's chances with Beadel-Muffet. Howard promised to produce Beadel-Muffet after his disappearance and before his reported suicide; Maud promised to marry Howard if he could do so. But the man's return baffles clever Howard, who now determines to quit journalism, to the delight of Maud, who has been further disillusioned by Mrs. Chorner's suppressed but now obvious desire for publicity herself.

Sir A. B. C. Beadel-Muffet, K. C. B., M. P., Lady Beadel-Muffet, Miss Miranda Beadel-Muffet, Miss Beadel-Muffet, Miss Beadel-Muffet, Beatrice Beaumont, Howard Bight, Maud Blandy, Mrs. Chorner, Guy Devereux, Mortimer Marshal, Lady Wispers, Lord Wispers.

"A Passionate Pilgrim," 1871.

The American narrator, arriving in London from Italy, meets sick Clement Searle, who is discouraged because his lawyer has failed to substantiate his claim to a Middleshire estate now owned by Richard Searle, a distant relative of Clement's. Visiting the estate, Clement and the narrator meet first Miss Searle, who is strange and supports Clement's claim, and then her suspicious brother Richard, who tells them unpleasant anecdotes which upset worsening Clement. The narrator and Clement proceed to Oxford, where dying Clement aids a fallen gentleman in his plans to go to America. Clement sends for Miss Searle, who comes in and announces that her brother has been fatally thrown from a horse. Clement soon dies and, mourned for a time by Miss Searle, is buried in England.

Mme. Bosio, Mrs. Horridge, Rawson, Clement Searle, Clement Searle, Cynthia Searle, Margaret Searle, Richard Searle, Miss Searle, Abijah Simmons, Tottenham.

"Paste," 1899.

Arthur Prime's country vicar father dies, and then two weeks later so does the father's second wife, former actress Miss Bradshaw. After the second funeral, Arthur tells his cousin Charlotte Prime that she may pick out any piece of paste jewelry she wishes to take from a collection which his step-mother left. Miss Prime selects a row of pearls, which she tells Arthur seem heavy enough to be real. He scoffingly wonders where an actress could get such pearls and seems to feel that his step-mother's reputation has been insulted. Miss Prime takes the pearls back to Bleet to her position as governess. At a party there, she aids in preparing guests for some tableaux vivants when Mrs. Guy recognizes the pearls as genuine, wears them at dinner, and offers to buy them. But Charlotte returns them to Arthur, who still pretends to believe that they are paste and later writes her to say that he smashed them to destroy any implied slur upon his family. Later, however, Charlotte at another party given by her employers sees Mrs. Guy with the same pearls. The woman explains that she bought them from a dealer to whom Arthur sold them. Charlotte is sick at her cousin's treachery.

Blanche, Lady Bobby, Mrs. Guy, Gwendolyn, Arthur Prime, Charlotte Prime, Rev. Mr. Prime, Mrs. Prime.

"The Patagonia," 1888.

Before sailing on the *Patagonia* for Liverpool, the narrator calls in Boston upon Mrs. Nettlepoint, who is to be a fellow passenger. While there he meets Grace Mavis, who is also going to Liverpool, to marry her long-engaged fiance David Porterfield, an architecture student. Mrs. Nettlepoint's rakish son Jasper sees Grace and decides at the last minute to become a passenger too. Aboard ship, the narrator soon senses trouble, especially after chatting with indulgent Mrs. Nettlepoint about her son and then with blatant gossip Mrs. Peck, who says that Grace is flirting outrageously with Jasper. The gossip increases, and even the captain is annoyed. The narrator warns, puzzles, and then intimidates Jasper. Now Grace feels lonely, insulted, and yet proud still, and then one night after Ireland is sighted she quietly drops overboard. In Liverpool harbor, the narrator has the task of explaining everything to Porterfield.

Mrs. Allen, Mrs. Amber, Mrs. Gotch, Mrs. Jeremie, Jasper Nettlepoint, Mrs. Nettlepoint, Grace Mavis, Mavis, Mrs. Mavis, Mrs. Peck, David Porterfield.

"The Path of Duty," 1884.

The narrator, an American woman, explains that her casual British friend Ambrose Tester is deeply in love with Lady Margaret Vandeleur, whose husband, however, is unfortunately still alive. Tester's father Sir Edmund wanting him to marry, the dutiful son becomes engaged to Joscelind Bernardstone. But then Lord Vandeleur dies. The narrator will not encourage Tester to break his honorable engagement, which crass London society hopes he will do. Tester marches to his wedding with the smile of a condemned prisoner. He and Joscelind have two children, and Sir Edmund dies happy. The world fancies that it appreciates the virtue of Tester and Lady Vandeleur, who are often thrown together socially; but the narrator judges their superior conduct to be smug. Poor Joscelind is puzzled by her inability to make her husband happy.

Lady Emily Bernardstone, Joscelind Bernardstone, General Bernardstone, Lord Clanduffy, Ambrose Tester, Sir Edmund Tester, Francis Tester, Tester, Miss Tester, Lady Margaret Vandeleur, Lord Vandeleur.

"The Pension Beaurepas," 1879.

The narrator, an American student in Geneva, observes life in Madame Beaurepas's pension. He sympathizes with American lumberman Ruck, whose wife and daughter Sophy dominate him and spend his money on shopping sprees. The narrator hears stories of cheap traveling through Europe from Miss Aurora Church, who is with her mother and who now interests a Frenchman named Pigeonneau. The narrator defends America against the charge of crudity leveled by Miss Church's mother. Madame Beaurepas tells him that Mrs. Church is trying to marry her daughter well in Europe. The narrator talks to the girl, who says that she hates Europe and prefers American society. He neatly resists Mrs. Church's suggestion that he accompany them to Chamouni, but nonetheless he is interested in Aurora. He learns that his brother, in England briefly on business, would like to see him; at his banker's he sees Ruck and learns of his serious financial reverses. The two then bump into the Ruck women on another shopping tour looking for jewelry; and the narrator, hearing Ruck explain that they must return to New York, goes alone to the pension and checks out.

Mme. Beaurepas, Mlle. Beaurepas, Celestine, Mme. Chamousset, Aurora Church, Mrs. Church, Pasteur Galopin, Mme. Galopin, Parker, Mrs. Parker, Pigeonneau, Sophy Ruck, Ruck, Mrs. Ruck.

"The Point of View," 1882.

At sea on her way home to America, Aurora Church writes a letter about a couple of fellow-American passengers, pro-European Louis Leverett and pro-American Marcellus Cockerel, and also about British Parliamentarian Edward Antrobus. Next her mother Mrs. Church writes from New York deploring American conditions and the limited prospects for her marriageable daughter. Miss Sturdy then writes of her impressions of vigorous, curious Antrobus, guest in her brother's Newport home, and of many changes in youthful America. Antrobus in Boston writes home about American women, the school system, and manners. Leverett in Boston writes of languishing there but of liking Miss Church. Gustave Lejaune in Washington writes home to Paris in criticism of almost everything American but the well-turned ladies. Cockerel writes from Washington to his sister praising everything American and running down European institutions and manners; he says that he liked Miss Church but that she was harmed by Europe. Finally, Miss Church writes again that, not married, she must return to her mother and go west with her in search of a husband.

> Charlotte Antrobus, Edward Antrobus, M.P., Mrs. Edward (Susan) Antrobus, Gwendolyn Antrobus, Lord Bottomley, Adolfe Bouche, Aurora Church, Mrs. Church, Marcellus Cockerel, Mrs. Cooler, Mrs. Draper, Mme. Galopin, Cecile Galopin, Susan Green, Miss Gulp, Gustave Lejaune, Louis Leverett, Plummeridge, Miss [Sophy] Ruck, Ruck, Mrs. Ruck, Miss Sturdy, Harvard Tremont, Miss Whiteside.

"Poor Richard," 1867.

Unstable and unpromising Richard Maule loves his well-to-do rural neighbor Gertrude Whittaker, who likes him well enough but loves Union Army Captain Edmund Severn. Richard and Major Robert Luttrel, the local recruiting officer, untruthfully tell Captain Severn on the last night of his convalescent leave before returning to battle that Miss Whittaker is not at home. Captain Severn is despondent at her not being there, reports for duty, and is later killed. In remorse, Richard resumes his habit of drinking, catches typhoid fever, and thus leaves Luttrel as Miss Whittaker's only suitor. Richard recovers in time to warn the girl of Luttrel, who remains brash, advances in the army to the rank of general, and later marries a wealthy Philadelphian. Miss Whittaker would accept Richard, who, however, remains ashamed, sells his farm, joins the army, and after the war plans to go west. Miss Whittaker travels in Europe and resolves to remain single.

> Miss Catching, Major Robert Luttrel, Mrs. Martin, Fanny Maule, Richard Maule, Miss Pendexter, Captain Edmund Severn, Miss Van Winkel, Gertrude Whittaker.

The Portrait of a Lady, 1880-1881.

Through the kindness of her aunt Lydia Touchett, Isabel Archer goes from Albany to Europe, first to the Touchett estate of Gardencourt near London, where Isabel meets her uncle Daniel Tracy Touchett, her sick but pleasant cousin Ralph, and his friend Lord Warburton; and second, after the death of her uncle provides her with wealth, to the Continent, where she is fatally introduced in Florence to expatriate American dilettante Gilbert Osmond, a friend of Madame Serena Merle, whom Isabel first met at Gardencourt through her aunt. Isabel has rejected not only Lord Warburton's proposal of marriage but also repeated proposals from rich American Caspar Goodwood, to the dismay of her traveling American journalist friend Henrietta Stackpole. However, to Ralph's disgust, she accepts the hand of Osmond, who, it is later revealed, was led to propose to Isabel through learning from Madame Merle of her wealth and naivete. The Osmonds settle in Rome and time passes, during which Isabel loses a baby boy but becomes more and more devoted to Pansy Osmond, her husband's gentle daughter presumably by his first marriage. When Pansy is sought in marriage by Ned Rosier, a shallow but sincere young American in Europe, Isabel, although rather numbed by her husband's increasingly critical attitude toward her, supports Rosier in spite of Lord Warburton's turning up in Rome and appearing anxious to wed Pansy — much to socially ambitious Osmond's delight. Ralph, visiting in Rome, grows fatally sick and is accompanied home to England by Goodwood, after one of his periodic interviews with Isabel, and by voluble Henrietta Stackpole. When Isabel learns from her aunt that Ralph is dying, she determines to go to comfort him. Osmond, blaming Isabel for Lord Warburton's decision not to propose to Pansy after all, selfishly opposes. Isabel learns from Countess Amy Gemini, Osmond's licentious but friendly sister, that Pansy is her brother's daughter by Madame Merle, with whom he had a liaison of several years' duration. Poor Isabel goes to England and is with Ralph until the end. Goodwood meets her once more and urges her to leave Osmond. But she resists his passionate embrace and soon returns to Rome.

Archer, Isabel Archer, Bob Bantling, Sister Catherine, Annie Climber, Miss Climber, Felicia, Flora, Countess Amy Gemini, Count Gemini, Caspar Goodwood, Lady Haycock, Lord Haycock, Hilary, Sir Matthew Hope, Sister Justine,

Mrs. Edith Archer Keyes, Luce, Mrs. Luce, Edmund Ludlow, Mrs. Edmund (Lilian Archer) Ludlow, Mme. Serena Merle, Miss Mildred Molyneux, Miss Molyneux, Gilbert Osmond, Pansy Osmond, Lady Pensil, Edward "Ned" Rosier, Rossiter, Henrietta Stackpole, Daniel Tracy Touchett, Mrs. Daniel Tracy (Lydia) Touchett, Ralph Touchett, Mrs. Varian, Lord Warburton.

The Princess Casamassima, 1885-1886.

Seamstress Amanda Pynsent has adopted Hyacinth Robinson, delicate illegitimate son of a French adventuress and a British lord whom she stabbed to death. Pinnie takes the boy to prison to visit his dying mother, whose identity he later reads about in old newspapers. Years pass, and Hyacinth is now working in a book-bindery. Visiting his friends the Poupins one day, he meets revolutionary Paul Muniment; later he meets Paul's crippled sister Rosy and philanthropic Lady Aurora Langrish, who pathetically likes Paul. Hyacinth takes his girl friend, coarse, warm, fickle Millicent Henning, to the theater, where Captain Sholto, remembering him from a political argument in a cafe, introduces him to the Princess Casamassima. Soon the radiant, enigmatic Princess meets Paul, his sister, and Lady Aurora, and is satisfactorily getting into the lower social orders. But her husband the Prince turns up and is displeased by the report from her companion Madame Grandoni, who also advises Hyacinth to resist the Princess. But he cannot. At the same time he suspects Millicent of becoming involved with Sholto. Hyacinth visits the Princess at the country estate of Medley which she rents, and he stays on and on, even giving up his bookbinding job, to practical Madame Grandoni's annoyance. Now trusted by the professional anarchists, he tells the Princess that he has promised to murder any nobleman named by revolutionary leader Diedrich Hoffendahl. Returning to London, Hyacinth finds Pinnie dying, with neighbor Anastasius Vetch and Lady Aurora caring for her. She wills Hyacinth a small sum, sufficient for a vacation to Paris and Venice. The experience changes him. He would now fight for old culture, but he will not seek release from his vow. Back home, he works again but is different, is suspicious of the Princess, and tries to confide in Paul. The Princess is unable to induce Paul to have Hyacinth relieved of his duty. When Prince Casamassima returns and observes his wife and Muniment, he cuts off her income at last. Hyacinth goes to the Poupins' home, where a fellow radical delivers the fatal summons. He meets a final time with the Princess but says nothing to her of the letter. Later Paul tells her that Hyacinth is trusted since he now has his orders to shoot a nobleman. She wants to be given the assignment instead. Feeling that the Princess, Paul, Millicent, and Lady Aurora are drifting from him, and unable either to commit murder or break his promise, Hyacinth goes to his room and shoots himself.

Assunta, Baskerville, Mrs. Bowerbank, Dr. Buffery, Bunbury, Mrs. Bunbury, Prince [Gennaro] Casamassima, Princess [Christina Light] Casamassima, Mrs. Chipperfield, Crookenden, Mrs. Crookenden, Miss Crookenden, Miss Crookenden, Miss Crookenden, Miss Crookenden, Miss Crookenden, Miss Crookenden, Delancey, Mme. Grandoni, Griffin, Grugan, Millicent Henning, Mrs. Henning, Diedrich Hoffendahl, Hotchkin, Earl of Inglefield, Lady Aurora Langrish, Mrs. Major, Lady Marchant, Miss Marchant, Miss Marchant, Miss Marchant, Millington, Mrs. Millington, Paul Muniment, Rosy Muniment, Muniment, Mrs. Muniment, Eustace Poupin, Mme. Poupin, Lord Frederick Purvis, Amanda "Pinnie" Pynsent, Hyacinth Robinson, Roker, Mrs. Ruffler, Schinkel, Captain Godfrey Gerald Sholto, Tripp, Mrs. Tripp. Anastasius Vetch, Florentine Vivier, Hyacinth Vivier, Lady Eva Warmington, Lord Warmington, Withers, Lord Whiteroy.

"The Private Life," 1892.

Vacationing at a Swiss hotel is a sociable group of successful people including the polished statesman Lord Mellifont and his wife, the quiet writer Clare Vawdrey, the actress Blanche Adney and her violinist husband Vincent Adney, and the writer-narrator. After dinner Vawdrey is to read from his new play, designed for Blanche; when he cannot find it, Lord Mellifont bridges the awkward gap with his windy eloquence. At the end of the evening the narrator, seeing Blanche and Vawdrey talking on the terrace, goes as requested to Vawdrey's room to pick up the play manuscript and eerily sees Vawdrey's alternate identity at his desk writing. The next evening the narrator discusses the matter with Blanche, and they conclude that Vawdrey has a dual personality; further, they reason that Lord Mellifont, with whom Blanche has taken Alpine walks, has no private life or identity — he is nothing but a public impression. It seems that once when Blanche left Lord Mellifont to return to the hotel, he simply disappeared until her seeking him caused him to spring up again. Learning next that Vawdrey has taken a walk outside, Blanche goes to his room and gratefully encounters his alter ego. Meanwhile the narrator goes toward Lord Mellifont's room to obtain his signature on a sketch; but when he meets embarrassed Lady Mellifont at the room door, he senses that she wishes him not to expose her husband's emptiness. Blanche later tells the narrator that the ghostly Vawdrey will write her play.

Vincent Adney, Mrs. Vincent (Blanche) Adney, Chafer, Lady Mellifont, Lord Mellifont, Lady Ringrose, Clarence "Clare" Vawdrey.

"A Problem," 1868.
David and Emma, young newlyweds, are shaken by an old Indian woman's prophecy that their first child will be a daughter and will die. When their baby turns out to be a girl who gets sick but then recovers, the parents recall earlier predictions, that they will marry twice. This supposed fact estranges them. Emma suddenly writes David that their little daughter has died. Attending the funeral, the unhappy parents are reconciled and in a sense remarry under the minister's benedictory hand.

Rev. Mr. Clark, David, Emma, Julia, Magawisca.

"Professor Fargo," 1874.
Delayed in the New England village of P—, the narrator goes to an entertainment put on by a spiritualist named Professor Fargo, a mathematician named Colonel Gifford, and the Colonel's deaf-mute daughter who has a talent for rapid arithmetical calculation. Later, in New York, the narrator sees Professor Fargo hypnotize Miss Gifford into leaving her father for him. Poor Colonel Gifford goes insane.

Professor Fargo, Colonel Gifford, Miss Gifford.

"The Pupil," 1891.

Pemberton, an impoverished American student from Oxford, obtains at Nice a position with a wandering American family named Moreen, to be the tutor of their precocious, sickly son Morgan, aged eleven. He soon becomes attached to the boy although he increasingly dislikes the parents, the toadying older son Ulick, and the husband-seeking daughters Paula and Amy. A year passes, and the group has moved to Switzerland, Florence, and Paris. Pemberton has not been paid, but he stays on through friendship with his ashamed pupil. Then Pemberton demands and receives a small sum. Back in Nice, Morgan, now fourteen, breaks out during a lesson one day with the advice that Pemberton should abandon the whole shabby family. Instead, now refusing pay, he puts his relationship with the parents on a franker footing, though he feels emotionally blackmailed to be doing so; he fears that if he leaves Morgan, the boy will suffer. But Morgan says that this is precisely what his shoddy parents are counting on and voices his preference for going away with his tutor. Pemberton is honorable in not exposing the boy's parents and promises to take any suitable job for money in the hope that he can later call Morgan to him. In Venice next and noting that the Moreen family fortunes are worsening, Pemberton accepts the offer of a tutoring job in England; soon, however, he returns to Morgan, now fifteen, upon receipt of a telegram that the youth is sick in Paris. At the end of a long winter walk, the two return to find the family ousted from the hotel; when the parents lugubriously agree that Pemberton can now take Morgan away with him, Pemberton hesitates and Morgan dies of a heart attack.

Mrs. Clancy, Lady Dorrington, Lord Dorrington, Granger, Amy Moreen, Morgan Moreen, Paula Moreen, Ulick Moreen, Moreen, Mrs. Moreen, Pemberton, Lord Verschoyle, Zenobie.

"The Real Right Thing," 1899.

Author Ashton Doyne's widow offers journalist George Withermore the chance to write Doyne's biography. Soon he is working away in the dead man's own study, and he senses the helpful ghost of Doyne aiding him in locating files and finding papers. However, papers later seem to be missing and the ghost seems to be warning Withermore away. One evening he actually sees an immense dim presence urging him to be off. He finally tells Mrs. Doyne that he is quitting but that she need not. Evidently she too sees the ghost at the study threshold, for she gives up as well.

Ashton Doyne, Mrs. Ashton Doyne, George Withermore.

"The Real Thing," 1892.

The painter-narrator agrees to hire as models Major and Mrs. Monarch, handsome, sociable, and destitute. But he soon finds these real things too inflexible to help him in his trial illustrations for a de luxe edition of Philip Vincent's works. So he relies more and more on Cockney model Miss Churm and, later, on a lithe Italian named Oronte, whose poses are eloquent. The real thing lacks plasticity. The narrator is harshly warned to this effect by his critical friend Jack Hawley. The impoverished Monarchs mutely ask to be retained as his servants; but, unwilling to assent to this demeaning, the narrator pays them liberally and they leave.

Artemisia, Miss Churm, Jack Hawley, Major Monarch, Mrs. Monarch, Oronte, Rutland Ramsey, Claude Rivet, Philip Vincent.

The Reverberator, 1888.

George Flack, who works in Paris for an American newspaper *The Reverberator*, talks in a hotel with his American friends rich old Whitney Dosson, his plain daughter Fidelia, and her pretty sister Francina. Flack convinces Francie that she should sit for a portrait to the American painter Charles Waterlow. With him in his studio one day is Gaston Probert, French born but of an American family from Carolina. He quickly falls in love with Francie, to whom Flack unsuccessfully proposes marriage. Gaston, more in love soon, introduces to Francie one of his Frenchified sisters, Suzanne de Brecourt, who disapprovingly says that the Probert family will never accept her. Nonetheless, Gaston asks Mr. Dosson, who is receptive and calm. The Parisian Proberts meet the Dossons in their hotel; Gaston's rigid father begins to accept the idea of the marriage. Gaston goes to America to check into some family property at about the time Flack returns from America to Paris. Flack takes Francie for an innocent drive, of which another of Gaston's sisters, Marguerite de Cliche, violently disapproves. Suddenly *The Reverberator* prints horrible but true stories about the Proberts; when Suzanne queries her, Francie admits telling Flack various items of family gossip which Gaston confided in her. A noisy family scene follows, with Francie simply not seeing the enormity of her conduct and with Suzanne surprisingly aiding the callow girl. Gaston returns from America and at first seems outraged. Flack professes innocence of any wrongdoing. To Gaston, Francie says that she will not put any blame upon Flack. After advice from the painter Waterlow, Gaston determines to follow his heart, support his fiancee, and quietly accept the predictable denunciation of his family.

Alphonse de Brecourt, Mme. Alphonse (Suzanne Probert) de Brecourt, Mme. de Brives, Carolus, Marquis Maxime de Cliche, Mme. Maxime (Marguerite Probert) de Cliche, Courageau, Blanche de Douves, Raoul de Douves, Mme. Raoul (Jeanne Probert) de Douves, M. de Douves, Fidelia "Delia" Dosson, Francina "Francie" Dosson, Whitney Dosson, Durand, George P. Flack, Galignani, M. de Grospre, D. Jackson Hodge, Mme. de Marignac, Munster, Mme. d'Outreville, Alphonse Probert, Gaston Probert, Probert, Probert, Mme. Probert, Cora Rosenheim, D. S. Rosenheim, Mrs. D. S. Rosenheim, Samuel Rosenheim, Mlle. de Saintonge, R. P. Scudamore, Florine (Dorine?) Topping, Lady Trantum, Lord Trantum, Mme. Leonie de Villepreux, Charles Waterlow.

Roderick Hudson, 1875.

Before returning to Europe, wealthy Rowland Mallet visits his Northampton cousin Cecilia, who introduces him to a talented young sculptor Roderick Hudson. Mallet offers to finance him during a long residence in Rome. Before leaving, the sculptor introduces his patron to his widowed mother Sarah Hudson and to his fiancee Mary Garland. Once the two men are in Rome, Hudson displays quickness at learning and even genius in his studio, but also emotional instability and fatal egocentricity. He goes off to Baden-Baden and foolishly gambles; worse, he breaks with a rich patron Mr. Leavenworth, who has ordered an expensive statue; worst, he cannot resist the beauty of enigmatic Christina Light, whom Mallet urges to stay away from Hudson and whose mercenary mother by revealing the daughter's illegitimacy forces her to marry rich Prince Casamassima of Naples. Mallet then takes the sculptor, together with his mother and his fiancee — who have by this time joined the group in Rome — with him to Florence; but Hudson's will to work does not revive, and the group goes on to Switzerland. Here Hudson is completely discouraged by seeing Christina, now the Princess Casamassima, with her husband at Interlaken and also by learning from the now angered Mallet that he has long unselfishly adored Miss Garland from afar. Hudson wanders dejectedly into an Alpine storm. The following morning Mallet, aided by a friendly American painter named Sam Singleton, finds the body of the sculptor, who has fallen or jumped to his death.

Assunta, Bessie, Augusta Blanchard, Prince Gennaro Casamassima, Cecilia, Mary Garland, Cavaliere Giuseppe Giacosa, Gloriani, Mme. Gloriani, Mme. Grandoni, Roderick Hudson, Mrs. Sarah Hudson, Leavenworth, Christina Light, Mrs. Light, Jonas Mallet, Mrs. Jonas Mallet, Rowland Mallet, Maddalena, Sam Singleton, Schafgans, Barnaby Striker, Miss Striker, Rev. Mr. Whitefoot.

"The Romance of Certain Old Clothes," 1868.

Mrs. Willoughby's son Bernard returns from Oxford University to Massachusetts, bringing with him a British friend Arthur Lloyd. Lloyd marries Bernard's sister Perdita, making the other sister, Rosalind, jealous. Perdita dies in giving birth to a daughter, whom Rosalind, aided by her mother, cares for while Lloyd visits in England. Upon his return, he marries Rosalind. She talks him into giving her the key to dead Perdita's chest of wedding clothes, which he has sacredly promised to keep locked up for his daughter. Lloyd later finds his wife in the attic dead and with two claw-like wounds inflicted by ghostly hands.

Arthur Lloyd, Mrs. Arthur (Perdita Willoughby) Lloyd,

Mrs. Arthur (Rosalind Willoughby) Lloyd, Miss Lloyd, Bernard Willoughby, Mrs. Bernard Willoughby, Mrs. Bernard Willoughby, Perdita Willoughby.

"Rose-Agathe," 1878.

Sanguinetti, a collector of bric-a-brac, is late in arriving to dine with the narrator because, as he can see from his balcony, his guest looked for a while into Anatole the hairdresser's shop at a pretty head there. The narrator jokes with his friend, who says that he might pick up what he was admiring. The narrator thinks that the object of his desire is Mme. Anatole; but when Sanguinetti buys "Rose-Agathe," the creature turns out to be Anatole's attractive dummy.

Anatole, Mme. Anatole, Clementine, Rose-Agathe, Sanguinetti.

"A Round of Visits," 1910.

Swindled by his absconding distant cousin Phil Bloodgood, Mark Monteith returns from Europe to New York in the winter, and promptly catches cold. Recovering by the following Sunday, he meets Mrs. Folliott, who has also lost money through Bloodgood's trickery and who speaks viciously of the swindler. Mark has lunch with her and thereby meets the sister-in-law of his old, unpleasant acquaintance Newton Winch, recently widowed. This woman asks Mark to visit Newton, who is depressed and sick, she explains. First Mark visits Florence Ash, who regales him with the story of her impossible husband. Beginning to feel that he is fated to hear the woes of others, he reluctantly goes on to Newton, only to find him sensitive and charming now, and even able to guess at Mark's worry over Phil. Mark defends the swindler, saying that he must be in remorseful misery after betraying his friends. Newton is surprised and shortly thereafter agitated, asking restless Mark to be seated. Suspecting Newton of not wanting him to see something nearby, Mark glances about and notices a gun under a chair and rug-edge. Newton wildly confesses his need for sympathy, since he is another Phil Bloodgood and is involved in larceny. He thanks Mark for helping him through the time of waiting for the authorities. The police ring his doorbell, and as Mark lets them in and speaks briefly to them, they hear the shot which ends poor Newton's life. The police criticize Mark, who admits his probable responsibility.

Bob Ash, Mrs. Bob (Florence) Ash, Phil Bloodgood, Mrs. Folliott, Lottie, Mark P. Monteith, Tim' Slater, Newton Winch, Mrs. Newton Winch.

The Sacred Fount, 1901.

On the train platform at Newmarch near London, the narrator sees Gilbert Long, who seems more suave and handsome, and Grace Brissenden, who though ten years older than her husband Guy Brissenden seems to be growing younger. Mrs. Briss tells the narrator that Long has been made wiser by Lady John, who is due with Briss at Newmarch on the next train. Before dinner, the narrator sees Briss but hardly recognizes the aging man. Long reluctantly and almost angrily admits that Briss seems older. The narrator impresses his painter friend Ford Obert by theorizing that Mrs. Briss grows younger by damagingly tapping her husband's "sacred fount." The next morning the narrator says that Lady John cannot be Long's source of vitality since she does not appear depleted, the way Briss does because of Mrs. Briss. Canceling other possibilities, Mrs. Briss suggests Mrs. May Server as Long's fount. The narrator seems shocked at perhaps compromising May, but Mrs. Briss will try to find out more. The narrator takes May from Mrs. Briss and goes with her to a picture gallery, where they find Long intelligently discoursing on art to Obert. They seek resemblances in real life about them to the face of a man and to his mask in one of the portraits. Later when Obert speaks critically of May, the narrator, still feeling responsible, defends her and is soon happy to hear Obert theorizing on May's possible source of vitality from another's fount. Then Obert suddenly tires of the search for supposedly shriveled founts. When Mrs. Briss gossips about May as Long's likely fount, the narrator tries to get her to abandon such a theory and even lets Mrs. Briss abuse him a bit. He goes so far as to suggest that May is perhaps after Briss because Mrs. Briss ignores him so much. But Mrs. Briss counters by saying that May might use Briss as a means of keeping people from thinking that she wants Long. The narrator now nervously tries

to avoid his friends for the afternoon. But taking a walk, he
happens to see Lady John and Briss, and immediately thinks
that Lady John, loving Long, is using Briss as a screen. When
Long appears, the narrator thinks that he is using Lady John
as a cover for his love of May. Next the narrator talks about
May with Briss, who admits to a fear of her but with it a
desire to help prevent her from breaking down. Alone again,
the narrator walks in the garden and meets May, who seems
pitifully dessicated — undoubtedly owing to Long — but lovable;
he then talks curiously and suggestively with her about Briss,
until she falters and vaguely smiles. Briss comes up. At dinner
the narrator wants to stop theorizing but soon is imaginatively
pairing various guests again. He particularly ponders Long's
and Mrs. Briss's improvement, doubtless at May's and Briss's
expense. Lady John tackles him and counters his comment
that she is free with Briss by accusing Mrs. Briss of liberality
with the narrator. They fence on, meanwhile viewing Mrs. Briss
and Long in close conversation; next the narrator sees Obert
talking with the eternally smiling May. A little later Obert
rather contemptuously tells the narrator that he is tired of
all this theorizing, but still the painter is intrigued. He praises
May. Fatigued Briss comes to tell the narrator that his wife
wants to see him. She tells him that May might seem to be the
source of Long's new radiance but is really not. This statement
surprises the narrator until he senses that Long urged Mrs.
Briss to protect May. Mrs. Briss denies knowing Long's source,
criticizes the narrator for his hyper-sensitiveness, and deplores
talking with him so much. She adds that she and Long both
now fear his intervention. Saying that he must feel at peace,
the narrator asks her to help him destroy his imagination.
She accuses him of being crazy on the whole subject. When
he presses her to say when she began thinking so, she says
that it was when she was talking with Long and suddenly
judged him to be dull. The narrator in a flash sees that this
comment is a subterfuge to cover her own draining of Briss.
The narrator now feels that Mrs. Briss and Long are evilly
shamming together to throw him off the track. In response to
his query about Lady John, Mrs. Briss says that she chattered
about that woman only to try to be sympathetic toward his
theory of founts. Finally, saying that she is driven to the wall,
she says that she has proof (from Briss) that there is a woman

in Long's life and that the woman is Lady John. The narrator is shocked: he did not want his theory to result in any humiliating exposure but only in a scurrying to cover. She adds that Briss took the train to Newmarch with Lady John in innocence but that the effect of his doing so was to screen Long. When the narrator wonders, then, why Mrs. Briss was annoyed to see Briss and May together, she denies any such anger, blames his imagination again, and adds that horrid May tried to make love to Briss. This seems to be more disproof of the theory of the narrator, whom Mrs. Briss now calls crazy again. He appears abashed and determines to leave Newmarch early in the morning.

> Guy "Briss" Brissenden, Mrs. Guy (Grace) Brissenden, Count de Dreuil, Countess de Dreuil, Mrs. Froome, Gilbert Long, Lady John Lutley, Lord John Lutley, Ford Obert, Mrs. May Server.

The Sense of the Past, 1917.
Wealthy young Ralph Pendrel of New York has written an admirable book on how to read history, which has so pleased an English relative, Philip Augustus Pendrel, that he wills Ralph an eighteenth-century house in London. Ralph proposes to the rich widow Aurora Coyne, who has traveled in Europe and should be delighted at his prospects now. But she rejects him, saying that she wants him to be intellectually great and suggesting that he go and sample the Old World. She suspects that he will never willingly return to America. Ralph now goes to London and delights in the evocative spirit of everything, especially that of his Mansfield Square house, crossing the threshold of which is like stepping back in time. The tenant in his house is a distant kinswoman, Mrs. Midmore of Hampshire, but her temporary absence enables him to wander about freely. One night a portrait on the wall, that of an ancestor named Ralph Pendrel also, young like himself but with averted face, turns in its frame: the face and figure in the portrait are exactly like Ralph's. The historical Ralph steps out of the frame, and the two commune. Feeling that he must share his extraordinary secret with someone, Ralph goes to the urbane American ambassador and tries to explain,

while the other Ralph is waiting in a cab outside. Ralph evidently now becomes his eighteenth-century alter ego, returns to his house, and meets Mrs. Midmore's older daughter Molly, then the mother, who is delighted that rich Ralph, Molly's fiance, has arrived safely from America to meet them. Next Ralph, intuitively feeling his way, meets Mrs. Midmore's surly son Perry, who reminds him that the family has a younger daughter also. She is Nan, and quickly Ralph shows a preternatural curiosity about her which distresses the Midmores who are present. They speak of Sir Cantopher, the man presumably interested in Nan; instantly Ralph guesses that he is Sir Cantopher Bland, who enters almost at once. They fence for a while, and Ralph is increasingly annoyed that all of them seem to want to use his wealth and presence. Sir Cantopher and Mrs. Midmore leave, and Perry immediately hints at financial embarrassment, which Ralph generously offers to alleviate. Then Nan enters, having daringly come alone from Hampshire to see him. Their immediate emotional rapport with one another, together with Ralph's continuing clairvoyance, annoys thick Perry. Ralph delights in Nan's fresh, direct, modern nature . . .

Sir Cantopher Bland, Townsend "Stent" Coyne, Mrs. Townsend (Aurora) Coyne, Coyne, Molly Midmore, Nancy "Nan" Midmore, Peregrine "Perry" Midmore, Mrs. Midmore, Philip Augustus Pendrel, Ralph Pendrel, Pendrel.

"The Siege of London," 1883.
Rich, bored widowed George Littlemore, with fellow-American Rupert Waterville, while at the Comedie Francaise sees a former acquaintance Mrs. Nancy Grenville Beck Headway. The attractive middle-aged American widow is devotedly attended by Sir Arthur Demesne. She soon asks Littlemore, who has a well-married sister in London, to help her get into British society. He refuses but is amused by observing her determined assault, which is partly motivated by a snub by New York society. Demesne, though puzzled by Mrs. Headway, is strongly attracted to her and introduces his widowed mother to her in Waterville's presence. In London during the next season, Waterville is invited to the Demesne estate at Longlands, where Mrs. Headway is also a guest. More successful now, she

accuses him of being a spy but still confides to him that Demesne's mother is a hateful cat. Lady Demesne seeks out Waterville but fails to elicit adverse information concerning the American woman. Mrs. Headway tells Littlemore in London that Demesne's mother will soon visit him to learn whether she is corrupt; she begs him not to give her away. Next his sister tells him that Lady Demesne has written her for information. Littlemore informs his sister that Mrs. Headway is not respectable but that he will say nothing to jeopardize her chances with Demesne. He maintains this position with Waterville, who seems to feel that Mrs. Headway is succeeding so well that she should be checked. In her presence, Littlemore refuses to say anything adverse to Demesne; the next day she writes him that she is engaged. Then his sister brings Lady Demesne, to whom he says only that Mrs. Headway is not respectable. But the marriage occurs anyway. Finally Littlemore suspects that irate Waterville is in love with her himself.

> Rev. Mr. April, Mrs. April, Mrs. Bagshaw, Philadelphus Beck, Davidoff, Sir Arthur Demesne, Sir Baldwin Demesne, Lady Demesne, Reggie Dolphin, Mrs. Reggie (Agnes) Dolphin, Lady Dovedale, Lord Edward, Headway, Mrs. Nancy Grenville Beck Headway, George Littlemore, Miss Littlemore, Lady Margaret, Max, Rupert Waterville.

"Sir Dominick Ferrand," 1892.
Peter Baron is a rather unsuccessful young writer whose material is not very interesting to Locket, editor of *The Promiscuous Review*. Baron buys an old desk, and when Sidney, the little son of his rooming-house neighbor widowed Mrs. Ryves, is playing about it, he discovers that it contains some secret papers. They are most damaging to the reputation of Sir Dominick Ferrand, a formerly renowned public figure now dead. Mrs. Ryves is a music teacher, and she and Baron write a song together. He proposes marriage, but she declines. When he shows the revealing Ferrand papers to Locket, the editor offers £300 for them and is also willing to accept some of the young man's fiction. But Baron soon feels that he has no right to injure Ferrand's fame and therefore burns the letters; the instant he does so, Mrs. Ryves almost occultly returns, reports

that their song is to be published, and accepts his renewed proposal. First she must tell him a family secret: she is the illegitimate daughter of Sir Dominick Ferrand.

Peter Baron, Mrs. Bundy, Sir Dominick Ferrand, Locket, Morrish, Sidney Ryves, Mrs. Ryves, Miss Teagle.

"Sir Edmund Orme," 1891.

At Brighton the narrator meets Mrs. Marden and her attractive daughter Charlotte. While they are talking, the mother inexplicably turns pale; later she drops a cup of tea handed to her, evidently not even seeing it. Then at Tranton, a nearby estate, the narrator, falling in love with Charlotte, sees a ghost sit beside her in church; Mrs. Marden sees it too, but the girl does not. The narrator proposes to aloof Charlotte that evening, while the ghost looks on. The girl retires to consider the proposal, and her mother proceeds to tell the narrator that Sir Edmund Orme loved her years ago but that she married elsewhere, upon which Orme poisoned himself; then after her husband's death, Orme's ghost began to haunt her. The next day the temporarily discouraged narrator, saying goodbye to Charlotte, sees the ghost again and feels that it is on his side. At Brighton three months later, the narrator again sees Charlotte; but before they can do much talking, they both see a darkened figure nearby. Perhaps it is the ghost. Charlotte quickly goes to her fainting mother inside. The following day the narrator is summoned to Mrs. Marden, who is dying but happily says that Charlotte wishes to marry him. The ghost stands near the mother. Charlotte sees it and leaps into the narrator's embrace. The mother dies, and the ghost is not seen again.

Teddy Bostwick, Charlotte Marden, Major Marden, Mrs. Marden, Sir Edmund Orme.

"The Solution," 1889-1890.

Outside Rome, callow American diplomat Henry Wilmerding goes for an innocent but unchaperoned stroll with Miss Veronica Goldie into a secluded grove. He is then made to feel, by some practical jokers, including the diplomat-narrator, that he has compromised her. So he honorably proposes marriage to the odious girl and is accepted. Conscience-stricken, the narrator asks the aid of his fiancee Mrs. Rushbrook. She and Wilmerding buy off Veronica and then marry each other.

Lord Bolitho, Augusta Goldie, Mrs. Blanche Goldie, Rosina Goldie, Veronica Goldie, Guy de Montaut, Rushbrook, Mrs. Rushbrook, Miss Rushbrook, Henry Wilmerding.

"The Special Type," 1900.

To provoke his wife into divorcing him, Frank Brivet, a friend of the painter-narrator, treats Mrs. Alice Dundene in public as his mistress. She loves but loses him after the resulting divorce, because Brivet planned everything in this fashion in order then to marry beautiful, smug Rose Cavenham, whom the narrator once painted. Mrs. Brivet then marries unpleasant Remson Sturch. As a signal of her success to come, Mrs. Cavenham commissioned the narrator to paint a full-length portrait of Brivet. The narrator shows it to long-suffering Alice, who when promised by grateful Brivet anything she wishes as payment for aiding him in the divorce action, meekly but successfully demands the portrait; it will partially make up for her never being alone with the man she passively loved.

Frank Brivet, Mrs. Frank Brivet, Rose Cavenham, Mrs. Alice Dundene, Remson Sturch.

The Spoils of Poynton, 1896.

Widowed Mrs. Gereth tells sensitive Fleda Vetch that she is afraid her son Owen is falling for crass Mona Brigstock, who with her mother visits Poynton, the Gereth home which is laden with wisely gathered art spoils. Fleda reproaches Mrs. Gereth for appearing to offer her to Owen, who soon reports his engagement to Mona and their plans to take over expropriated Mrs. Gereth's Poynton. Owen asks Fleda to persuade his mother to vacate without a scene. Taking Fleda with her as a guest, Mrs. Gereth goes to Ricks, the other family estate, and soon thinks that something can be made of it. Fleda feels uncomfortable, sympathizing with both Mrs. Gereth and her embarrassed, oppressed son; so she returns to London, where her sister is being married. Fleda and Owen chance to meet: he goes shopping with her, buying her a pincushion for being nice to mummy; and he seems to like her too well for an engaged man. Returning to Ricks, she disapprovingly sees that Mrs. Gereth has furnished the place with the finest pieces from Poynton. Owen comes to report Mona's anger at the "theft"; Fleda feels that she could wreck the engagement simply by urging Mrs. Gereth to hold the spoils. But, respecting honor, Fleda advises Owen to honor his pledge and even tries to deny to his mother her increasing devotion to his cause. Owen looks up Fleda at her father's home in London, and when they discuss matters she honorably tells him that his mother is stalling to bluff Mona out of the engagement. Owen now prefers fine Fleda to sulking Mona. Mrs. Brigstock calls on Fleda and is so annoyed at finding Owen there that he defends the girl. He follows bewildered Fleda to her sister's home and professes his love; momentarily responding, she soon insists that he be the fiance of Mona until she breaks with him. Ten days later Mrs. Gereth tells Fleda that Mrs. Brigstock feels that Mona has lost Owen; so Mrs. Gereth returns the spoils to Poynton. Mrs. Gereth admires Fleda but is critical of her sensitive scruples. Three days later Owen and massive Mona are reported married; and soon they go abroad. Reconciled to Mrs. Gereth, Fleda later receives a letter from Owen begging her to select any one fine treasure from the spoils to keep. She goes to Poynton, only to find it burning to the ground.

Mona Brigstock, Mrs. Brigstock, Mrs. Firmin, Mrs. Adela Gereth, Owen Gereth, Col. Gereth, Mme. de Jaume, Fleda Vetch, Maggie Vetch, Vetch.

"The Story in It," 1902.

In her rainy country home Mrs. Dyott is entertaining a sweet young widow named Maud Blessingbourne. While her hostess writes letters, Maud is reading a dull French novel until the arrival of married Colonel Voyt, at which time she leaves for a while. Mrs. Dyott and the rather rakish colonel talk intimately of old times. Maud returns, and soon she and Voyt are discussing French novels, which, routine though they are, says Voyt, he still prefers to evasive Anglo-American fiction. Maud counters with her theory that a completely moral and inactive woman can provide an interesting plot for a novel. Voyt critically browbeats her, but she remains serene in her happy fancy. When he leaves, Mrs. Dyott extracts the suggestion that Maud silently loves Voyt, who after Maud's departure returns later to Mrs. Dyott and appears to be her lover. They discuss Maud's curiously tender position, and soon they agree both that Maud's theory concerning fiction gains plausibility by virtue of her untold, unrewarded love and that an author might make more money writing up their own more passionate affair.

Mrs. Maud Blessingbourne, Mrs. Dyott, Col. Voyt, Mrs. Voyt.

"The Story of a Masterpiece," 1868.

John Lennox, a rich and childless widower, meets Miss Marian Everett in Newport. While she was traveling in Europe with Mrs. Denbigh, an invalid widow, she met a painter named Stephen Baxter, who fell far more deeply in love with her than she with him. They quarreled, and the affair ended. She and Lennox are now engaged to each other, when Lennox through a painter friend meets Baxter, who is painting a work which reminds Lennox of Miss Everett. He commissions Baxter to paint his fiancee. He dislikes the finished work, however, because of the frivolity and cynicism it reveals in the original. Meeting Baxter's fiancee, Lennox concludes that his own prospective wife is thoroughly hard; nonetheless, he goes through with the marriage, but permits himself the satisfaction of hacking up the painting.

Stephen Baxter, Mrs. Denbigh, Marian Everett, Gilbert, Goupil, King, John Lennox, Sarah, Frederic Young, Mrs. Young.

"The Story of a Year," 1865.

Lieutenant John Ford becomes quietly engaged to Miss Elizabeth Crowe, informs his disapproving mother of the fact, and soon leaves for the South with the Union Army. At a neighboring town Lizzie, who has grown restless and critical while living with Mrs. Ford, meets Robert Bruce. While she is beginning to fall in love with Bruce, they learn that Lt. Ford has been grievously wounded by the Confederate forces. His mother goes south to nurse him and bring him home, where, dying, he releases confused Lizzie.

Jane Bruce, Robert Bruce, Dr. James Cooper, Miss Cooper, Elizabeth "Lizzie" Crowe, Miss Dawes, Lt. John "Jack" Ford, Mrs. Ford, Littlefield, Mrs. Littlefield, George Mackenzie, Robertson, Simpson.

"The Sweetheart of M. Briseux," 1873.

While the narrator is visiting the picture gallery in the French city of M—, he sees a woman viewing a skillful work of which she when younger was the original. When questioned, she tells him how while she was unhappily engaged some years ago to ineffectual painter Harold Staines, Pierre Briseux invaded the studio and brilliantly painted over Harold's mediocre painting of her. Harold was so furious that she had to sacrifice her engagement to let Briseux continue with a work which began his illustrious career.

Pierre Briseux, Martinet, Harold Staines, Staines, Mrs. Lucretia Staines.

"The Third Person," 1900.

Miss Susan Frush, a water-colorist, and her younger second cousin Miss Amy Frush, an amateur writer, are bequeathed property at Marr in southern England. The two go there and meet for the first time, discovering that they like each other and want to remain together in the home rather than sell it. Rummaging in the basement, they find a chest full of old papers which they ask the Rev. Mr. Patten, the local vicar, to decipher. As they are retiring that night, Susan sees the ghost of a young man with his neck twisted to one side. Later they learn from Mr. Patten that according to the papers loaned him an ancestor of theirs, Cuthbert Frush, was hanged. Amy next reports seeing the neck-twisted ghost. Mr. Patten now adds that the handsome young ancestor was hanged for the formerly aristocratic and even necessary crime of smuggling. Susan happily sees the ghost again and seems reluctant to share her story with Amy, who becomes jealous and wants an experience with the ancestor also. The two remain suspicious of one another, however, only a short while. Then Susan admits sending £20 to the government to ease the ghost's conscience. Saying that such a procedure would never do, Amy goes to France and smuggles a Tauchnitz volume into England on her return. Now the ghost leaves in peace.

Amy Frush, Cuthbert Frush, Susan Frush, Mrs. Frush, Rev. Mr. Patten.

"The Tone of Time," 1900.

The painter-narrator turns over to fellow-painter Miss Mary J. Tredick the commission for a portrait of an imaginary, handsome man. The order came to him from Mrs. Bridgenorth, and the painting is to have the tone of about twenty years of time. Miss Tredick agrees. When the narrator as intermediary returns and compliments her for a brilliant portrait of an insolent, unsuffering man, she cries out that it was painted in hate, implying that she knew and was hurt by the original. The narrator takes the work to his home and shows it to Mrs. Bridgenorth, who recognizes the original: it appears that she also knew him well. She now desperately wants the portrait, but when Miss Tredick on hearing details from the narrator suspects that Mrs. Bridgenorth is the one for whom the original left her and whom he would have married but for his sudden death, the painter refuses to sell her work for any sum. Both women later die, and the narrator, now old, now owns the portrait.

Mrs. Bridgenorth, Mary Juliana Tredick.

"A Tragedy of Error," 1864.

Hortense Bernier loses the support of her lover Vicomte Louis de Meyrau when she tells him that her crippled husband Charles is returning home to the French port city of H—. So she hires a murderous boatman to kill her husband. But through a mix-up Louis is drowned instead and Charles limps back to her after all.

Charles Bernier, Mme. Charles (Hortense) Bernier, Mme. Bernier, Josephine, Vicomte Louis de Meyrau, M. de Saulges, Valentine.

The Tragic Muse, 1889-1890.

Nick Dormer prefers painting to politics, to the annoyance of his widowed mother Lady Agnes, his older sister Grace, and his fiancee widowed Julia Sherringham Dallow, whose diplomat brother Peter Sherringham becomes attracted in Paris to actress Miriam Rooth, to the sorrow of Nick's sweet younger sister Biddy. If Nick runs for election in the county of Harsh, Julia will back him and he will undoubtedly inherit great wealth from sonless old Charles Carteret. But Nick is encouraged to rebel for art by Oxford friend Gabriel Nash, a talkative aesthete. Nick wins the election and proposes to generous but domineering Julia, but they decide to wait; when he advises with Carteret, that man's promises and advice make him feel that he is losing all independence. Meanwhile Peter in Paris is torn between his diplomatic career and love of Miriam, who is improving rapidly in acting ability under the tutelage of Madame Honorine Carre. In London Julia leaves Nick free to paint a few days, and Nash wanders in to encourage and yet upset him. Miriam, now seeking engagements in London through actor-agent Basil Dashwood, comes to Nick for a sitting; he wonders if artistic success like hers would make him surer of himself. Julia returns to the studio, sees Miriam (and Nash), is angered, and after offering to release Nick from their engagement leaves for Paris. There she advises her brother Peter to marry Biddy; but instead he rushes to London and at the theater recognizes Miriam's impressive ability, is attracted to her more than ever, but is reconciled to final disappointment. Nick visits dying Carteret and gently refuses to quit art; his subsequent loss of £60,000 enrages his selfish mother Lady Agnes. Nash theorizes to Peter that Nick and Miriam are unconsciously in love with each other; Peter applies for and receives a Central American post, to the annoyance of Biddy's mother and sister. The careers of Peter and Miriam must separate them. Much time passes. Nick in London and briefly in Paris plugs away at his painting without material progress and is made to feel responsible for serious family reverses. Miriam discontinues her sittings for him, and after a while so does Nash; next Biddy reveals that Julia wishes to pose for her portrait by him. Miriam with Dashwood returns to London to play Juliet; Peter suddenly turns up and attends the drama, only to learn part way through it that Miriam is now married to Dashwood. Later Julia gives

a party to announce Biddy's betrothal to Peter. Nick paints
Julia and successfully exhibits the results. Will the two marry?

Mrs. Billinghurst, Lord Bottomley, Mme. Honorine Carre,
Charles Carteret, Chayter, George Dallow, Mrs. George
(Julia Sherringham) Dallow, Basil Dashwood, Lord Daven-
ant, Mrs. Delamere, Lady Agnes Dormer, Bridget "Biddy"
Dormer, Grace Dormer, Sir Nicholas Dormer, Nicholas
"Nick" Dormer, Percival Dormer, Mlle. Dunoyer, Durand,
Lord Egbert, Gresham, Mrs. Gresham, Goodwood Grindon,
Gushmore, Sir Matthew Hope, Hoppus, Hutchby, Kings-
bury, Mrs. Kingsbury, Mrs. Urania Lendon, Edmund
Lovick, Mrs. Edmund Lovick, Laura Lumley, Macgeorge,
Muriel Macpherson, Mitton, Gabriel Nash, Percy, Pinks,
Miriam Rooth, Mrs. Rudolph Rooth (Roth), Rudolph
Roth, Fanny Rover, Ruggieri, Lady St. Dunstans, Peter
Sherringham, Edith Temple, Florence Tressilian, Gladys
Vane, Maud Vavasour, Mlle. Voisin, Lady Windrush.

"Travelling Companions," 1870.
American narrator Mr. Brooke while touring in Italy meets
Mark Evans and his attractive daughter Charlotte in Milan;
they meet again in Venice. When Mr. Evans returns to Milan
to visit a sick friend, the young couple go to Padua and
pleasantly talk so long that they miss their return train. Miss
Evans feels embarrassed and perhaps a little compromised, but
her father believes their reasonable explanation. Later Evans
dies, and his daughter accepts Brooke's fervent but not forced
proposal of marriage.

Signora B—, B—, Brooke, Charlotte Evans, Mark Evans,
L—, Mrs. L—, Munson.

"The Tree of Knowledge," 1900.
From a decent distance Peter Brench hopelessly loves the
pretty, rather vain, seemingly uncomprehending wife of Morgan
Mallow, the slow, kindly, unproductive sculptor of Carrara
Lodge in a London suburb. The Mallows' son Lance reveals
that he wants to quit Cambridge and study painting in Paris.
The Mallows josh Peter, who regularly dines with them on
Sundays, for having presumed to advise Lance not to study

in France. But within a year the abashed young man returns to confess that he knows now why Peter did not want him to go — it was because he knew that Lance had no talent. Further, Lance now sees that Peter also feared that the young man would discover that his sculptor father had no talent either. Peter is surprised that Lance should learn so much so fast in Paris and makes the young man promise not to reveal to his mother the professional worthlessness of Mallow. When, six months later, Lance almost argues with his complacent father about art and its demands upon the artist to produce, Peter bribes the young man into silence. Then Lance tells Peter that he almost had a scene with his father but that his mother appeared later in order to tell him to be quiet, as she had learned to do, through love. This revelation surprises Peter, who always thought that Mrs. Mallow believed her husband to be a genius.

Peter Brench, Egidio, Lancelot "Lance" Mallow, Morgan Mallow, Mrs. Morgan Mallow.

"The Turn of the Screw," 1898.

To a group of Griffin's guests, Douglas reads the following story in manuscript. Shortly after arriving at the country estate of Bly, the narrator, a young governess who is to have complete charge of her absent employer's orphaned nephew Miles and niece Flora, sees a couple of times the ghost of Peter Quint, the dead valet of her employer, and then the ghost of Miss Jessel, the governess's predecessor. The housekeeper Mrs. Grose talks with the governess about Quint and Miss Jessel, who evidently were intimate with each other and with Miles and Flora. The governess becomes increasingly distraught in the eerie environment, feeling that the children see the ghosts but pretend not to. Late one night the governess is aroused while reading, finds Quint on the stairs and outfaces him, then returns to find Flora at the window. During another night she awakens to find Flora at the window again and this time Miles in the yard. After other incidents, the governess tells Mrs. Grose that she believes the ghosts are corrupting the children. Mrs. Grose to no avail suggests informing the governess's employer. Miles wants to return to school, from which he was evidently expelled for perhaps unsavory reasons. The governess prefers to have him stay at Bly where she can protect him from Quint, and can protect Flora from Miss Jessel. Writing a letter at last to her employer but then not mailing it at once, the governess closely questions Miles until he screams to be let alone. Then she and Mrs. Grose seek Flora and find her by the lake; the governess sees Miss Jessel again, and her pointing at the ghost drives frightened Flora into the housekeeper's arms. Now Mrs. Grose is to take Flora to the girl's uncle. Alone with Miles, whom she suspects of stealing the letter which she wrote but did not mail, the governess tries to save the boy by encouraging him to confess all wickedness. Quint suddenly appears at the window; the governess shields Miles from the apparition while the boy says that he took the letter and also behaved improperly at school. The governess mockingly tells Quint that he cannot have the penitent boy now. Miles strains apparently to see Quint and dies in the governess's arms.

Douglas, Flora, Griffin, Mrs. Grose, Miss Jessel, Luke, Miles, Peter Quint.

"The Two Faces," 1900.

Mr. Shirley Sutton watches as May Grantham receives Lord Gwyther, her former lover, who enters to report his marriage to Valda, English-born daughter of a Britisher and a German countess. Gwyther begs Mrs. Grantham to conduct his naive wife through the English social labyrinth. Sutton later tells Mrs. Grantham that Gwyther has placed his wife in her charge to put her on her honor not to wreck the girl socially. At an important social gathering at Burbeck soon thereafter, Sutton watches the entrance of poor little Lady Gwyther, hideously and fatally overdressed by vindictive Mrs. Grantham. Lady Gwyther's face is pathetic but beautiful, whereas Mrs. Grantham's face has hardened horribly.

Miss Banker, Bates, Mrs. May Grantham, Lady Valda Gwyther, Lord Gwyther, Countess Kremnitz, Shirley Sutton.

"The Velvet Glove," 1909.

In Gloriani's garden one April in Paris, novelist John Berridge meets a certain half-remembered lord, whom he slowly recollects when the lord introduces him to a beautiful girl whom

Berridge assuredly remembers seeing with the lord in Italy once. The girl turns out to be Amy Evans, authoress of trashy novels. She spoils everything by enticing Berridge to her home, hoping thereby to induce him to write a preface for her latest book, *The Velvet Glove.* He refuses, kissing her gently and telling her that she is romance and should therefore not meddle in art. She cries uncomprehendingly.

John Berridge, Amy Evans, Gloriani, Mme. Gloriani.

"The Visits," 1892.

Visiting at a country home, the woman narrator meets Louisa Chantry, the daughter of a former school friend. The girl is nervous, and the narrator senses that something is amiss between her and Jack Brandon, who is sitting nearby. Later, in the garden, the narrator comes upon distraught Louisa, who cries hysterically in her arms and then exacts a promise of silence. A couple of days later the narrator pays a visit to the mother of Louisa, who is now discovered to be dying — of secret shame. It seems that she was sexually attracted to Jack, made improper advances to him, then was remorseful, irrationally reviled him, and now is mortally ashamed. Because of her vow, the narrator never tells Louisa's parents the true account.

Jack Brandon, Christopher Chantry, Mrs. Christopher (Helen) Chantry, Louisa Chantry.

Washington Square, 1880.

Wealthy widower Dr. Austin Sloper lives in Washington Square, New York City, with his stolid daughter Catherine and his busybody widowed sister Lavinia Penniman. At a party given by his other sister, Mrs. Almond, Catherine meets Morris Townsend, who sweeps her off her feet but whom Dr. Sloper does not trust. While Townsend calls on enamoured Catherine, her father is checking on the impoverished and parasitic young man. Townsend asks for Catherine's hand, and Dr. Sloper volubly disapproves. Meanwhile Mrs. Penniman espouses the couple's cause and begins to meet Townsend privately, to Catherine's annoyance. Dr. Sloper enjoys testing

his daughter, whom he now takes to Europe for six months.
Catherine angers him in the Alps by announcing her continued
determination. Back home again, she learns that Townsend
wants her to placate her father so that she will not be cut off
penniless. She will not, nor could she; the two quarrel, and
Townsend leaves the city. Feeling that the couple may be only
waiting, Dr. Sloper, mocking and boastful though he is, never
feels secure. Seventeen years pass. Catherine refuses to promise
not to marry Townsend after the death of her father, who
soon dies leaving his daughter badly cared for financially.
Through Mrs. Penniman, Townsend, now a fat, bald widower,
sees Catherine again; but she refuses even to be his friend.

   Jefferson Almond, Mrs. Jefferson (Elizabeth) Almond,
   Marian Almond, John Ludlow, Macalister, Mrs. Mont-
   gomery, Rev. Mr. Penniman, Mrs. Lavinia Penniman,
   Dr. Austin Sloper, Mrs. Austin (Catherine Harrington)
   Sloper, Catherine Sloper, Sloper, Miss Sturtevant, Arthur
   Townsend, Morris Townsend, Mrs. Morris Townsend.

Watch and Ward, 1871.
   Roger Lawrence, about thirty, is rejected again, presumably
in Boston, by Isabel Morton. When he hears a stranger whom
he refused financial help shoot himself in a hotel room, in
lonely remorse he decides to adopt the stranger's daughter
Nora Lambert, aged twelve. Roger carefully supervises her
education, hoping to marry her in a half-dozen years, as he
writes Isabel, now Mrs. Keith in Rome. Traveling in South
America, Roger decides against proposing to a Peruvian beauty
when Nora writes him from home that she likes him. Finished
with her formal education, Nora now travels a while with her
guardian, who later reluctantly lets her cousin, worthless but
attractive George Fenton, come calling. Visiting from New York,
Parson Hubert Lawrence, Roger's younger cousin, who has
also taken an interest in Nora, advises Roger to woo and wed
his ward quickly; but he lets Mrs. Keith take her to Rome for
a year instead. Remaining loyal in her absence to Nora, who,
however, is attracted somewhat more to Hubert now than to
anyone else, Roger next resists the charms of lovely Miss
Sands. When he contracts a fever through sleeping in a damp

room, Nora, back from Europe, attends him in spite of her growing affection for Hubert, whom militant Mrs. Keith ejects by threatening to expose his engagement in New York. Well again and encouraged by Mrs. Keith, Roger proposes to Nora, whom he now sincerely loves but who rejects him. When Mrs. Keith, hoping to help, shows Nora a letter written her years before by Roger saying that he hopes to rear Nora as a perfect wife, the bewildered girl makes her way to opportunistic Fenton, now a junk dealer in New York. Fenton hides her in his rooming house and tries unsuccessfully to extort money from Roger, who has followed the girl. Nora forces the somewhat abashed Fenton to let her go, and she proceeds to Hubert, who is vainly posing for a picture and whose fiancee in addition enters. Nora leaves in embarrassment, sees Roger approaching, and is soon happy to return home with him.

Amy, Mrs. Lucinda Brown, Mrs. Chatterton, George Fenton, Franks, Mrs. Isabel Morton Keith, Mrs. Keith, Nora Lambert, Lambert, Mrs. Lambert, Rev. Mr. Hubert Lawrence, Roger Lawrence, Mrs. Lawrence, Abbe Leblond, Miss Lilienthal, Mrs. Middleton, Morton, Mrs. Morton, Miss Morton, Miss Murray, Mrs. Paul, Miss Sands, Lisa Stamm, Mlle. Stamm, Teresa, Vose.

What Maisie Knew, 1897.

Beale and Ida Farange are divorced, and their little daughter Maisie shuttles between them. After Beale marries Maisie's pretty nurse Miss Overmore, whom Ida hired (then replacing her by ugly Mrs. Wix), Ida marries Sir Claude. Maisie meets likable Claude, while he is having a nice chat with Beale's wife, whom Ida soon senses Claude loves. Ida leaves Claude and Mrs. Wix and Maisie, and goes off with a series of lovers — Perriam, Lord Eric, a captain, then Tischbein. Claude's seeing Beale's wife distresses moral Mrs. Wix, but Maisie likes both of her foster parents and is happy to bring them together. She bumps into her father, who takes her to the apartment of his American "countess" and distresses Maisie by so talking that she declines an invitation to accompany them to America, then feels guilty. Later she learns that they lied about their plans. After Ida saddens Maisie by talking lugubriously of going to South

Africa, Claude takes the girl to Boulogne, where Mrs. Wix soon joins them. Against Mrs. Wix's advice and wishes, he soon returns to England and to Beale's wife, who is evidently now free. Maisie and Mrs. Wix argue about the propriety of men paying women: when Mrs. Wix reveals that Claude pays Beale's wife, Maisie counters by saying that he also pays Mrs. Wix. But by the time Claude and Beale's wife return to them in Boulogne, Maisie has accepted Mrs. Wix's lecture that the pair are sinful. Claude returns to England, and Beale's wife behaves so considerately that Mrs. Wix is almost persuaded that she has morally improved. Beale's wife says that after their divorces she and Claude will marry and keep Maisie; but Claude too swiftly returns to Beale's wife, which angers Mrs. Wix. Claude asks Maisie if she will go to southern France with Beale's wife and himself but without Mrs. Wix. Maisie asks for a little time to ponder. When all four confront each other, Maisie learns that Claude and Beale's wife will assuredly make a unit and therefore determines to stay only with Mrs. Wix. What Maisie now knows is the moral sense.

> Susan Ash, Sir Claude, Mrs. Cuddon, Lord Eric, Beale Farange, Mrs. Beale (Ida) Farange, Maisie Farange, Moddle, Miss Overmore, Perriam, Tischbein, Mrs. Tucker, Clara Matilda Wix, Wix, Mrs. Wix.

"The Wheel of Time," 1892-1893.

Lady Greyswood fails to induce her third son, useless Maurice Glanvil, to pay much attention to plain Fanny Knocker. Twenty years later, Maurice, now a widower, returns to London with his daughter Vera, bright but plain and diminutive. They meet Arthur Tregent, the handsome son of Fanny Knocker, who is now widowed Mrs. Tregent. Fanny agrees to ask her son Arthur to try to like Vera, but he simply cannot. Poor Vera becomes sick at the Tregent summer estate of Blankley and later dies of a broken heart. Thus the wheel of time gives unintending Fanny a kind of revenge.

> Crisford, Mrs. Crisford, Maurice Glanvil, Mrs. Maurice Glanvil, Vera Glanvil, Lady Greyswood, Lord Greyswood, Lord Greyswood, General Blake Knocker, Mrs. Blake(Jane) Knocker, Knocker, Knocker, Knocker, Knocker, Miss Knocker, Arthur Tregent, Mrs. Fanny Knocker Tregent.

The Wings of the Dove, 1902.

Lionel Croy agrees that his daughter Kate should appear to ignore him, go to her aunt Maud Lowder, and let that massive woman negotiate a fine marriage for her. Then Kate visits her widowed sister Marian Condrip, who urges her to drop Merton Densher, a London journalist soon to visit America temporarily, in favor of Lord Mark, Maud's choice. Rich, dying Milly Theale and her traveling companion Mrs. Susan Stringham go from New York, where the girl chanced to meet Densher, to Italy and Switzerland, then on to London. Mrs. Stringham soon introduces Milly to her old school-friend Mrs. Lowder, at whose home the girl quickly becomes friendly with Kate and attracts Lord Mark, whom Maud, however, still wants for her niece Kate. Through Kate, Milly meets Marian and learns from her of Densher's love for Kate; Milly says nothing about it, however, because Maud does not want Densher mentioned. Nor does Kate ever speak of him. Lord Mark is intrigued by Milly when he points out her resemblance to a Bronzino portrait. Milly enlists Kate's confidence by having Kate accompany her to the eminent physician Sir Luke Strett, who tells the girl to make the best of her short time remaining. Densher returns to London; Milly is puzzled by seeing him with Kate in an art gallery since soon thereafter (at Kate's instigation) he calls upon and is most attentive to Milly. Kate hopes that he can marry rich, dying Milly, inherit her money at her death, and then defiantly marry Kate. On Sir Luke's advice, Milly goes for the winter to Venice, accompanied by Mrs. Stringham, in addition Kate and her aunt briefly, and Densher somewhat hesitantly. To assure himself of Kate after the consummation of their unsavory plan, he gets her to visit him in his room privately. He is later so charming to Milly that she quickly falls in love with him. However, Lord Mark, also in Venice now, has proposed to Milly, been rejected, and later in bitterness and frustration — Mrs. Stringham soon tells tardily remorseful Densher — informs worsening Milly of Kate's permanent liaison with Densher, which somehow he learned of. Back in London, Densher cannot bring himself to go and see Kate. He hears on Christmas Day through Maud at Sir Luke's home of Milly's death in Venice. He then receives a letter in Milly's hand, takes it unopened to Kate; ill at ease, they burn it, sensing that it contains an offer of money so that they can marry. Later a letter comes to Densher from a New York law firm. He sends it unopened to Kate, who comes to him with it. He will marry her without the money but not with it; she will not marry him without it. Kate now knows that Densher loves Milly's memory, wants no other love, and like her has changed.

Lady Aldershaw, Lord Aldershaw, Dr. Buttrick, Bertie Condrip, Guy Condrip, Kitty Condrip, Maudie Condrip, Rev. Mr. Condrip, Mrs. Marian Croy Condrip, Miss Condrip, Miss Condrip, Kate Croy, Lionel Croy, Mrs. Lionel Croy (nee Manningham), Croy, Croy, Merton Densher, Rev. Mr. Densher, Mrs. Densher, Eugenio, Dr. Finch, Mrs. Maud Manningham Lowder, Lord Mark, Pasquale, Sir Luke Strett, Mrs. Susan Shepherd Stringham, Dr. Tacchini, Milly Theale, Lady Wells.

CHARACTERS

Acton, Lizzie. *The Europeans*. A cousin of Gertrude, Charlotte, and Clifford Wentworth; she is Robert Acton's sister.

Acton, Robert. *The Europeans*. A cousin of Gertrude, Charlotte, and Clifford Wentworth; he is Lizzie Acton's brother; he decides against proposing to Baroness Eugenia Munster.

Acton, Mrs. *The Europeans*. Robert and Lizzie Acton's gentle mother.

Addard, C. P. "Fordham Castle." The pseudonym of Abel F. Taker, which see.

Adney, Vincent. "The Private Life." Blanche Adney's violinist husband.

Adney, Mrs. Vincent (Blanche). "The Private Life." The competent actress who admires Clare Vawdrey and sees through Lord Mellifont.

Adolph of Silberstadt-Schreckenstein. *The Europeans*. The husband of Baroness Eugenia Munster.

Agnesina "Aggie." *The Awkward Age*. The sheltered niece of Duchess Jane of Naples, who is a friend of Mrs. Brookenham.

Alcibiade. "Four Meetings." A waiter at the inn at Le Havre seen by Caroline Spencer.

Alden, Bessie. "An International Episode." Kitty Westgate's

unmarried sister; she loves Lord Lambeth, but prejudice prevents their marrying.

Aldershaw, Lady. *The Wings of the Dove*. Lord and Lady Aldershaw live at Matcham, where a Bronzino portrait is located; they entertain Milly Theale there.

Aldershaw, Lord. *The Wings of the Dove*. Lord and Lady Aldershaw live at Matcham, where a Bronzino portrait is located; they entertain Milly Theale there.

Aldis, Margaret. "De Grey, A Romance." An orphan girl adopted into the De Grey family; she is the object of Paul De Grey's affection.

Allen, Mrs. "The Patagonia." A neighbor of the Mavises in Boston.

Almond, Jefferson. *Washington Square*. Prosperous New York merchant; he is Dr. Austin Sloper's brother-in-law.

Almond, Mrs. Jefferson (Elizabeth). *Washington Square*. Dr. Austin Sloper's sister.

Almond, Marian. *Washington Square*. Dr. Austin Sloper's niece.

Alsager. "Nona Vincent." Wealthy husband of playwright Allan Wayworth's adviser.

Alsager, Mrs. "Nona Vincent." Playwright Allan Wayworth's generous adviser and financial support.

Altemura, Contessa. "The Aspern Papers." Supposedly high-society former friend of the Bordereaus.

Amanda. "Georgina's Reasons." The parlor maid of Georgina Gressie's parents.

Amber, Mrs. "The Patagonia." A neighbor of the Mavises in Boston.

Ambient, Dolcino. "The Author of Beltraffio." The delicate little son of Mark and Beatrice Ambient; he is the victim of their animosity.

Ambient, Gwendolyn. "The Author of Beltraffio." Mark Ambient's pre-Raphaelitesque sister.

Ambient, Mark. "The Author of Beltraffio." A gifted novelist, the author of *Beltraffio*.

Ambient, Mrs. Mark (Beatrice). "The Author of Beltraffio." Novelist Mark Ambient's unsympathetic wife; she withholds her dying son Dolcino's medicine.

Amerigo, Prince. *The Golden Bowl.* The husband of Maggie Verver, son-in-law of Adam Verver, and lover of Charlotte Stant.

Amy. *Watch and Ward.* The Rev. Mr. Hubert Lawrence's fiancee.

Anatole. "Rose-Agathe." A barber, the owner of Rose-Agathe.

Anatole, Mme. "Rose-Agathe." The wife of Anatole the barber.

Antrim, Mary. "The Altar of the Dead." The dead love of altar-keeping George Stransom.

Antrobus, Charlotte. "The Point of View." The daughter of Edward and Susan Antrobus.

Antrobus, Edward, M.P. "The Point of View." A British political figure who travels in America.

Antrobus, Mrs. Edward (Susan). "The Point of View." The recipient of her husband's letters concerning life in America.

Antrobus, Gwendolyn. "The Point of View." The daughter of Edward and Susan Antrobus.

Anvoy, Ruth. "The Coxon Fund." The American niece of Lady Coxon; her management of the Coxon Fund, after Lady Coxon's death, costs her marriage to George Gravener.

Anvoy. "The Coxon Fund." The New York father of Ruth Anvoy; he suffers financial reverses and soon thereafter dies.

April, Rev. Mr. "The Siege of London." A British clergyman at Longlands, the estate of the Demesne family.

April, Mrs. "The Siege of London." The wife of the British clergyman at Longlands.

Archer. *The Portrait of a Lady.* Convivial, liberal, traveling father of Isabel Archer; he is now deceased.

Archer, Edith. *The Portrait of a Lady.* See Keyes, Mrs.

Archer, Isabel. *The Portrait of a Lady.* Sponsored to England by her Aunt Lydia Touchett, she rejects the proposal of Lord Warburton and repeated proposals of the American textile industrialist Caspar Goodwood, marries Gilbert Osmond in Florence, and slowly settles into a stifling life with him in Rome.

Archer, Lilian. *The Portrait of a Lady.* See Ludlow, Mrs. Edmund.

Armiger, Rose. *The Other House.* The strong-minded object of Denis Vidal's affection; she loves Tony Bream and drowns his daughter Effie.

Artemisia. "The Real Thing." A fictional character in Philip Vincent's *Rutland Ramsey*, which novel the narrator is commissioned to illustrate.

Ash, Bob. "A Round of Visits." The husband of Florence Ash, who intends to divorce him.

Ash, Mrs. Bob (Florence). "A Round of Visits." A casual friend of Mark Monteith, who visits her in New York; she intends to divorce her husband.

Ash, Susan. *What Maisie Knew.* A housemaid in Beale Farange's employ.

Ashbury, Maud. "Lord Beaupre." A casual friend of Guy Firminger.

Ashbury, Mrs. "Lord Beaupre." The mother of Maud Ashbury and a casual friend of Guy Firminger.

Ashmore, Arthur. "The Liar." The son of Sir David Ashmore, whose portrait Oliver Lyon paints while visiting at the estate of Stayes.

Ashmore, Sir David. "The Liar." The genial old subject of the portrait which Oliver Lyon paints while visiting at the estate of Stayes.

Aspern, Jeffrey. "The Aspern Papers." The deceased American poet whose papers Juliana Bordereau, his former mistress, has treasured through the years.

Assingham, Colonel Robert "Bob." *The Golden Bowl.* The patient husband of Fanny Assingham; he is a close friend of Adam Verver, Maggie Verver, Prince Amerigo, and Charlotte Stant.

Assingham, Mrs. Robert (Fanny). *The Golden Bowl.* The long-winded, well-meaning friend of Adam Verver, Maggie Verver, Prince Amerigo, and Charlotte Stant; she breaks the golden bowl.

Assunta. *Roderick Hudson, The Princess Casamassima.* The maid of Christina Light, who becomes the Princess Casamassima.

Aubert, Abbe. *The American.* Lizzie Tristram's friend who tells her that Claire de Bellegarde de Cintre has become a Carmelite nun.

Augustine. *The Europeans.* The maid of Baroness Eugenia Munster.

Austin, Maxim "Max." "A Light Man." A worthless adventurer, the "light man" whose journal comprises the story; he is a friend of Theodore Lisle.

Austin, Mrs. "A Light Man." The deceased mother of Max Austin and a former friend of Frederick Sloane.

Azarina. *The Europeans.* An old Negro maid at the Wentworth estate whom Baroness Eugenia Munster cannot make talk.

B, Mrs. "At Isella." The woman from Philadelphia who is to be the narrator's mother-in-law.

B, Miss. "At Isella." The woman from Philadelphia who is to be the narrator's wife.

B —, Signora. "Travelling Companions." A Neapolitan lady whom Brooke the narrator meets.

B —. "Travelling Companions." The child of a Neapolitan lady whom Brooke the narrator meets.

Babcock, Rev. Mr. Benjamin "Dorchester." *The American.* A Unitarian minister from Dorchester, Massachusetts, who experiences moral reactions to art in Europe; he is a traveling friend of Christopher Newman briefly.

Babe. "A London Life." A member of the Rifles whom Lady Davenant introduces to Laura Wing.

Bagger. *The Awkward Age.* A casual friend named by the Brookenhams.

Bagger, Mrs. *The Awkward Age.* A casual friend named by the Brookenhams.

Bagley, Sir Bruce, Bart. "Mora Montravers." A man loved by Mora Montravers.

Bagshaw, Mrs. "The Siege of London." A woman who is to visit Mrs. Nancy Grenville Beck Headway and help her into British society.

Bald (or Bold), Miss. "A London Life." A former governess of Lionel Berrington.

Bamborough, Lord. "A London Life." A former lover of Mrs. Selina Wing Berrington.

Banker, Miss. "The Two Faces." A gossip who chats with Shirley Sutton about the awaited entrance of Valda Gwyther.

Banks. *The Outcry.* Lord Theign's butler at Dedborough.

Bannister, Alfred. "A Landscape Painter." The man whom Miriam Quarterman decides not to marry.

Bantling, Bob. *The Portrait of a Lady.* The Britisher who escorts Henrietta Stackpole about Europe and eventually is to marry her.

Baptiste. *The Ambassadors.* The servant of Chad Newsome in Paris.

Barbara, Lady. *The American.* A relative of Lord Deepmere.

Bardi. *The Outcry.* The art expert from Milan who says that the controversial painting owned by Lord Theign is by Mantovano and not Moretto.

Bernard, Clara. "A Bundle of Letters." A friend of Miranda Hope, who mentions her in a letter to her mother.

Baron, Peter. "Sir Dominick Ferrand." A writer who discovers the Ferrand papers, destroys them, and marries Mrs. Ryves, deceased Sir Dominick Ferrand's illegitimate widowed daughter.

Barrace, Miss. *The Ambassadors.* A casual friend of Chad Newsome, Little Bilham, and members of their group in Paris.

Bartram, May. "The Beast in the Jungle." The woman who loves John Marcher, the beast in whose life she identifies.

Baskerville. *The Princess Casamassima.* A real actor performing in *The Pearl of Paraguay,* attended by Hyacinth Robinson and Millicent Henning.

Bates. "The Two Faces." Mrs. May Grantham's butler.

Battledown, Lady. "A Bundle of Letters." A friend of Evelyn Vane; Miss Vane mentions her in a letter to Lady Augusta Fleming.

Baxter, Stephen. "The Story of a Masterpiece." The painter whose portrait of Marian Everett disturbs her fiance John Lennox.

Bayswater, Duchess of. "An International Episode." Lord Lambeth's mother, whose prejudice contributes to spoiling the relationship between Lambeth and Bessie Alden.

Bayswater, Duke of. "An International Episode." Lord Lambeth's father, whose supposed sickness obliges Lambeth to return from America.

Beadle, Dr. "Crawford's Consistency." An old physician who once attended Elizabeth Ingram.

Beadel-Muffet, Sir A. B. C., K.C.B., M.P. "The Papers." The publicity-seeker whose reported disappearance is sensational; he is Mrs. Chorner's fiance.

Beadel-Muffet, Lady. "The Papers." Sir A. B. C. Beadel-Muffet's recently deceased wife.

Beadel-Muffet, Miranda. "The Papers." The daughter of Sir A. B. C. Beadel-Muffet who is reported not to be marrying Guy Devereux.

Beadel-Muffet, Miss. "The Papers." Another daughter of Sir A. B. C. Beadel-Muffet.

Beadel-Muffet, Miss. "The Papers." Another daughter of Sir A. B. C. Beadel-Muffet.

Beati, Angelo. "Adina." The handsome Italian who discovered and lost the Tiberian topaz but won Sam Scrope's fiancee Adina Waddington in the process.

Beatrice. "A New England Winter." Mrs. Susan Daintry's maid.

Beauchemin, Lady Lucretia. "Lady Barbarina." The London lady who introduces Dr. Jackson Lemon to her sister Lady Barbarina, whom he marries.

Beauchemin, Lord. "Lady Barbarina." Lady Beauchemin's husband and a son-in-law of Lord Canterville, Lady Barbarina's father.

Beaumont, Beatrice. "The Papers." An actress playing in *Corisande;* she is mentioned as a possibility for a part in a play by Mortimer Marshal.

Beaumont, Percy. "An International Episode. " The close friend of Lord Lambeth who fears that Lambeth is falling in love with Bessie Alden.

Beaumont. "Nona Vincent." The actor-manager of the Legitimate Theater.

Beaumont, Mrs. "Nona Vincent." The wife of actor-manager Beaumont.

Beaupre, Lord. "Lord Beaupre." Guy Firminger, whom family deaths convert into the titled lord and hence into the target for husband-seeking society ladies.

Beaupre, Lord. "Lord Beaupre." The father of Guy Firminger's cousin; he dies.

Beaupre. "Lord Beaupre." Guy Firminger's cousin, the son of the elder Lord Beaupre; he dies.

Beauprey. "Lord Beaupre." The original name in the magazine publication for Beaupre, which see.

Beaurepas, Mme. "The Pension Beaurepas." The keeper of Pension Beaurepas.

Beaurepas. Mlle. "The Pension Beaurepas." The niece of Mme. Beaurepas.

Beck, Mrs. Clara. "Guest's Confession." The widowed duenna to Miss Laura Guest and the object of her own rich cousin Crawford's affections; she is evidently related to John Guest.

Beck, Philadelphus. "The Siege of London." The previous husband of Nancy Grenville Beck Headway.

Becky. "A Day of Days." The maid of Herbert and Adela Moore.

Beever, Paul. *The Other House.* A deceased banker, the former partner of Paul Bream and the husband of Kate Beever.

Beever, Mrs. Paul (Kate). *The Other House.* The widow of banker Paul Beever and now the head of the house near that of Tony Bream; she is the mother of Paul Beever, whom she wants to marry Jean Martle.

Beever, Paul. *The Other House.* The son of Kate Beever, who wants him to marry Jean Martle.

Beldonald, Lady Nina. "The Beldonald Holbein." A hard beauty who wants a plain foil and hence hires Mrs. Louisa Brash for a while.

Belfield, Diana. "Longstaff's Marriage." The initially hard beauty who refuses the hand of the supposedly dying Reginald Longstaff and then when she is dying wants him.

Belfield, Mrs. "Longstaff's Marriage." Diana Belfield's mother, whose death unites Diana and her companion Agatha Josling.

Belinda. "The Ghostly Rental." Captain Diamond's Negro maid.

Bellamy, D. F. "Pandora." The fiance of Pandora Day, who obtains a consular appointment to Holland for him.

Bellegarde, Blanche. *The American.* The daughter of Urbain de Bellegarde and his wife.

Bellegarde, Claire. *The American.* See Cintre, Claire de Bellegarde de.

Bellegarde, Marquis Henri-Urbain. *The American.* The murdered husband of Mme. de Bellegarde, Christopher Newman's implacable foe.

Bellegarde, Mme. Emmeline de. *The American.* The widow of murdered Marquis Henri-Urbain de Bellegarde, and the mother of Urbain, Claire, and Valentin de Bellegarde; she is Christopher Newman's implacable foe.

Bellegarde, Urbain (Henri-Urbain) de. *The American.* The older son of Mme. de Bellegarde and now the nominal head of the family.

Bellegarde, Mme. de. *The American.* The wife of Urbain de Bellegarde, whom she loathes.

Bellegarde, Valentin de. *The American.* The younger son of Mme. de Bellegarde; he is a friend of Christopher Newman and is killed in a duel with Stanislas Kapp.

Bellevue, Lady Beatrice. "An International Episode." A fashionable lady seen in Hyde Park.

Bellhouse, Lady. "Mrs. Medwin." A lady of fashion who, according to Mamie Cutter, has approved of Mrs. Medwin.

Beltram, Dr. *The Awkward Age.* Agnesina's physician.

Bender, Breckenridge. *The Outcry.* The well-financed American purchaser of British art treasures; he is the cause of "the outcry."

Benton, Laura. "A Day of Days." An affianced friend of Adela Moore.

Benvolio. "Belvolio." An allegorical poetic personality torn between love of society (the Countess) and learning (Scholastica).

Benyon, Georgina. "Georgina's Reasons." See Roy, Mrs.

William (Georgina Gressie Benyon).

Benyon, Captain Raymond. "Georgina's Reasons." An American naval officer; he is the first husband of bigamous Georgina Gressie Benyon Roy.

Benyon. "Georgina's Reasons." Unlocatable infant son of Raymond and Georgina Benyon; he was abandoned in Italy by Georgina.

Bergerac, Gabrielle de. "Gabrielle de Bergerac." The young maiden aunt of the narrator; she elopes with and marries the narrator's boyhood tutor Pierre Coquelin and dies with him during the French Revolution.

Bergerac, Baron de. "Gabrielle de Bergerac." The grandfather of the narrator.

Bergerac, Baron de. "Gabrielle de Bergerac." The offensive brother of Gabrielle de Bergerac; his conduct precipitates his sister's elopement with Pierre Coquelin.

Bergerac, Baroness de. "Gabrielle de Bergerac." The wife of Baron de Bergerac and the mother of the narrator.

Bergerac, Chevalier de. "Gabrielle de Bergerac." The narrator; he is the nephew of Gabrielle de Bergerac and the pupil of Pierre Coquelin.

Bernardstone, Lady Emily. "The Path of Duty." The wife of General Bernardstone and the mother of Joscelind Bernardstone.

Bernardstone, Joscelind. "The Path of Duty." The fiancee and then the wife of Ambrose Tester, who all along has loved Lady Margaret Vandeleur.

Bernardstone, General. "The Path of Duty." The father of Joscelind Bernardstone.

Bernier, Charles. "A Tragedy of Error." The crippled husband of Hortense Bernier.

Bernier, Mme. Charles (Hortense). "A Tragedy of Error." The wife of Charles Bernier and the mistress of Vicomte Louis de Meyrau.

Bernier, Mme. "A Tragedy of Error." The mother-in-law of Hortense Bernier.

Berridge, John. "The Velvet Glove." A successful and competent novelist who refuses to write a preface for a trashy novel by Amy Evans.

Berrington, Ferdy "Parson." "A London Life." The son of Lionel and Selina Berrington.

Berrington, Geordie "Scratch." "A London Life." The son of Lionel and Selina Berrington.

Berrington, Lionel. "A London Life." The outraged husband of Selina Berrington; he is the brother-in-law of Laura Wing.

Berrington, Mrs. Lionel (Selina "Lina" Wing). "A London Life." The adulterous American wife of Lionel Berrington; she is the sister of Laura Wing.

Berrington, Mrs. "A London Life." The expropriated mother of Lionel Berrington.

Bessie. *Roderick Hudson.* The little daughter of Cecilia, Rowland Mallet's cousin.

Bessie. "Georgina's Reasons." Presumably the daughter of Agnes Theory's aunt Harriet; she receives gifts from Agnes.

Beston. "John Delavoy." The conservative and opinionated publisher of the *Cynosure,* a popular magazine; his crassness loses him Miss Delavoy.

Bestwick, Raymond. "Mrs. Temperly." The patient and perennially unrewarded suitor of his cousin Maria Temperly's oldest daughter, Dora Temperly.

Betterman, Frank B. *The Ivory Tower.* The former business associate of Abel Gaw and the uncle of Graham Fielder; Betterman's death makes Fielder wealthy but changes his life.

Betterman, Mrs. *The Golden Bowl.* A London hostess of Charlotte Stant.

Betty. "Glasses." Mrs. Meldrum's niece; she refused Geoffrey Dawling.

Bight, Howard. "The Papers." The tardily disgusted journalist who caters to publicity-seekers like Sir A. B. C. Beadel-Muffet and Mortimer Marshal; he is a close friend of Maud Blandy.

Bilham, John Little "Little Bilham." *The Ambassadors.* A dilettante painter-friend of Chad Newsome in Paris.

Billinghurst, Mrs. *The Tragic Muse.* A casual friend of Mrs. Julia Sherringham Dallow, who is to see her at Versailles.

Bingham, George. "My Friend Bingham." The man who accidentally kills the son of widowed Mrs. Lucy Hicks; later they marry.

Birdseye, Miss. *The Bostonians.* An ineffectual but sweet old feminist; she dies.

Blackborough, Marquis de. "An International Episode." A swell observed in Hyde Park.

Blanchard, Augusta. *Roderick Hudson.* An American flower painter in Rome; she is seemingly attracted to Rowland Mallet; in frustration she takes up with Leavenworth.

Blanche. "Paste." Charlotte Prime's pupil.

Bland, Sir Cantopher. *The Sense of the Past.* A family friend of the Midmores; he is suspicious of Ralph Pendrel.

Bland, Rev. Mr. "My Friend Bingham." The minister at the funeral of Mrs. Lucy Hicks's son.

Blandy, Maud. "The Papers." A sensitive and finally disgusted journalist who likes Howard Bight and is also liked by Mortimer Marshal.

Blankenberg, Miss. "A Landscape Painter." A minor friend of Miriam Quarterman.

Blessingbourne, Mrs. Maud. "The Story in It." The sweet young widow whose quietly exciting love for Colonel Voyt he does not suspect until Mrs. Dyott tells him.

Blint. *The Golden Bowl.* The sleek, civil little lover of Lady Castledean.

Bloodgood, Phil. "A Round of Visits." A former trusted friend of Mark Monteith; he absconded with some of Monteith's money.

Blumenthal, Mme. Anastasia. "Eugene Pickering." A youngish widow who is the temporary object of Eugene Pickering's infatuation.

Blumenthal. "Eugene Pickering." The unpleasant Jewish husband of Anastasia Blumenthal; he is now deceased.

Blunt, Esther. "A Landscape Painter." The original name in the magazine publication for Miriam Quarterman, which see.

Bobby, Lady. "Paste." A woman whose becoming sick at a party necessitates the substitution for her by Mrs. Guy, who thus meets Charlotte Prime.

Bogle, Miss. *The Golden Bowl.* The nurse of the Principino, the infant son of Prince Amerigo and his wife Maggie Verver.

Bolitho, Lady. "The Modern Warning." The sister of Sir Rufus Chasemore.

Bolitho, Lord. "The Solution." The deceased father of Mrs. Blanche Goldie.

Bolton-Brown. "Lord Beaupre." The New Yorker who loves and tardily wins Mary Gosselin, the sister of his friend Hugh Gosselin.

Bolton-Brown, Mrs. "Lord Beaupre." The mother of Bolton-Brown, Hugh Gosselin's friend.

Bolton-Brown, Miss. "Lord Beaupre." A sister of Bolton-Brown, Hugh Gosselin's friend.

Bolton-Brown, Miss. "Lord Beaupre." A sister of Bolton-Brown, Hugh Gosselin's friend.

Bombici, Cavaliere. "The Aspern Papers." A supposedly high-society former friend of the Bordereaus.

Bonifazio. "At Isella." The host of the inn at Isella visited by the narrator.

Bonnycastle, Alfred. "Pandora." A charming host in Washington; at one of his parties Pandora Day meets the President.

Bonnycastle, Mrs. Alfred. "Pandora." A charming hostess in Washington; at one of her parties Pandora Day meets the President.

Bonus, Alfred. "Collaboration." A casual American friend of Herman Heidenmauer and Felix Vendemer.

Booker. "A London Life." A casual friend of Wendover, who loves but is puzzled by Laura Wing.

Boquet, Mlle. "An International Episode." A former governess of Lord Lambeth.

Bordereau, Juliana. "The Aspern Papers." The aged former mistress of the deceased poet Jeffrey Aspern, whose papers the narrator wishes to obtain.

Bordereau, Tina. "The Aspern Papers." The spinster niece of Juliana Bordereau; at the end she says that she has burned the Aspern papers.

Bordereau, Tita. "The Aspern Papers." The original name in the magazine and book publication for Tina Bordereau, which see.

Borealska, Princess. *The American.* A Polish princess whose invitation Christopher Newman declines.

Bosio, Mme. "A Passionate Pilgrim." An opera singer at Covent Garden.

Bostwick, Captain Teddy. "Sir Edmund Orme." An unimportant friend of the narrator.

Bottomley, Lord. "The Point of View." A friend back in England of Edward Antrobus.

Bottomley, Lord. *The Tragic Muse.* A friend of Charles Carteret.

Bouche, Adolfe. "The Point of View." The recipient of Gustave Lejaune's letter.

Bounder. "The Death of the Lion." A person involved in a divorce scandal.

Bourde, Mlle. "Mrs. Temperly." The French governess of the Temperly children in Paris.

Bousefield. "The Next Time." The owner of the magazine which Ray Limbert edited briefly.

Bowerbank, Mrs. *The Princess Casamassima.* A prison official who visits Amanda Pynsent to tell her that Hyacinth Robinson's unwed mother Florentine Vivier is dying in prison.

Bowles, William. "A Most Extraordinary Case." The servant to whom Colonel Ferdinand Mason leaves some money.

Boyer. "The Beast in the Jungle." A casual friend of John Marcher and May Bartram.

Boyer, Mrs. "The Beast in the Jungle." A casual friend of John Marcher and May Bartram.

Braby, Mrs. "The Death of the Lion." The subject of a sensational article in Pinhorn's magazine.

Bracken, Mrs. "Flickerbridge." The subject of one of Frank Granger's portraits.

Braddle, Bertram. "The Great Condition." The man who loves but is suspicious of Mrs. Damerel and hence loses her to the older and less demanding Henry Chilver.

Bradeen, Lady. "In the Cage." A woman who is to marry

Captain Count Philip Everard; she receives one of his telegrams, which was processed by the unnamed girl "in the cage."

Bradeen, Lord. "In the Cage." The recently deceased husband of Lady Bradeen.

Bradham, Davey. *The Ivory Tower.* The middle-aged husband of Gussy Bradham and a friend of Graham Fielder and Rosanna Gaw.

Bradham, Mrs. David (Gussy). *The Ivory Tower.* A friend of Graham Fielder and Rosanna Gaw.

Bradshaw, Mrs. "A Most Extraordinary Case." The hostess at a dance attended by Caroline Hofmann and Dr. Horace Knight, to the discomfiture of Colonel Ferdinand Mason.

Bradshaw, Miss. "Paste." See Prime, Mrs.

Bradshaw. *The Golden Bowl.* Presumably a servant of Prince Amerigo.

Brady, Dr. *The Golden Bowl.* The physician of the Principino, the infant son of Prince Amerigo and his wife Maggie Verver.

Brand, Rev. Mr. *The Europeans.* The young New England minister who eventually is to marry Charlotte Wentworth.

Brandon, Jack. "The Visits." The puzzled object of Louisa Chantry's sudden passion.

Bransby, Adam P. "Miss Gunton of Poughkeepsie." The fiance of Lily Gunton after she has dropped the Roman Prince.

Bransby, Mrs. "Miss Gunton of Poughkeepsie." Adam P. Bransby's mother.

Bransby, Miss. "Miss Gunton of Poughkeepsie." Adam P. Bransby's sister.

Bransby, Miss. "Miss Gunton of Poughkeepsie." Adam P. Bransby's sister.

Brash, Mrs. Louisa. "The Beldonald Holbein." The lovable, ugly, Holbein-like foil to hard, beautiful Lady Beldonald.

Bray, Mrs. "The Chaperon." The rich sister of Lady Maresfield; she unsuccessfully tries to invite Rose Tramore to a ball while ignoring Rose's mother.

Bread, Mrs. Catherine. *The American.* Mme. de Bellegarde's English-born servant who reveals the Bellegarde family secret to Christopher Newman.

Bream, Anthony "Tony." *The Other House.* The widower-father of Effie Bream and the object of the passion of Rose Armiger; he loves Jean Martle.

Bream, Mrs. Anthony (Julia Grantham). *The Other House.* The dying wife of Tony Bream, who promises her not to remarry while their daughter Effie lives; Julia has memories of an unpleasant step-mother.

Bream, Effie. *The Other House.* The little daughter of Tony and Julia Bream; she is drowned by Rose Armiger to nullify Tony Bream's promise to his dying wife Julia not to remarry while Effie lives.

Bream, Paul. *The Other House.* A deceased banker, the former partner of Paul Beever and the father of Tony Bream.

Brecourt, Alphonse de. *The Reverberator.* The husband of Suzanne de Brecourt, a sister of Gaston Probert.

Brecourt, Mme. Alphonse de (Suzanne [Susan] Probert). *The Reverberator.* A sister of Gaston Probert.

Brench, Peter. "The Tree of Knowledge." The friend of Morgan Mallow; he is harmlessly in love with Mallow's wife.

Bride, Julia. "Julia Bride." The often-engaged young New York girl who aids her innocent step-father Pitman and then loses Murray Brush to May Lindeck, who has a better reputation than Julia.

Bride, Mrs. "Julia Bride." See Connery, Mrs.

Bridgenorth, Mrs. "The Tone of Time." The woman who commissions Mary J. Tredick to paint the portrait of a supposedly imaginary person; the painting turns out to be that of a mutual friend.

Bridget, Lady. *The American.* Lord Deepmere's mother.

Brigstock, Mona. *The Spoils of Poynton.* The unpleasant fiancee and then the wife of Owen Gereth, who has come to love Fleda Vetch.

Brigstock, Mrs. *The Spoils of Poynton.* The unpleasant, unyielding mother of Mona Brigstock.

Brinder, Sir John. *The Golden Bowl.* An ambassador's aide in London.

Brindes, Paule de. "Collaboration." The young lady who loves

Felix Vendemer but is too anti-German to marry him after he begins to associate with Herman Heidenmauer.

Brindes, Mme. Marie de. "Collaboration." Paule de Brindes's anti-German mother; she is the widow of a casualty of the Franco-Prussian War.

Brine. "Miss Gunton of Poughkeepsie." The American husband of Mrs. Brine, Lily Gunton's traveling companion.

Brine, Mrs. "Miss Gunton of Poughkeepsie." Lily Gunton's American traveling companion.

Briseux, Pierre. "The Sweetheart of M. Briseux." An inspired French painter, for whom at the outset of his career the female narrator gives up Harold Staines to let Briseux use her as a model and paint over Staines's poor portrait of her.

Brissenden, Guy "Briss." *The Sacred Fount.* The apparently fast-aging husband of Grace Brissenden and hence, according to the narrator, her "sacred fount."

Brissenden, Mrs. Guy (Grace) "Mrs. Briss." *The Sacred Fount.* The wife of guy Brissenden, who according to the narrator is depleted while Grace seems to be growing younger.

Brives, Marquise de. "Mrs. Temperly." A supposedly high-society friend of Mrs. Temperly in Paris.

Brives, Mme. de. *The Reverberator.* A friend of Suzanne de Brecourt, Gaston Probert's sister.

Brivet, Frank. "The Special Type." The lover of Rose Cavenham who incites his wife to divorce him by appearing in public with Alice Dundene as though she were his mistress.

Brivet, Mrs. Frank. "The Special Type." The woman who divorces her husband Frank Brivet and then marries Remson Sturch.

Broderip. *The Europeans.* A former Harvard Law School friend of William Wentworth.

Brohan, Madeleine. "At Isella." An actress seen by the narrator at the Theatre Francais.

Brooke. "Travelling Companions." The narrator; he is a young American tourist who seems to compromise Charlotte Evans in Padua; later they marry in Rome.

Brookenham, Edward. *The Awkward Age.* The husband of Mrs. Brook, the father of Nanda and Harold, and the cousin of Duchess Jane of Naples.

Brookenham, Mrs. Edward "Mrs. Brook." *The Awkward Age.* The center of an effete social circle observed by Longdon, a friend of her lovely and now deceased mother Lady Julia.

Brookenham, Harold. *The Awkward Age.* The ever-borrowing wastrel son of Edward Brookenham and Mrs. Brook; he is Nanda's brother.

Brookenham, Fernanda "Nanda." *The Awkward Age.* The daughter of Edward Brookenham and Mrs. Brook; the god-daughter of Longdon; she loves Vanderbank.

Brooks. "A Light Man." The lawyer of rich, dying Frederick Sloane.

Brooksmith. "Brooksmith." The impeccable butler of the late Oliver Offord.

Brooksmith, Mrs. "Brooksmith." Brooksmith's mother; she dies.

Brown, Mrs. Lucinda. *Watch and Ward.* Roger Lawrence's faithful housekeeper.

Brown. "The Great Good Place." Author George Dane's servant.

Brownrigg, Miss. "Collaboration." An authoress whom Alfred Bonus admires but whom Herman Heidenmauer does not admire.

Bruce, Jane. "The Story of a Year." Robert Bruce's sister.

Bruce, Robert. "The Story of a Year." A young man from Leatherborough who does not join the Union Army during the Civil War but stays home; Lizzie Crowe falls in love with him after her fiance Lieutenant John Ford enters the Union Army.

Brush, Murray. "Julia Bride." A young man whom Julia Bride loves; stories of her lead him away and into an engagement with Mary Lindeck.

Brydon, Spencer. "The Jolly Corner." An expatriate American who late in life returns to New York and confronts his alter ego; he is comforted by Alice Staverton.

Bubb, Mrs. "In the Cage." A customer of Mrs. Jordan, who arranges flowers.

Buckton. "In the Cage." A man who works in the store where

the unnamed telegraphist's "cage" is located.

Buffery, Dr. *The Princess Casamassima.* The conscientious little physician of dying Amanda Pynsent.

Bunbury. *The Princess Casamassima.* A neighbor of the Princess Casamassima, from Broome.

Bunbury, Mrs. *The Princess Casamassima.* A neighbor of the Princess Casamassima, from Broome.

Bundy, Mrs. "Sir Dominick Ferrand." Peter Baron's landlady.

Burfield, "In the Cage." A name mentioned in one of Captain Everard's telegrams.

Burrage, Henry, Jr. *The Bostonians.* A Harvard Law School student and an unsuccessful admirer of Verena Tarrant.

Burrage, Mrs. Henry, Sr. *The Bostonians.* A rather domineering New York widow, the mother of Henry Burrage, Jr.

Butterworth. "Madame de Mauves." Euphemia Cleve de Mauves's New York uncle.

Butterworth. "An International Episode." An American host for the Duke of Green-Erin.

Butterworth, Mrs. "An International Episode." An American hostess for the Duke of Green-Erin.

Buttons. "In the Cage." A person from Thrupp's apartment.

Buttons, Mrs. "In the Cage." A person from Thrupp's apartment.

Buttrick, Dr. *The Wings of the Dove.* Milly Theale's Boston physician.

Buzzard, Dr. "In the Cage." Perhaps a code name for Lady Bradeen in Captain Everard's telegrams.

Calderoni. *The Golden Bowl.* Prince Amerigo's lawyer.

Caliph. "The Impressions of a Cousin." The unscrupulous handler of the financial affairs of Eunice, the cousin of the narrator Catherine Condit; he is the half-brother of Adrian Frank, Eunice's fiance.

Camerino, Count. "The Diary of a Man of Fifty." The killer of the husband of Countess Salvi in a duel; he let another claim the victory and married her.

Canterville, Lord Philip. "Lady Barbarina." The father of Lady

Barbarina, who marries Dr. Jackson Lemon, and of many other children.

Canterville, Lady. "Lady Barbarina." The mother of Lady Barbarina, who marries Dr. Jackson Lemon, and of many other children.

Capadose, Amy. "The Liar." The young daughter of Colonel Clement Capadose and his wife Everina Brant Capadose.

Capadose, Colonel Clement. "The Liar." The liar whose inner nature is revealed by Oliver Lyon's portrait of him.

Capadose, Mrs. Clement (Everina Brant). "The Liar." The wife of Colonel Clement Capadose, the liar; she was formerly the object of Oliver Lyon's affection.

Capadose. "The Liar." The Dean of Rockingham and the brother of Colonel Clement Capadose.

Capadose, General. "The Liar." The father of Colonel Clement Capadose.

Cardew, Mary. "Crapy Cornelia." The original of a memory-evoking photograph which Cornelia Rasch shows to White-Mason.

Carolus. *The Reverberator.* A friend of Charles Waterlow, a painter friend of Gaston Probert.

Carpenter, Mrs. "Osborne's Revenge." A hostess who gives plays and once invites Philip Osborne to a picnic.

Carre, Mme. Honorine. *The Tragic Muse.* A grand retired actress, the coach of Miriam Rooth in Paris.

Carteret, Charles. *The Tragic Muse.* A wealthy, aged friend of Nick Dormer; he unsuccessfully tries to bribe Nick into continuing in a political career.

Casamassima, Prince Gennaro. *Roderick Hudson.* A wealthy Neapolitan who marries Christina Light; this marriage stops Roderick Hudson's career as a sculptor. *The Princess Casamassima.* He pursues his thrill-seeking wife to London, spies on her activities with various anarchistic friends, including Paul Muniment.

Casamassima, Princess (Christina Light). *Roderick Hudson.* As Christina Light she intrigues sculptor Roderick Hudson; her marriage to Prince Gennaro Casamassima ends Hudson's career. *The Princess Casamassima.* She goes to London to associate with members of the international anarchistic movement, and becomes a friend of Hyacinth Robinson, Paul Muniment, and others.

Cashmore, Lady Fanny. *The Awkward Age.* The wife of Lord Cashmore, who gives Harold Brookenham money; she is Lord Petherton's sister.

Cashmore, Lord. *The Awkward Age.* A member of Mrs. Brook's circle; he gives Harold Brookenham money.

Castillani. "Adina." A Roman expert on antiquities.

Castledean, Lady. *The Golden Bowl.* A guest at Matcham whose stay on with Blint emboldens Charlotte Stant and Prince Amerigo to stay also.

Castledean, Lord. *The Golden Bowl.* A guest at Matcham who leaves ahead of his wife.

Catching, Mrs. "Poor Richard." The nurse at Richard Maule's farm home.

Catching, Miss. *The Bostonians.* A librarian at Harvard College.

Catherine, Sister. *The Portrait of a Lady.* One of Pansy Osmond's convent teachers.

Cecilia. *Roderick Hudson.* Rowland Mallet's cousin and confidante; she is Bessie's mother.

Celestine. "The Pension Beaurepas." The cook at the Pension Beaurepas.

Chafer. "The Private Life." A reviewer gossiped about by the author Clare Vawdrey.

Chalais, Marie de. "Gabrielle de Bergerac." The gracious young friend of Gabrielle de Bergerac.

Chalais, Marquis de. "Gabrielle de Bergerac." The grandfather of Marie de Chalais.

Chalumeau. "Madame de Mauves." An old roue friendly to Marie Clairin, the sister-in-law of Mme. de Mauves.

Chamousset, Mme. "The Pension Beaurepas." A competitor of Mme. Beaurepas in a rival pension.

Champer, Lady. "Miss Gunton of Poughkeepsie." A woman who is sympathetic to the Roman Prince when she learns that Miss Gunton seems only to be leading him on.

Chancellor, Olive. *The Bostonians.* A spinster feminist from Boston, the sponsor of Verena Tarrant, friend of Miss Birdseye, bitter enemy of Basil Ransom, and sister of Adelina Luna.

Chantry, Christopher. "The Visits." The husband of Helen
   Chantry and father of Louisa Chantry.

Chantry, Mrs. Christopher (Helen). "The Visits." The mother
   of Louisa Chantry and friend of the woman narrator.

Chantry, Louisa. "The Visits." The young lady who through
   apparently uncontrollable passion proposes to Jack Brandon and later sickens and dies because of shock and
   remorse.

Charles. "My Friend Bingham." The narrator and friend of
   George Bingham.

Chart, Adela. "The Marriages." The young lady who blackens
   her deceased mother's reputation in an effort to prevent
   her father from marrying Mrs. Churchley.

Chart, Basil. "The Marriages." Adela Chart's brother who is
   away in the army in India.

Chart, Beatrice. "The Marriages." A young sister of Adela
   Chart.

Chart, Godfrey. "The Marriages." The brother of Adela Chart
   whose studies for examinations for acceptance in the
   diplomatic service are interrupted by marriage to a
   floozy, whom his father pays off.

Chart, Mrs. Godfrey. "The Marriages." The middle-aged floozy
   who marries Godfrey Chart and then accepts money from
   her father-in-law to stay away.

Chart, Muriel. "The Marriages." A young sister of Adela
   Chart.

Chart, Colonel. "The Marriages." The father of Adela Chart;
   she tries to protect him by lying about her mother to Mrs.
   Churchley, whom the father, a widower, wishes to marry.

Chasemore, Sir Rufus, K.C.B., M.P. "The Modern Warning."
   The anti-American Britisher who marries the American
   Agatha Grice.

Chasemore, Lady Agatha. "The Modern Warning." See Grice,
   Agatha.

Chataway, Ronald. "The Married Son." The husband of a
   healer and medium.

Chataway, Mrs. Ronald. "The Married Son." The New York
   healer and medium; she is a friend of Elizabeth (Aunt

Eliza) Talbert (introduced earlier in *The Whole Family*).

Chatterton, Mrs. *Watch and Ward.* A talkative New York friend of Mrs. Isabel Morton Keith.

Chayter. *The Tragic Muse.* Charles Carteret's austerely splendid butler.

Chew, Mrs. "Lady Barbarina." A woman who attends Lady Barbarina Lemon's New York salon.

Chilver, Henry. "The Great Condition." The gentleman who through trust succeeds in winning Mrs. Damerel where the younger Bertram Braddle fails through suspicion.

Chipperfield. *The Princess Casamassima.* Mrs. Bowerbank's sick brother-in-law, who is an undertaker and lives in Amanda Pynsent's neighborhood.

Chipperfield, Mrs. *The Princess Casamassima.* Mrs. Bowerbank's sister, who lives in Amanda Pynsent's neighborhood.

Chivers. "Covering End." Captain Clement Yule's butler at the estate of Covering End.

Chorner, Mrs. "The Papers." Sir A. B. C. Beadel-Muffet's fiancee; it is ultimately revealed that she too likes publicity.

Chumleigh. "The Wheel of Time." See Greyswood, Lord.

Church, Aurora. "The Pension Beaurepas." An American girl traveling frugally through Europe with her mother; she is attractive to M. Pigeonneau of the Pension Beaurepas. "The Point of View." She returns to America with her mother, meeting Louis Leverett on shipboard but not being proposed to by him.

Church, Mrs. "The Pension Beaurepas." Aurora Church's mother, who travels frugally through Europe seeking a son-in-law. "The Point of View." She returns to America with her daughter, whom she allows a brief independence in New York before requiring her to go west with her.

Churchley, Mrs. "The Marriages." The widow whom Colonel Chart loves but fails to win owing to his daughter Adela Chart's lies about his first wife.

Churm, Miss. "The Real Thing." The painter-narrator's adept Cockney model.

Churton. "The Aspern Papers." A supposedly high-society former friend of the Bordereaus.

Churton, Mrs. "The Aspern Papers." A supposedly high-society former friend of the Bordereaus.

Cintre, Blanche de. *The American.* The young daughter of Mme. Claire de Bellegarde de Cintre.

Cintre, Mme. Claire de Bellegarde de. *The American.* The attractive young widow who loves Christopher Newman but is forced by family pressure to deny him; she enters a Carmelite convent.

Cissy. "In the Cage." The recipient of a telegram from Captain Everard.

Clairin, Mme. Marie de Mauves. "Madame de Mauves." The sister of Richard de Mauves and sister-in-law of Mme. Euphemia de Mauves.

Clairin. "Madame de Mauves." The druggist husband of Marie de Mauves Clairin, the sister-in-law of Mme. Euphemia de Mauves.

Clancy, Mrs. "The Pupil." The sister of Mr. Moreen.

Clanduffy, Lord. "The Path of Duty." The father-in-law of General Bernardstone.

Clare, Richard. "Poor Richard." The original name in the magazine publication for Richard Maule, which see.

Clarisse, Mamselle. *The American.* A former maid of Mme. Emmeline de Bellegarde.

Clark, Rev. Mr. "A Problem." Emma's favorite clergyman; he aids in her reconciliation with David, her husband.

Claude, Lady. "Broken Wings." Mrs. Harvey's friend, who also wants to write.

Claude, Sir. *What Maisie Knew.* Ida Farange's second husband; he is a friend of Maisie Farange and the lover of Miss Overmore after her marriage to Beale Farange.

Claudia, Donna. "Miss Gunton of Poughkeepsie." The sister of the Roman Prince, Lily Gunton's estranged fiance.

Claudine. "Madame de Mauves." The wife or girl-friend of a painter; both are seen by envious Longmore.

Clement, Lady Agnes. "Lady Barbarina." A younger sister of

Lady Barbarina Lemon; she is wooed and won by the cowboy Herman Longstraw.

Clement, Lady Barbarina. "Lady Barbarina." See Lemon, Mrs. Jackson (Lady Barbarina).

Clement, Lady Barberina. "Lady Barberina." The original name in the magazine publication for Mrs. Jackson (Lady Barbarina) Lemon, which see.

Clementine, Mlle. "Rose-Agathe." The name given to the hair-dresser's second dummy.

Clementine. "A Bundle of Letters." A dressmaker named in a letter from Violet Ray to Agnes Rich.

Cleve, Euphemia. "Madame de Mauves." See Mauves, Countess Euphemia Cleve de.

Cleve, Mrs. "Madame de Mauves." The mother of Mme. Euphemia Cleve de Mauves.

Cliche, Marquis Maxime de. *The Reverberator.* The husband of Marguerite, a sister of Gaston Probert.

Cliche, Mme. Maxime de (Marguerite [Margaret, "Maggie," "Margot"] Probert). *The Reverberator.* A sister of Gaston Probert.

Climber, Annie. *The Portrait of a Lady.* A social climber from Wilmington traveling with her sister in Europe.

Climber, Miss. *The Portrait of a Lady.* A social climber from Wilmington traveling with her sister in Europe.

Cocker. "In the Cage." The owner of the store in which the unnamed telegraphist's cage is located.

Cockerel, Marcellus C. "The Point of View." The pro-American friend of Louis Leverett.

Collingwood. "A London Life." A minor friend of Mrs. Selina Berrington.

Collingwood, Mrs. "A London Life." A minor friend of Mrs. Selina Berrington.

Collop, Miss. "The Death of the Lion." The real name of the popular authoress whose pen name is Guy Walsingham.

Condit, Catherine. "The Impressions of a Cousin." The painter-narrator; she has just returned from Europe to New York; Adrian Frank, her cousin Eunice's fiance, falls in love with her.

Condrip, Bertie. *The Wings of the Dove.* A son of Marian Croy Condrip.

Condrip, Guy. *The Wings of the Dove.* A son of Marian Croy Condrip.

Condrip, Kitty. *The Wings of the Dove.* A daughter of Marian Croy Condrip.

Condrip, Maudie. *The Wings of the Dove.* A daughter of Marian Croy Condrip.

Condrip, Rev. Mr. *The Wings of the Dove.* The deceased minister husband of Marian Croy Condrip.

Condrip, Mrs. Marian Croy. *The Wings of the Dove.* The sister of Kate Croy; she is the widowed mother of four small children.

Condrip, Miss. *The Wings of the Dove.* An unmarried sister of the late Rev. Mr. Condrip.

Condrip, Miss. *The Wings of the Dove.* An unmarried sister of the late Rev. Mr. Condrip.

Congreve, Henrietta. "Osborne's Revenge." The innocent girl wrongly accused of jilting Philip Osborne's friend Robert Graham, who committed suicide.

Connery. "Julia Bride." A step-father of Julia Bride.

Connery, Mrs. Bride Pitman. "Julia Bride." Julia Bride's often-wed and evidently promiscuous mother, about whom Julia Bride tells the truth to help Pitman.

Considine, Lady. "Glasses." The mother of Lord Iffield, whom Flora Saunt wishes to marry but does not.

Considine, Lord. "Glasses." The father of Lord Iffield, whom Flora Saunt wishes to marry but does not.

Considine, Lord. "Mrs. Medwin." A dinner partner of Mamie Cutter once.

Cookham, Kate. "The Bench of Desolation." The victimizer of Herbert Dodd, for whom she invested for years his breach of promise payment.

Cooler, Mrs. "The Point of View." The sister of Marcellus C. Cockerel, to whom he writes.

Cooper, Dr. James. "The Story of a Year." The physician at Glenham who treats Lieutenant John Ford.

Cooper, Miss. "The Story of a Year." The daughter of Dr. Cooper and friend of Lizzie Crowe.

Cooper. "In the Cage." A name mentioned in one of Lady Bradeen's telegrams.

Coote, Charley. "The Bench of Desolation." A friend whom Herbert Dodd sees outside Kate Cookham's hotel window.

Cope. "Master Eustace." A businessman who returns from an extended time spent in India and marries Mrs. Garnyer; Eustace Garnyer is their illegitimate son.

Cope, Mrs. "Master Eustace." See Garnyer, Mrs. Henry.

Coquelin, Pierre. "Gabrielle de Bergerac." The tutor of little Chevalier de Bergerac; he is the lover and then the husband of Gabrielle de Bergerac; they die together during the French Revolution.

Coquelin, Mme. "Gabrielle de Bergerac." Pierre Coquelin's mother, who remarried after her first husband's death.

Corvick, George. "The Figure in the Carpet." A literary critic friend of the critic-narrator; he claims to have traced out "the figure in the carpet" of Hugh Vereker's works; he marries Gwendolyn Erme and dies before he can publish his discovery concerning Vereker's works.

Corvick, Mrs. George (Gwendolyn Erme). "The Figure in the Carpet." See Erme, Gwendolyn.

Costello, Mrs. "Daisy Miller." Frederick Forsyth Winterbourne's Europeanized aunt who disapproves of Daisy Miller's conduct.

Courageau, M. de. *The Reverberator.* An elderly friend of Suzanne de Brecourt, Gaston Probert's sister.

Coventry, Mrs. "The Madonna of the Future." The American woman in Florence who upbraids the painter Theobald for not being productive.

Coxon, Lord Gregory. "The Coxon Fund." The deceased husband of Lady Coxon, who established the Coxon Fund at her husband's request.

Coxon, Lady. "The Coxon Fund." The widow of Lord Gregory Coxon and the founder of the Coxon Fund at her husband's request; she is the aunt of Ruth Anvoy.

Coyle, Spencer. "Owen Wingrave." The coach of aspirants for
    military careers, including Owen Wingrave and young
    Lechmere; he and his wife are guests at the Wingrave
    estate of Paramore.

Coyle, Mrs. Spencer. "Owen Wingrave." The wife of Spencer
    Coyle, who accompanies him to the Wingrave estate of
    Paramore.

Coyne, Townsend "Stent." *The Sense of the Past.* The deceased
    husband of Aurora Coyne.

Coyne, Mrs. Townsend (Aurora). *The Sense of the Past.* A
    wealthy young anti-European New York widow whom
    historian Ralph Pendrel loves but who only admires him.

Coyne. *The Sense of the Past.* The elderly Wall Street father-
    in-law of Aurora Coyne.

Crawford. "Guest's Confession." A silver-millionaire who likes
    Clara Beck, Laura Guest's companion.

Crawford. "Crawford's Consistency." The man who marries
    a vicious low-brow when Elizabeth Ingram is forced by
    her parents to renounce him; he loses his fortune and
    becomes a druggist; he is crippled by his wife.

Crawford, Mrs. "Crawford's Consistency." The vicious low-
    brow whom Crawford marries on the rebound; she brow-
    beats and even cripples him when he loses his fortune.

Creston, Paul. "The Altar of the Dead." The man who dis-
    pleased George Stransom by remarrying after the death
    of his first wife.

Creston, Mrs. Paul (Kate). "The Altar of the Dead." The de-
    ceased first wife of Paul Creston, George Stransom's
    friend.

Creston, Mrs. Paul. "The Altar of the Dead." The present
    wife of Paul Creston, George Stransom's friend.

Crichton. *The Golden Bowl.* A museum curator friendly to
    Adam Verver; through him Maggie Verver checks into
    the lineage of her husband Prince Amerigo.

Crick. *The Ivory Tower.* The lawyer of the estate of Frank B.
    Betterman; he advises with Betterman's heir Graham
    Fielder.

Crimble, Hugh. *The Outcry.* An art devotee and friend of Lady

Grace; he thinks that the so-called Moretto owned by Lord Theign is really a Mantovano.

Crisford. "The Wheel of Time." A minor host; he paints.

Crisford, Mrs. "The Wheel of Time." A minor hostess.

Crispin, Captain Charley, "A London Life." One of Mrs. Selina Berrington's lovers.

Crookenden "Old Crook." *The Princess Casamassima.* The London bookbinder for whom Hyacinth Robinson works.

Crookenden, Mrs. *The Princess Casamassima.* The wife of the London bookbinder for whom Hyacinth Robinson works; he visits the Crookenden home for Sunday tea.

Crookenden, Miss. *The Princess Casamassima.* One of six Crookenden daughters; Hyacinth Robinson is led to believe that it is hoped he will propose.

Crookenden, Miss. *The Princess Casamassima.* One of six Crookenden daughters; Hyacinth Robinson is led to believe that it is hoped he will propose.

Crookenden, Miss. *The Princess Casamassima.* One of six Crookenden daughters; Hyacinth Robinson is led to believe that it is hoped he will propose.

Crookenden, Miss. *The Princess Casamassima.* One of six Crookenden daughters; Hyacinth Robinson is led to believe that it is hoped he will propose.

Crookenden, Miss. *The Princess Casamassima.* One of six Crookenden daughters; Hyacinth Robinson is led to believe that it is hoped he will propose.

Crookenden, Miss. *The Princess Casamassima.* One of six Crookenden daughters; Hyacinth Robinson is led to believe that it is hoped he will propose.

Crotty. *The Princess Casamassima.* The paroled convict husband of Susan Crotty.

Crotty, Mrs. Susan. *The Princess Casamassima.* A woman gossiped about by the Princess Casamassima in imitation of Lady Aurora Langrish; her husband is a paroled convict.

Croucher, Mrs. *The Bostonians.* A New Yorker in whose home feminists gather and talk.

Crowe, Elizabeth "Lizzie," "Liz." "The Story of a Year." The light-headed girl in Glenham who forgets her fiance Lieutenant John Ford and falls in love with Robert Bruce.

Croy, Kate. *The Wings of the Dove.* The daughter of Lionel Croy, the sister of Mrs. Marian Croy Condrip, and the niece of Mrs. Maud Manningham Lowder; she loves Merton Densher and plots with him to have him obtain money by marrying dying Milly Theale.

Croy, Lionel. *The Wings of the Dove.* The conniving father of Kate Croy and Marian Croy Condrip.

Croy, Mrs. Lionel (nee Manningham). *The Wings of the Dove.* The deceased sister of Mrs. Maud Manningham Lowder, the wife of Lionel Croy, and the mother of Kate Croy and Marian Croy Condrip.

Croy. *The Wings of the Dove.* The brother of Kate Croy who died of typhoid.

Croy. *The Wings of the Dove.* The brother of Kate Croy who drowned.

Cuddon, Mrs. *What Maisie Knew.* One of Beale Farange's mistresses.

Cumnor, John. "The Aspern Papers." The editor friend of the critic-narrator; a British admirer of the works of Jeffrey Aspern.

Curd, Susan. *The Awkward Age.* Mrs. Brookenham's maid.

Cutter, Mamie. "Mrs. Medwin." The half-sister of Homer Scott; she supports herself by getting people into British social circles.

Cynthia. "A Landscape Painter." Captain Quarterman's aged Negro maid.

Dadd, Miss. "The Beldonald Holbein." The deceased companion of Lady Beldonald; Mrs. Louisa Brash is her successor.

Daintry, Florimond. "A New England Winter." The dilettante painter who visits his mother in Boston after a period of art-study in Paris.

Daintry, Lucretia. "A New England Winter." The sister of Florimond Daintry's father; she correctly judges her nephew's pretentiousness.

Daintry, Mrs. Susan. "A New England Winter." The mother of Florimond Daintry who foolishly wishes Rachel Torrance to visit Boston to make her son's stay pleasant.

Dallow, George. *The Tragic Muse.* The deceased husband of Julia Sherringham Dallow, who loves Nick Dormer.

Dallow, Mrs. George (Julia Sherringham). *The Tragic Muse.* The sister of Peter Sherringham, who loves Miriam Rooth; she loves Nick Dormer but will marry him only if he enters politics.

Damerel, Mrs. "The Great Condition." The American widow who loves Bertram Braddle but marries Henry Chilver because Braddle is groundlessly suspicious of her past.

Dandelard. *The American.* A brutal wife-beating Frenchman.

Dandelard, Mme. *The American.* An Italian who entered French society by marrying a brutal Frenchman.

Dane, George. "The Great Good Place." An oppressedly busy writer who dreams of a "great good place" of rest.

Dangerfield, Mrs. "Pandora." A shipboard companion of Count Otto Vogelstein who lectures him on social customs in America.

Dashwood, Basil. *The Tragic Muse.* A competent actor who helps Miriam Rooth into London theatrical circles and later marries her.

Dashwood, Mrs. Basil. *The Tragic Muse.* See Rooth, Miriam.

Davenant, Lady. "A London Life." The companion of Mrs. Berrington, the expropriated mother of Lionel Berrington; she is the hard-headed confidante of Laura Wing.

Davenant, Lord. *The Tragic Muse.* An embassy official in the youth of Mrs. Rooth.

David. "A Problem." Emma's husband; according to Magawisca's prophecy and that of others, their child dies and they remarry (to each other).

David. "Guest's Confession." The narrator and step-brother of Edgar Musgrave; he falls in love with Laura Guest.

Davidoff. "The Siege of London." An ambassador invited by the Demesnes to their estate of Longlands.

Davis, Dr. "Daisy Miller." The Schenectady physician for the Miller family.

Dawes, Miss. "The Story of a Year." A neighbor of the Ford family.

Dawling, Geoffrey. "Glasses." The seemingly hopeless admirer of Flora Saunt; he marries her when she goes blind.

Dawling. "Glasses." The father of Geoffrey Dawling; he is employed in the Treasury.

Dawling, Miss. "Glasses." A sister of Geoffrey Dawling; she lives in Bournemouth.

Dawling, Miss. "Glasses." A sister of Geoffrey Dawling; she lives in Bournemouth.

Dawling, Miss. "Glasses." A sister of Geoffrey Dawling; she lives in Bournemouth.

Dawling, Miss. "Glasses." A sister of Geoffrey Dawling; she lives in Bournemouth.

Dawson. "A Landscape Painter." The storekeeper at Chowderville, where Locksley goes to recover after being jilted by Miss Leary.

Day, P. W. "Pandora." Pandora Day's sleepy father from Utica.

Day, Mrs. P. W. "Pandora." Pandora Day's sleepy mother from Utica.

Day, Pandora. "Pandora." The self-made girl who impresses Count Otto Vogelstein aboard ship and again in Washington but who will marry D. F. Bellamy, whose position as Minister to Holland she obtains from the President.

Day. "Pandora." Pandora Day's young brother.

Day, Miss. "Pandora." Pandora Day's young sister.

Dean. "The Bench of Desolation." The crooked partner of Drury, Nan Drury's father.

Deane, Drayton. "The Figure in the Carpet." The third-rate literary critic who marries Gwendolyn Erme Corvick but who can tell the critic-narrator nothing about "the figure in the carpet" of Hugh Vereker's works.

Deane, Mrs. Drayton (Gwendolyn Erme Corvick). "The Figure in the Carpet." See Erme, Gwendolyn.

Deborah. "De Grey, A Romance." Mrs. De Grey's servant.

Deborah, Miss. "The Ghostly Rental." The local gossip who tells the narrator part of Captain Diamond's story.

Dedrick, Maud-Evelyn. "Maud-Evelyn." The long-deceased daughter of Mr. and Mrs. Dedrick, who with Marmaduke gradually build up an imaginary life in which he becomes their son-in-law, although he never saw Maud-Evelyn Dedrick.

Dedrick. "Maud-Evelyn." The father of the deceased Maud-Evelyn, who is made into the imaginary wife of Marmaduke.

Dedrick, Mrs. "Maud-Evelyn." The mother of the deceased Maud-Evelyn, who is made into the imaginary wife of Marmaduke.

Deedy. "The Death of the Lion." The deceased owner and editor of the weekly periodical taken over by Pinhorn, the critic-narrator's employer.

Deedy, Mrs. "The Death of the Lion." The widow of the late owner of the weekly periodical taken over by Pinhorn, the critic-narrator's employer.

Deepmere, Lord. *The American.* The shallow young Irish nobleman who is the cousin of Mme. de Bellegarde and who is interested in her daughter Mme. Claire de Bellegarde de Cintre.

De Grey, George. "De Grey, A Romance." An ancestor of Paul De Grey who loved and hence caused the death of Antonietta Gambini, according to the family curse.

De Grey, George. "De Grey, A Romance." An ancestor of Paul De Grey who loved and hence caused the death of Mary Fortescue, according to the family curse.

De Grey, George. "De Grey, A Romance." The deceased father of Paul De Grey; he died after one year of marriage.

De Grey, Mrs. George. "De Grey, A Romance." The widow of George De Grey and the mother of Paul De Grey; she was spared from the De Grey family curse because her husband did not love her.

De Grey, John. "De Grey, A Romance." An ancestor of Paul De Grey who loved and hence caused the death of Henrietta Spencer, according to the family curse.

De Grey, John. "De Grey, A Romance." An ancestor of Paul De Grey who loved and hence caused the death of Blanche Ferrars, according to the family curse.

De Grey, Paul. "De Grey, A Romance." An ancestor of Paul De Grey who loved and hence caused the death of Lucretia Lefevre, according to the family curse.

De Grey, Paul. "De Grey, A Romance." An ancestor of Paul De Grey who loved and hence caused the death of Magdalen Scrope, according to the family curse.

De Grey, Paul. "De Grey, A Romance." The scion of the De Grey family who loves Margaret Aldis; he dies because of a reversal of the family curse which usually kills the first loves of De Greys; his estranged fiancee died in Italy.

Delamere, Mrs. *The Tragic Muse*. A friend of Miriam Rooth; exceptionally, she could tell Miriam something.

Delancey. *The Princess Casamassima*. An anarchistic hairdresser whose general accusation of cowardice Hyacinth Robinson oratorically answers.

Delavoy, John. "John Delavoy." The recently deceased author whose sister Miss Delavoy the narrator pleases by writing an interpretive rather than a chatty essay on him.

Delavoy, Miss. "John Delavoy." The sister of John Delavoy, the recently deceased author; the narrator pleases her by writing an interpretive rather than a chatty essay on him.

Demesne, Sir Arthur. "The Siege of London." An aristocratic Britisher of Longlands who wishes to marry Nancy Grenville Beck Headway but is suspicious of her past; he marries her.

Demesne, Sir Baldwin. "The Siege of London." The deceased father of Sir Arthur Demesne.

Demesne, Lady. "The Siege of London." The mother of Sir Arthur Demesne; she is most suspicious of Mrs. Nancy Grenville Beck Headway, whom her son loves.

Demesne, Lady Nancy. "The Siege of London." See Headway, Mrs. Nancy Grenville Beck.

Denbigh, Mrs. "The Story of a Masterpiece." A woman distantly related to the painter Stephen Baxter, who falls in love with Marian Everett while the two women are traveling in Europe together.

Dence, Sir Digby. *The Awkward Age.* Vanderbank's governmental superior.

Dencombe. "The Middle Years." The dying novelist who has no second chance.

Densher, Merton. *The Wings of the Dove.* The lover of Kate Croy, whose plan to have him love Milly Theale long enough to obtain money from her backfires.

Densher, Rev. Mr. *The Wings of the Dove.* The deceased chaplain father of Merton Densher.

Densher, Mrs. *The Wings of the Dove.* The deceased copyist mother of Merton Densher.

Desmond. "A Bundle of Letters." A friend of Evelyn Vane.

Desmond, Mrs. "A Bundle of Letters." A friend of Evelyn Vane.

Despard, Colonel. "The Given Case." The philandering husband of Kate Despard; the cad returns.

Despard, Mrs. Kate. "The Given Case." The married object of lawyer Barton Reeve's affections; her philandering husband returns.

Devereux, Guy. "The Papers." The young man who it is reported will not marry Miranda Beadel-Muffet, daughter of Sir A. B. C. Beadel-Muffet.

Diamond, Captain. "The Ghostly Rental." A demented man who cursed his daughter and now receives a rental from her "ghost."

Diamond, Mrs. "The Ghostly Rental." The deceased wife of Captain Diamond.

Diamond, Miss. "The Ghostly Rental." The daughter of Captain Diamond; according to the legend, she was cursed to death; in reality she provides "the ghostly rental" for her demented father.

Dodd, Herbert. "The Bench of Desolation." The man who broke his engagement to Kate Cookham and was forced to pay a sum for breach of promise; he married Nan Drury, now deceased; he renews his friendship with Kate Cookham.

Dodd, Mrs. Herbert (Nan Drury). "The Bench of Desolation." The woman who married Herbert Dodd, had two daughters by him, and died; her daughters are also dead.

Dodd, Mrs. Maria. "Osborne's Revenge." The woman who believes the untrue story that Henrietta Congreve jilted Robert Graham and thus caused his suicide.

Dodd, Major. "Osborne's Revenge." The cousin of Mrs. Maria Dodd; he tells Philip Osborne that Henrietta Congreve was not the cause of Robert Graham's suicide.

Dolman, Miss. "In the Cage." A recipient of telegrams from Lady Bradeen and Captain Everard.

Dolphin, Reggie. "The Siege of London." The brother-in-law of George Littlemore.

Dolphin, Mrs. Reggie(Agnes Littlemore). "The Siege of London." The sister of George Littlemore; at her friend Lady Demesne's request, she futilely asks him to state publicly that Mrs. Nancy Grenville Beck Headway is not respectable.

Donner, Beach. *The Awkward Age.* The husband of Carrie Donner, who is the sister of Tishy Grendon, whom Nanda Brookenham visits.

Donner, Mrs. Beach (Carrie). *The Awkward Age.* The shy, pretty sister of Mrs. Tishy Grendon, whom Nanda Brookenham visits.

Donovan, Mrs. "The Chaperon." An Irish woman who offers to aid Rose Tramore socially; Rose refuses because Mrs. Donovan wants to help her alone first and only thereafter help Rose's socially ostracized mother.

Dora. "Osborne's Revenge." This name is mentioned as not that of Philip Osborne's wife.

Doria, Prince. "Adina." A nobleman reported by Mrs. Waddington as staying at a villa in Albano, outside Rome.

Dorimont, Lord. "The Death of the Lion." This nobleman and Lady Augusta Minch lose Neil Paraday's priceless last manuscript between them.

Dormer, Lady Agnes. *The Tragic Muse.* The mother of Percy, Nick, Grace, and Biddy Dormer; she is Mrs. Julia Sherringham Dallow's cousin; she is anguished because Nick prefers painting to politics.

Dormer, Bridget "Biddy." *The Tragic Muse.* The daughter of Lady Agnes Dormer and the sister of Nick Dormer;

she loves Peter Sherringham.

Dormer, Grace. *The Tragic Muse.* The older of Nick Dormer's two sisters, Biddy being the younger.

Dormer, Sir Nicholas. *The Tragic Muse.* The deceased husband of Lady Agnes Dormer and the father of Percy, Nick, Grace, and Biddy Dormer.

Dormer, Nicholas "Nick." *The Tragic Muse.* The man whose preference for painting over politics upsets his mother Lady Agnes Dormer and causes widowed Mrs. Julia Sherringham Dallow to cancel their engagement; he paints Miriam Rooth's portrait; he is a friend of Gabriel Nash.

Dormer, Percival "Percy." *The Tragic Muse.* The older brother of Nick Dormer; he is a disappointment to the family.

Dorrington, Lady. "The Pupil." A casual friend of the Moreen family; her son Lord Verschoyle does not propose to Amy or Paula Moreen.

Dorrington, Lord. "The Pupil." A casual friend of the Moreen family; his son Lord Verschoyle does not propose to Amy or Paula Moreen.

Dosson, Fedelia "Delia." *The Reverberator.* Francie Dosson's older sister who stands by Francie when she is in trouble.

Dosson, Francina "Francie." *The Reverberator.* The younger daughter of Whitney Dosson and the fiancee of Gaston Probert; she is in trouble with all her prospective in-laws when George Flack publishes Probert family gossip which she innocently told him.

Dosson, Whitney. *The Reverberator.* A rich, retired American whose daughter Francie Dosson's plight with the Proberts would perplex him if he ever worried.

Douglas. "The Turn of the Screw." The man who prepares the group at Griffin's home for the story which is "The Turn of the Screw"; he is now deceased.

Douves, Blanche de. *The Reverberator.* The kleptomaniac sister of Raoul de Douves, the husband of Jeanne de Douves, Gaston Probert's sister.

Douves, Raoul de. *The Reverberator.* The husband of Jeanne de Douves, a sister of Gaston Probert.

Douves, Mme. de (Jeanne [Jane] Probert). *The Reverberator.* A sister of Gaston Probert.

Douves, M. de. *The Reverberator.* Raoul de Douves's father.

Dovedale, Lady. "The Siege of London." A minor friend of Mrs. Reggie Dolphin, George Littlemore's sister.

Dovedale, Lord. "The Marriages." A nobleman who is to marry Mrs. Churchley, the object of the affections of Colonel Chart, Adela Chart's widower father.

Doyne, Ashton. "The Real Right Thing." The deceased author whose ghostly presence convinces George Withermore that he should not write the man's biography.

Doyne, Mrs. Ashton. "The Real Right Thing." The widow who commissions George Withermore to write her distinguished husband's biography.

Drack, Mrs. David E. "Julia Bride." The fat widow who is the object of the affection of Pitman, one of Julia Bride's step-fathers.

Drake. "In the Cage." The former butler of Lord Rye and the present butler of Lady Bradeen; he will marry Mrs. Jordan, a flower arranger.

Draper, Maggie. "Madame de Mauves." The young daughter of Mrs. Draper, who is a friend of Longmore.

Draper. "Madame de Mauves." The Wall Street husband of Mrs. Draper.

Draper, Mrs. "Madame de Mauves." A friend of Longmore, to whom she introduces Mme. Euphemia Cleve de Mauves.

Draper, Mrs. "The Point of View." The recipient of a letter from Miss Sturdy, the sister of the Newport host of Edward Antrobus.

Draper. "Georgina's Reasons." A name seen by Agnes Theory in a hotel book in Rome.

Draper, Mrs. "Georgina's Reasons." A name seen by Agnes Theory in a hotel book in Rome.

Dreuil, Comte de. *The Sacred Fount.* The husband of a casual friend of Gilbert Long.

Dreuil, Comtesse de. *The Sacred Fount.* The American wife of Comte de Dreuil; she is a casual friend of Gilbert Long.

Drury, Nan. "The Bench of Desolation." See Dodd, Mrs. Herbert.

Drury. "The Bench of Desolation." The father of six children, including Nan Drury, who marries Herbert Dodd; he is impoverished by the defection of his partner Dean.

Dundene, Mrs. Alice. "The Special Type." An innocent woman named correspondent in the divorce of Frank Brivet; the narrator paints a portrait of Brivet which she claims and takes.

Dunderton, Lord. "Fordham Castle." The fiance of Mattie Magaw, who sent her mother out of England with the pseudonym Mrs. Vanderplank to make a social catch in her mother's absence.

Dunn, Mrs. "Flickerbridge." A London woman whose portrait Frank Granger paints.

Dunoyer, Mlle. *The Tragic Muse.* A Theatre Francais actress seen and met by Miriam Rooth and Peter Sherringham.

Durand. *The Reverberator. The Tragic Muse.* A Paris cafe owner.

Dyott, Mrs. "The Story in It." The hostess of Mrs. Maud Blessingbourne; she is the object of Colonel Voyt's affections.

Edward, Lady. "Mrs. Medwin." A lady of fashion who, according to Mamie Cutter, has approved of Mrs. Medwin.

Edward, Lord. "The Siege of London." A fellow-guest with Mrs. Headway at the Demesne estate of Longlands.

Egbert, Lady. "The Lesson of the Master." A woman gossiped about by Mrs. Henry St. George, wife of the master novelist.

Egidio. "The Tree of Knowledge." The Italian servant of the untalented British sculptor Morgan Mallow.

Eleonore. "Mrs. Temperly." A friend of Marquise de Brives; she admires Mrs. Maria Temperly.

Elizabeth, Lady. *The Tragic Muse.* A friend of Charles Carteret.

Emma. "A Problem." David's wife; according to Magawisca's prophecy and that of others, their child dies and they remarry (to each other).

Emma, Lady. "Maud-Evelyn." The narrator; the daughter of her governess is Lavinia, who rejected Marmaduke.

Eric, Lord. *What Maisie Knew.* One of Ida Farange's many lovers.

Erme, Gwendolyn. "The Figure in the Carpet." The fiancee, then wife, and then widow of George Corvick, the critic who claims to have discovered "the figure in the carpet" of Hugh Vereker's works; she marries the third-rate critic Drayton Deane and then dies without revealing the figure.

Erme, Mrs. "The Figure in the Carpet." Gwendolyn Erme's mother, who dies.

Ermine, William. "The Impressions of a Cousin." The husband in New York of matchmaker Lizzie Ermine.

Ermine, Mrs. William (Lizzie). "The Impressions of a Cousin." A matchmaker who wants Eunice and Caliph to marry.

Ernesto. "At Isella." The lover of the Signora whom the narrator befriends at the inn at Isella.

Esther. "Adina." The narrator's aunt in Boston.

Eugene, Mrs. "The Modern Warning." A New York society friend of Agatha Grice, Lady Chasemore.

Eugenio. "Daisy Miller." The courier for the Miller family in Europe.

Eugenio. *The Wings of the Dove.* The knowledgeable guide and servant for Milly Theale in Venice.

Eunice. "The Impressions of a Cousin." The cousin of the painter-narrator Catherine Condit; she is the fiancee of Adrian Frank, whose half-brother Caliph unscrupulously handles her financial affairs.

Evans, Amy. "The Velvet Glove." The pseudonym of the writer who unsuccessfully tries to wheedle the novelist John Berridge into writing a preface for her novel *The Velvet Glove.*

Evans, Charlotte. "Travelling Companions." A young woman who travels in Italy with her father; she meets the narrator Brooke in Milan and again in Venice; alone they go to Padua and lose the last train; she temporarily rejects his proposal, thinking that it is prompted only by honor.

Evans, Mark. "Travelling Companions." A widower who travels

in Italy with his daughter Charlotte; he leaves her with the narrator Brooke, a traveling companion, to visit a sick friend in Milan; he accepts their explanation of their being in Padua overnight together; he later dies.

Everard, Captain Count Philip. "In the Cage." The mysterious sender of telegrams through the unnamed girl "in the cage," who helps him greatly once by remembering the contents of a telegram; he will marry Lady Bradeen.

Everett, Marian. "The Story of a Masterpiece." The fiancee of John Lennox, who slashes the portrait of her painted by Stephen Baxter.

Evers, Blanche. *Confidence.* A friend of Angela Vivian and her mother; she marries Gordon Wright and is escorted much by Captain Augustus Lovelock.

Fancourt, Marian. "The Lesson of the Master." The object of Paul Overt's incipient affections until he is advised to write by Henry St. George, who when his own wife dies marries her.

Fancourt, General. "The Lesson of the Master." The father of Marian Fancourt and the friend of Henry St. George and his wife.

Fane, Greville. "Greville Fane." The pseudonym of Mrs. Stormer, who writes innumerable potboilers to support her useless daughter Lady Ethel Stormer Luard and her pretentious son Leolin Stormer.

Farange, Beale. *What Maisie Knew.* The philandering father of Maisie Farange; after his divorce from Ida Farange, Maisie's mother, he marries Maisie's governess Miss Overmore; later he consorts with Mrs. Cuddon and others.

Farange, Mrs. Beale. *What Maisie Knew.* See Overmore, Miss.

Farange, Ida. *What Maisie Knew.* The philandering mother of Maisie Farange; after her divorce from Beale Farange, Maisie's father, she marries Sir Claude; later she consorts with Perriam, Lord Eric, and Tischbein, among others.

Farange, Maisie, *What Maisie Knew.* The pathetic daughter of divorced Beale and Ida Farange; she admires her governess Miss Overmore and Sir Claude; she learns moral consciousness from Mrs. Wix, her latest governess.

Fargo, Professor. "Professor Fargo." The New England medium who entices the deaf-mute daughter of his partner Colonel Gifford to go away with him.

Farrinder, Amariah. *The Bostonians.* The husband of the militant feminist friend of Miss Birdseye.

Farrinder, Mrs. Amariah. *The Bostonians.* The militant feminist friend of Miss Birdseye.

Featherstone, Miss. "Daisy Miller." An English lady who wonders why Daisy Miller's brother Randolph has no teacher.

Feeder, Dr. Sidney. "Lady Barbarina." A serious friend of Dr. Jackson Lemon, who marries Lady Barbarina Clement.

Felicia, Lady. *The Portrait of a Lady.* A name mentioned as possibly that of Lord Warburton's fiancee.

Fenton, George. *Watch and Ward.* The cousin of Nora Lambert; he tries to compromise her in order to blackmail her guardian Roger Lawrence.

Ferrand, Sir Dominick. "Sir Dominick Ferrand." Mrs. Ryves's deceased natural father whose compromising papers Peter Baron discovers and destroys.

Ferrars, Blanche. "De Grey, A Romance." A woman loved and hence destroyed by John De Grey in accordance with the De Grey family curse.

Fielder, Graham "Gray." *The Ivory Tower.* The nephew of Frank B. Betterman, who wills him great wealth; he is the friend of Rosanna Gaw, the daughter of Betterman's business foe; he is also the friend of Horton Vint.

Filer. *The Bostonians.* An agent hired by Olive Chancellor to promote Verena Tarrant's lecturing.

Filomena. *Roderick Hudson.* Mme. Grandoni's washwoman.

Finch, Dora. *The American.* An unimportant American seen by Christopher Newman at a party.

Finch, Dr. *The Wings of the Dove.* The physician consulted in New York by Milly Theale.

Finucane, Lord. *The American.* The grandfather of the foolish Irish nobleman Lord Deepmere.

Firmin, Mrs. *The Spoils of Poynton.* A woman who talks to Owen Gereth after a dinner party.

Firminger, Charlotte "Lottie." "Lord Beaupre." A cousin of Guy
    Firminger, later Lord Beaupre; they marry in spite of his
    love for Mary Gosselin.

Firminger, Major Frank. "Lord Beaupre." An uncle of Lord
    Beaupre and the father of Charlotte Firminger.

Firminger, Mrs. Frank. "Lord Beaupre." The wife of Major
    Frank Firminger and the mother of Charlotte Firminger.

Firminger, Guy. "Lord Beaupre." See Beaupre, Lord.

Firminger, Miss. "Lord Beaupre." A sister of Charlotte Firmin-
    ger, later Lady Beaupre.

Firminger, Miss. "Lord Beaupre." A sister of Charlotte Firmin-
    ger, later Lady Beaupre.

Firminger, Miss. "Lord Beaupre." A sister of Charlotte Firmin-
    ger, later Lady Beaupre.

Fitzgibbon, Lady Laura. "The Modern Warning." Sir Rufus
    Chasemore's Irish grandmother.

Flack, George P. *The Reverberator.* The American newspaper-
    man who violates the confidence of naive Francie Dos-
    son and invades the privacy of the Probert family by
    publishing Probert family gossip told him by Francie.

Fleming, Lady Augusta. "A Bundle of Letters." The Brighton
    recipient of a letter from Evelyn Vane.

Flora, Lady. *The Portrait of a Lady.* A name mentioned as pos-
    sibly that of Lord Warburton's fiancee.

Flora. *The Tragic Muse.* A friend of Charles Carteret.

Flora. "The Turn of the Screw." The niece of the governess's
    employer and the sister of Miles; she is perhaps victimized
    by the spirit of Miss Jessel.

Floyd-Taylor. "Glasses." The husband of Fanny Floyd-Taylor,
    a friend of Flora Saunt.

Floyd-Taylor, Mrs. Fanny. "Glasses." A friend of Flora Saunt.

Flynn, Mrs. "The Marriages." The housekeeper at Brinton,
    the country estate of the Chart family.

Foat, Ada T. P. *The Bostonians.* A distinguished feminist speaker
    in Boston.

Folliott, Mrs. "A Round of Visits." A self-centered friend of
    Mark Monteith; she also lost money because of Phil
    Bloodgood's defection.

Forbes, Dora. "The Death of the Lion." The pen-name of a bushy-browed and moustached popular novelist.

Ford, Lieutenant John "Jack." "The Story of a Year." The fiance of Lizzie Crowe in Glenham who is mortally wounded in the Civil War and is brought home to die.

Ford, Mrs. "The Story of a Year." Lieutenant John Ford's mother in Glenham who rightly but coldly distrusts his fiancee Lizzie Crowe.

Fortescue, Mary. "De Grey, A Romance." A woman loved and hence destroyed by George De Grey in accordance with the De Grey family curse.

Foy, Cecelia "Cissy." *The Ivory Tower.* A friend of the Bradhams; she perhaps had a liaison with Northover, Graham Fielder's step-father, in Europe earlier; she has supposedly set her cap for Fielder now.

Francois. *The Ambassadors.* A waiter in Paris for Strether and Waymarsh.

Frank, Adrian. "The Impressions of a Cousin." The half-brother of Caliph, who impoverishes Frank's fiancee Eunice; Frank makes restitution to please the painter-narrator Catherine Condit, Eunice's cousin.

Frankle, Bill. "The Bench of Desolation." Kate Cookham's former friend, of whom Herbert Dodd was jealous.

Franks. *Watch and Ward.* A junkman in business with George Fenton.

Freddy. "The Impressions of a Cousin." A young man whom Mrs. Lizzie Ermine wants Eunice to marry.

Freer, Dexter. "Lady Barbarina." A rich American who watches the passing parade of mounted society in Hyde Park.

Freer, Mrs. Dexter. "Lady Barbarina." The wife of a rich American; they watch the passing parade of mounted society in Hyde Park.

French, Basil. "Julia Bride." A young man who likes Julia Bride but refuses to propose because of stories concerning her.

Fritz. "In the Cage." A name mentioned in one of Lady Bradeen's telegrams processed by the unnamed girl "in the cage."

Froome, Mrs. *The Sacred Fount.* A woman who is to arrive later at Newmarch with Lord Lutley.

Frothingham, Miss. "A London Life." Lady Davenant's maid.

Frush, Amy. "The Third Person." An amateur writer who smuggles a Tauchnitz volume into England to appease the ghost of Cuthbert Frush, an ancestor hanged for smuggling; she is the second cousin of older Susan Frush.

Frush, Cuthbert. "The Third Person." The ancestor of Amy and Susan Frush; he was hanged for smuggling; his ghost haunts the Frush home at Marr.

Frush, Susan. "The Third Person." An amateur water-colorist; she is the second cousin of younger Amy Frush.

Galignani. *The Reverberator.* A place in Paris where Americans register.

Galopin, Cecile. "The Point of View." The daughter of M. le Pasteur Galopin and his wife of Geneva; Mrs. Church writes Mme. Galopin about Cecile's engagement.

Galopin, M. le Pasteur. "The Pension Beaurepas." A minister in Geneva who is to show Mrs. Church and her daughter Aurora some Reformation documents.

Galopin, Mme. "The Pension Beaurepas." The wife of M. le Pasteur Galopin of Geneva; Mrs. Church is more impressed by her society than her daughter Aurora Church is. "The Point of View." Mrs. Church writes her about her daughter Cecile's engagement.

Gambini, Antonietta. "De Grey, A Romance." A woman loved and hence destroyed by George De Grey in accordance with the De Grey family curse.

Garland, Mary. *Roderick Hudson.* The object of Roderick Hudson's affections until Christina Light appears; Rowland Mallet, Hudson's sponsor, hopelessly loves Miss Garland also.

Garlick. *The Awkward Age.* The teacher of a course of light literature taken by Agnesina.

Garnyer, Eustace. "Master Eustace." The spoiled illegitimate son of Mrs. Henry Garnyer and Cope; when Eustace learns the identity of his father, he tries to commit suicide.

Garnyer, Henry. "Master Eustace." The idolized supposed father, now deceased, of Eustace Garnyer, the illegitimate son of Mrs. Henry Garnyer and Cope.

Garnyer, Mrs. Henry. "Master Eustace." The indulgent mother of Eustace Garnyer by Cope; later she marries Cope.

Gaw, Abel. *The Ivory Tower.* The mortally sick father of Rosanna Gaw, the friend of Graham Fielder; he was formerly a business associate of Frank B. Betterman.

Gaw, Rosanna. *The Ivory Tower.* The elephantine but charming daughter of Abel Gaw and the friend of Graham Fielder.

Geddes, David. "The Bench of Desolation." Herbert Dodd's uncle.

Gedge, Morris. "The Birthplace." The initially too-scholarly lecturer at The Birthplace who becomes a commercially successful barker there.

Gedge, Mrs. Morris (Isabel). "The Birthplace." Morris Gedge's wife, who is afraid that his critical qualms at The Birthplace will cost him his job.

Gelsomina. *The Awkward Age.* The old nurse of Agnesina.

Gemini, Count. *The Portrait of a Lady.* The brutal Florentine husband of Amy Gemini, Gilbert Osmond's sister.

Gemini, Countess Amy. *The Portrait of a Lady.* The promiscuous sister of Gilbert Osmond, the husband of Isabel Archer, to whom she tells the secret of Pansy Osmond's natural mother.

Geraldine, Miss. "The Liar." The tipsy model who calls at the studio of Oliver Lyon while he paints Colonel Clement Capadose, who says that the model's real name is Harriet Pearson; she is also known as Miss Grenadine.

Gereth, Mrs. Adela. *The Spoils of Poynton.* The widowed collector of "the spoils of Poynton," and the mother of Owen Gereth; she unsuccessfully urges Fleda Vetch to become her daughter-in-law.

Gereth, Owen. *The Spoils of Poynton.* The stolid, likable son of Adela Gereth; Fleda Vetch urges him to be honorable in his relationship with his fiancee Mona Brigstock.

Gereth, Colonel. *The Spoils of Poynton.* The brother-in-law of Adela Gereth.

Gerome. "Four Meetings." The art teacher of Caroline Spencer's cousin, mentioned in the unrevised version only.

Giacosa, Cavaliere Giuseppe "Giuseppino." *Roderick Hudson.* Mrs. Light's Italian attendant; he was her former lover and is the natural father of Christina Light.

Gifford, Colonel. "Professor Fargo." The mathematician partner of the New England medium Professor Fargo, who entices Gifford's deaf-mute daughter away.

Gifford, Miss. "Professor Fargo." The deaf-mute daughter of Colonel Gifford who leaves her father to go with Professor Fargo.

Gilbert. "The Story of a Masterpiece." An artist friend of John Lennox.

Gilman, Rev. Mr. *The Europeans.* The minister of the congregation which includes the Wentworths.

Gimingham. "Louisa Pallant." The man who eventually marries Linda Pallant.

Gimingham, Mrs. "Louisa Pallant." See Pallant, Linda.

Giovanelli. "Daisy Miller." Daisy Miller's smooth little Roman escort.

Girolamo, Padre. "Adina." Angela Beati's priest uncle at Lariccia.

Giuseppino. "At Isella." The runaway Signora's brother whose face at death her lover Ernesto drew.

Glanvil, Maurice. "The Wheel of Time." The third son of Lady Greyswood; he fails to like ugly Fanny Knocker; twenty years later Fanny's son fails to like Vera, Maurice Glanvil's plain little daughter.

Glanvil, Mrs. Maurice. "The Wheel of Time." Maurice Glanvil's Russian wife who died giving birth to Vera.

Glanvil, Vera. "The Wheel of Time." Maurice Glanvil's plain little daughter who fails to interest Arthur Tregent, Fanny Knocker Tregent's handsome son.

Gloriani. *Roderick Hudson.* The successful sculptor in Rome who admires the work of Roderick Hudson. *The Ambassadors.* In his Paris garden Lambert Strether is introduced to Marie de Vionnet by Chad Newsome. "The Velvet Glove."

In his Paris salon novelist John Berridge meets attractive but meretricious Amy Evans.

Gloriani, Mme. *Roderick Hudson, The Ambassadors.* "The Velvet Glove." The wife of the sculptor Gloriani, in Rome and Paris.

Gobain, Prosper. "A Bundle of Letters." The recipient of a letter from Leon Verdier.

Goldie, Augusta "Gussy." "The Solution." The youngest daughter of Mrs. Blanche Goldie, in Rome.

Goldie, Mrs. Blanche. "The Solution." The daughter of deceased Lord Bolitho; she is now a widow with three daughters, in Rome; her daughter Veronica Goldie almost snares Henry Wilmerding.

Goldie, Rosina "Rosy." "The Solution." The oldest daughter of Mrs. Blanche Goldie, in Rome.

Goldie, Veronica. "The Solution." The middle of the three daughters of Mrs. Blanche Goldie, in Rome; she almost snares Henry Wilmerding.

Goldie. "The Aspern Papers." A supposedly high-society former friend of the Bordereaus.

Goldie, Mrs. "The Aspern Papers." A supposedly high-society former friend of the Bordereaus; perhaps she is Blanche Goldie, which see.

Goodenough, Miss. *The Ivory Tower.* This woman, Miss Mumby, and Miss Ruddle are Frank B. Betterman's nurses.

Goodwood, Caspar. *The Portrait of a Lady.* A wealthy American textile industrialist; he is the tireless suitor of Isabel Archer.

Gorham, Mrs. *The Other House.* Effie Bream's redoubtable nurse.

Gorton, Mrs. "The Given Case." The sister of Margaret Hamer; she is the hostess visited by Barton Reeve, who wants Miss Hamer's help.

Gosling, Agatha. "Longstaff's Marriage." The original name in the magazine publication for Agatha Josling, which see.

Gosselin, Hugh. "Lord Beaupre." The brother of Mary Gosselin and the friend of Bolton-Brown, who loves and tardily wins Mary.

Gosselin, Mary. "Lord Beaupre." The young woman who loves Lord Beaupre and did so while he was the untitled Guy Firminger; she reluctantly agrees to let the false rumor be started that they are engaged; she later marries Bolton-Brown.

Gosselin, Mrs. "Lord Beaupre." The mother of Hugh and Mary Gosselin; she foolishly starts the rumor that Mary is engaged to Lord Beaupre to protect him from husband-seeking society ladies.

Gostrey, Maria. *The Ambassadors.* The knowledgeable confidante of Lambert Strether, who meets her in Chester and often sees her in Paris; she was a former schoolmate of Marie de Vionnet.

Gotch, Mrs. "The Patagonia." A gossip aboard the *Patagonia;* she contributes to Grace Mavis's misery.

Gotch. *The Outcry.* Lady Amy Sandgate's butler.

Goupil. "The Story of a Masterpiece." The framer of Stephen Baxter's portrait of Marian Everett.

Grace, Lady. *The Outcry.* The daughter of Lord Theign and the younger sister of Kitty Imber; she loves Hugh Crimble.

Gracedew, Mrs. "Covering End." The rich young American widow whose sympathy and money rescue not only Captain Clement Yule and his mortgaged home Covering End, but also Cora Prodmore, the daughter of the mortgage-holder.

Gracie. *The Bostonians.* The friend of Henry Burrage, Jr., and a fellow Harvard Law School student.

Graham, Robert. "Osborne's Revenge." A suicide; his friend Philip Osborne at first wrongly thinks that Henrietta Congreve was responsible.

Grandoni, Mme. *Roderick Hudson.* A friend of Christina Light; she tells Rowland Mallet about Miss Light. *The Princess Casamassima.* She accompanies Christina Light, now the Princess Casamassima, to England; she finally leaves the Princess Casamassima.

Granger, Frank. "Flickerbridge." An American portrait painter and the fiance of Addie Wenham; he visits the estate of Flickerbridge owned by Adelaide Wenham.

Granger. "The Pupil." A rich American who does not propose to Amy or Paula Moreen.

Grant-Jackson. "The Birthplace." The spokesman for the company running The Birthplace; he hires Morris Gedge and later warns him when his critical honesty jeopardizes The Show.

Grantham, Mrs. May. "The Two Faces." The former mistress of Lord Gwyther who overdresses Gwyther's wife Lady Valda for revenge; Mrs. Grantham's face seems hard to Shirley Sutton.

Grantham, Mrs. *The Other House.* Julia Bream's step-mother; she was once married to Rose Armiger's uncle.

Gravener, George. "The Coxon Fund." A man elected to Parliament from Clockborough; he loves Ruth Anvoy but breaks with her when she gives Frank Saltram the Coxon Fund; on his brother's death and his nephew's death he becomes Lord Maddock.

Green, Susan. "The Point of View." A woman mentioned as a celebrated American authoress in a letter by Gustave Lejaune.

Green-Erin, Duke of. "An International Episode." A British visitor to America entertained by Mr. and Mrs. Butterworth.

Greenstreet, Abraham. *The Bostonians.* The father of Mrs. Selah Tarrant, who is the mother of feminist orator Verena Tarrant.

Greenstreet, Mrs. Abraham. *The Bostonians.* The mother of Mrs. Selah Tarrant, who is the mother of feminist orator Verena Tarrant.

Gregorini. "Mrs. Temperly." A woman singer at a party given in Paris by Mrs. Maria Temperly.

Gregory, Dr. "A Most Extraordinary Case." A physician recommended to Colonel Ferdinand Mason by Mrs. Maria Mason as a fine local doctor.

Grenadine, Miss. "The Liar." According to Colonel Clement Capadose, Miss Grenadine is a pseudonym of Miss Harriet Pearson, the tipsy model who calls herself at Oliver Lyon's studio Miss Geraldine, which see.

Grendon, Harry. *The Awkward Age.* The husband of Tishy Grendon, a frequent hostess of Nanda Brookenham.

Grendon, Mrs. Harry (Tishy). *The Awkward Age.* The sister of Carrie Donner; she is a frequent hostess of Nanda Brookenham.

Gresham. *The Tragic Muse.* The absent husband of Mrs. Julia Sherringham Dallow's secretary.

Gresham, Mrs. *The Tragic Muse.* Mrs. Julia Sherringham Dallow's secretary.

Gressie, Georgina. "Georgina's Reasons." See Roy, Mrs. Georgina Gressie Benyon.

Gressie. "Georgina's Reasons." Mrs. Georgina Gressie Benyon Roy's father.

Gressie, Mrs. "Georgina's Reasons." Mrs. Georgina Gressie Benyon Roy's mother.

Grey, Violet. "Nona Vincent." An actress whose portrayal of the title role of *Nona Vincent* by Allan Wayworth is improved by Mrs. Alsager's example; Wayworth and Miss Grey marry.

Greyswood, Lady. "The Wheel of Time." The mother of Maurice Glanvil; she cannot persuade him to like plain Fanny Knocker.

Greyswood, Lord. "The Wheel of Time." Lady Greyswood's deceased husband.

Greyswood, Lord. "The Wheel of Time." Lady Greyswood's oldest son; he was formerly Chumleigh.

Grice, Agatha. "The Modern Warning." An American girl who loves and marries Sir Rufus Chasemore, whom her brother Macarthy Grice loathes; their animosity forces her to commit suicide.

Grice, Macarthy. "The Modern Warning." The brother of Agatha Grice, who marries Sir Rufus Chasemore; the animosity of the two men forces Agatha to commit suicide.

Grice, Mrs. "The Modern Warning." The mother of Macarthy and Agatha Grice and hence the mother-in-law of Sir Rufus Chasemore; she dies.

Griffin. *The Princess Casamassima.* A London shoemaker radical; he is an associate of Paul Muniment and other anarchists.

Griffin. "The Turn of the Screw." The host to whose guests Douglas reads the governess's manuscript which is "The Turn of the Screw."

Grindon, Goodwood. *The Tragic Muse.* A rich young industrialist known to Lady Agnes Dormer, whose daughter Biddy is not interested in him; he is later won by Lady Muriel Macpherson.

Grose, Mrs. "The Turn of the Screw." The simple, well-meaning housekeeper at Bly, and the companion of the governess-narrator.

Grosjoyeux, M. de. *The American.* A second, with Ledoux, at Valentin de Bellegarde's duel with Stanislas Kapp.

Grospre, M. de. *The Reverberator.* A friend of Suzanne de Brecourt, Gaston Probert's sister.

Grove-Stewart, John. "The Given Case." The nominal fiance of Margaret Hamer; for a long time he has been in India.

Grugan. *The Princess Casamassima.* A fellow-bookbinder with Hyacinth Robinson in Crookenden's shop.

Guest, John. "Guest's Confession." The father of Laura Guest and the confessed swindler of Edgar Musgrave.

Guest, Laura. "Guest's Confession." The daughter of John Guest, swindler; she is a friend of Mrs. Clara Beck and the object of the affections of the narrator David.

Gulp, Miss. "The Point of View." The teacher of Gwendolyn and Charlotte Antrobus.

Gunton, Lily. "Miss Gunton of Poughkeepsie." The Poughkeepsie girl who repudiates her engagement to the Roman Prince and plans to marry Adam P. Bransby.

Gunton. "Miss Gunton of Poughkeepsie." The wealthy grandfather in Poughkeepsie of Lily Gunton.

Gushmore. *The Tragic Muse.* A play rewriter who is a friend of Basil Dashwood.

Guterman-Seuss. *The Golden Bowl.* A dealer in Brighton who sells Adam Verver some oriental tiles; he is the father of eleven children.

Guy, Mrs. "Paste." The woman who recognizes the supposedly paste pearls as real when shown them by Charlotte Prime.

Gwendolyn. "Paste." Charlotte Prime's pupil.

Gwyther, Lady Valda. "The Two Faces." The daughter of Countess Kremnitz; she is the wife of Lord Gwyther and is the over-dressed victim of Mrs. May Grantham; her pathetic, innocent face is appealing to Shirley Sutton.

Gwyther, Lord. "The Two Faces." The former lover of Mrs. May Grantham; having later married Valda, the daughter of Countess Kremnitz, he daringly asks Mrs. Grantham to lead Lady Valda into British society.

H—. "The Madonna of the Future." The narrator; he is the friend of the ineffectual painter Theobald and of Mrs. Coventry.

H—, Lady. "The Diary of a Man of Fifty." The hostess in London where the narrator sees Edmund Stanmer after his marriage.

Hack, Mrs. "The Chaperon." A former governess of Rose Tramore.

Haddon. "In the Cage." A name mentioned in one of Lady Bradeen's telegrams processed by the unnamed girl "in the cage."

Hague, Acton. "The Altar of the Dead." The public figure, recently deceased, who wronged George Stransom and the unnamed woman; her forgiveness finally inspires Stransom.

Hale. "Guest's Confession." Edgar Musgrave's lawyer; he is a partner in Stoddard and Hale.

Hamer, Margaret. "The Given Case." The sister of Mrs. Gorton; Barton Reeve's appeal to her makes her realize the force of her lover Phil Mackern's affection.

Hardman. "Lady Barbarina." The lawyer of Lord Canterville and his daughter Lady Barbarina; he arranges the terms of her dowry before her marriage to Dr. Jackson Lemon.

Harriet. "Georgina's Reasons." The aunt of Agnes Theory, who sends gifts to Harriet.

Harry. "The Impressions of a Cousin." A young man whom Lizzie Ermine wants Eunice to marry.

Harvey, Mrs. "Broken Wings." The unsuccessful writer friend of the unsuccessful painter Stuart Straith.

Hatch, C. P. *The American.* An unimportant American mentioned by Christopher Newman as one of his friends in Paris.

Hatch, Dr. *The Ivory Tower.* Frank B. Betterman's physician, with Dr. Root.

Hathaway. "Europe." With his wife he takes Jane Rimmle to Europe.

Hathaway, Mrs. "Europe." With her husband she takes Jane Rimmle to Europe.

Hauff. "Master Eustace." Eustace Garnyer's tutor.

Hawley, Jack. "The Real Thing." The unproductive critic friend of the painter-narrator.

Haycock, Lady. *The Portrait of a Lady.* One of Lord Warburton's sisters.

Haycock, Lord. *The Portrait of a Lady.* Lord Warburton's brother-in-law.

Hayes, B. D. "The Birthplace." A rich young American who with his pretty wife visits The Birthplace twice and notes the change in Morris Gedge's lectures.

Hayes, Mrs. B. D. "The Birthplace." The pretty wife of a rich young American; they visit The Birthplace twice and note the change in Morris Gedge's lectures.

Headway, Mrs. Nancy Grenville Beck. "The Siege of London." An often-married American woman, the object of the affections of Sir Arthur Demesne and of the suspicions of his mother; she marries Sir Arthur Demesne.

Headway. "The Siege of London." Nancy Grenville Beck Headway's latest husband.

Heidenmauer, Herman. "Collaboration." A German composer friend of and collaborator on an opera with Felix Vendemer.

Henning, Millicent. *The Princess Casamassima.* The undependable girl-friend of Hyacinth Robinson who finally prefers Captain Godfrey Sholto.

Henning, Mrs. *The Princess Casamassima.* The deceased mother of Millicent Henning; Hyacinth Robinson as a child knew her in the neighborhood.

Herbert, Father. "De Grey, A Romance." The English-born confessor of Mrs. George De Grey, Paul's mother.

Hicks, Mrs. Lucy. "My Friend Bingham." The widowed mother of the boy whom George Bingham accidentally kills; they later marry.

Hicks. "My Friend Bingham." The sickly little son of Mrs. Lucy Hicks; George Bingham accidentally kills him.

Highmore, Dr. Cecil. "The Next Time." A former British army surgeon; he is the novelist Jane Highmore's husband.

Highmore, Mrs. Cecil (Jane Stannace). "The Next Time." The popular novelist wife of former army surgeon Cecil Highmore; she is the sister of Maud Stannace Limbert, the wife of the novelist Ray Limbert.

Hilary. *The Portrait of a Lady.* Daniel Tracy Touchett's lawyer; he prepares the papers for the bequest to Isabel Archer.

Hirsch, Dr. Julius. "A Bundle of Letters." The scientist recipient of the pro-German letter of Dr. Rudolph Staub.

Hodge, D. Jackson. *The Reverberator.* A name on luggage in a Paris hotel.

Hoffendahl, Diedrich. *The Princess Casamassima.* The shadowy anarchist behind the scenes in London and on the Continent; through Paul Muniment he gives Hyacinth Robinson his fatal orders.

Hofmann, Caroline. "A Most Extraordinary Case." The niece of Mrs. Maria Mason; she is the object of the affections of Colonel Ferdinand Mason, who dies when he learns that she has become engaged to Dr. Horace Knight.

Holland, George. "Osborne's Revenge." The object of the affections of Henrietta Congreve, who at one time preferred him to Robert Graham.

Homer, Scott. "Mrs. Medwin." The witty, penniless, sponging half-brother of Mamie Cutter; his shady past intrigues Lady Wantridge.

Hope, Mrs. Abraham C. "A Bundle of Letters." The recipient in Bangor, Maine, of her daughter Miranda Hope's letters from Paris.

Hope, Sir Matthew. *The Portrait of a Lady.* The physician who attends Daniel Tracy Touchett during his fatal sickness. *The Tragic Muse.* He attends Charles Carteret during his fatal sickness.

Hope, Miranda. "A Bundle of Letters." The naive but spirited girl from Bangor, Maine, who writes effusive letters home from the Pension Maisonrouge about Paris and persons in Paris; her boy-friend at home is William Platt.

Hope, Warren. "The Abasement of the Northmores." A sick man who dies after attending the funeral of Lord John Northmore, his generally more successful friend.

Hope, Mrs. Warren. "The Abasement of the Northmores." The widow of Warren Hope; she furnishes the widow of Lord John Northmore some letters from him to her husband, whose love letters to her she prefers.

Hoppus. *The Tragic Muse.* A political writer mentioned by Nick Dormer and Mrs. Julia Sherringham Dallow.

Horner, Margaret. "My Friend Bingham." The second cousin of Mrs. Lucy Hicks; Mrs. Hicks lives with her for a while.

Horridge, Mrs. "A Passionate Pilgrim." Richard Searle's housekeeper at Lockley.

Hotchkin. *The Princess Casamassima.* A fellow-bookbinder with Hyacinth Robinson in Crookenden's shop.

Hudson, Roderick. *Roderick Hudson.* The American sculptor befriended by Rowland Mallet, loved by Mary Garland, and ruined because of his love for Christina Light in Rome.

Hudson, Mrs. Sarah. *Roderick Hudson.* The gentle, ineffectual, widowed mother of the sculptor Roderick Hudson.

Hugh, Dr. "The Middle Years." The literature-loving physician who leaves his wealthy, sick countess to minister to the dying novelist Dencombe.

Hume-Walker, Captain. "Owen Wingrave." A deceased British soldier, the brother of Mrs. Julian; he was once engaged to Jane Wingrave.

Hurter, Fanny. "The Death of the Lion." An American girl whom the critic-narrator persuades to respect novelist Neil Paraday's privacy; she marries the narrator.

Hutchby. *The Tragic Muse.* A political organizer mentioned by Nick Dormer and Mrs. Julia Sherringham Dallow.

Iffield, Lord. "Glasses." The son of Lord and Lady Considine; he would marry Flora Saunt but for her blindness.

Imber, Lady Kitty. *The Outcry.* The older daughter of Lord

Theign and the sister of Lady Grace; she has amassed gambling debts.

Inglefield, Earl of. *The Princess Casamassima.* The father of Lady Aurora Langrish.

Ingram, Elizabeth. "Crawford's Consistency." The daughter of Peter and Sabrina Ingram, who force her to reject Crawford; her beauty is later wrecked by smallpox.

Ingram, Peter. "Crawford's Consistency." The father of Elizabeth Ingram; he is socially ambitious for her.

Ingram, Mrs. Peter (Sabrina). "Crawford's Consistency." The mother of Elizabeth Ingram; she is socially ambitious for her daughter.

Jane. "Osborne's Revenge." The maid of Mrs. Wilkes, Henrietta Congreve's sister.

Jane, Lady. "The Lesson of the Master." A woman gossiped about by Mrs. Henry St. George, the wife of the master novelist.

Jane, Lady. "The Figure in the Carpet." The hostess at whose home the critic-narrator meets Hugh Vereker, the celebrated novelist.

Jane, Duchess. *The Awkward Age.* Edward Brookenham's cousin from Naples; she is Agnesina's aunt and Mrs. Brookenham's friend.

Jaume, Mme. de. *The Spoils of Poynton.* A witty, ugly friend of Mrs. Adela Gereth.

Jay, Captain Bertram. "The Chaperon." The finally loyal friend of Rose Tramore, who marries him.

Jay, Mrs. Bertram. "The Chaperon." See Tramore, Rose.

Jeremie, Mrs. "The Patagonia." A mutual friend of Mrs. Peck and Grace Mavis.

Jessel, Miss. "The Turn of the Screw." The female ghost seen by the governess-narrator and perhaps by Flora.

Jex, Mrs. "Maud-Evelyn." A medium whom Mr. and Mrs. Dedrick use to communicate with their daughter Maud-Evelyn but whom Marmaduke avoids.

John, Lord. *The Outcry.* The rather materialistic friend of

Lord Theign; he admires Lady Grace, Theign's younger daughter.

Johnson. "A Bundle of Letters." The pseudonym of governesses in the Battledown family.

Johnson. "The Abasement of the Northmores." A person asked by Lady Northmore for letters from Lord John Northmore.

Jones, Dr. "A Light Man." The physician of rich, dying Frederick Sloane.

Jordan, Mrs. "In the Cage." A clergyman's widow who supports herself by arranging flowers in the homes of the wealthy; she will marry Drake, Lady Bradeen's new butler.

Josephine. "A Tragedy of Error." Mme. Hortense Bernier's maid.

Josling, Agatha. "Longstaff's Marriage." The companion of Diana Belfield and the go-between for her and Reginald Longstaff.

Julia. "A Problem." A friend of David; she helps reconcile David and his wife Emma.

Julia, Lady. "An International Episode." Lord Lambeth's unmarried sister.

Julia, Lady. *The Awkward Age.* The deceased mother of Mrs. Brookenham; she was once the object of Longdon's unrequited affections and is now a sacred memory to Longdon.

Julian, Kate. "Owen Wingrave." The daughter of widowed Mrs. Julian; she taunts Owen Wingrave, who loves her.

Julian, Mrs. "Owen Wingrave." The widow of a soldier and the sister of Captain Hume-Walker, who was once engaged to Miss Jane Wingrave, with whom she now lives; she is the mother of Kate Julian.

Justine, Sister. *The Portrait of a Lady.* One of Pansy Osmond's convent teachers.

Kapp, Stanislas. *The American.* The son of a Strasbourg brewer; he kills Valentin de Bellegarde in a duel over Noemie Nioche.

Keith, Mrs. Isabel Morton. *Watch and Ward.* As Miss Morton, she is the unresponsive object of Roger Lawrence's affections; as the widowed Mrs. Keith, she is the friend of his ward Nora Lambert.

Keith, Mrs. *Watch and Ward.* The mother-in-law of Mrs. Isabel Morton Keith.

Kenyon, Lady. "Brooksmith." A member of Oliver Offord's social circle.

Keyes, Mrs. Edith Archer. *The Portrait of a Lady.* One of Isabel Archer's sisters.

King. "The Story of a Masterpiece." An admirer in Europe of Marian Everett; he is mentioned in conversation between Mrs. Denbigh and Stephen Baxter.

Kingsbury. *The Tragic Muse.* Nick Dormer's political opponent; he is discussed by Nick Dormer and Mrs. Julia Sherringham Dallow.

Kingsbury, Mrs. *The Tragic Muse.* The attractive wife of Nick Dormer's political opponent; she is discussed by Nick Dormer and Mrs. Julia Sherringham Dallow.

Knight, Dr. Horace. "A Most Extraordinary Case." A casual army friend of wounded Colonel Ferdinand Mason, who has a fatal relapse upon learning that Dr. Knight and Caroline Hofmann have become engaged.

Knight, Mrs. "A Most Extraordinary Case." The person with whom at one point Caroline Hofmann stays; she is probably Dr. Horace Knight's mother.

Knocker, General Blake. "The Wheel of Time." The father of Mrs. Fanny Knocker Tregent.

Knocker, Mrs. Blake (Jane). "The Wheel of Time." The mother of Mrs. Fanny Knocker Tregent.

Knocker, Fanny. "The Wheel of Time." See Tregent, Mrs. Fanny Knocker.

Knocker. "The Wheel of Time." The brother of General Blake Knocker; he dies.

Knocker. "The Wheel of Time." A son of General and Mrs. Blake Knocker.

Knocker. "The Wheel of Time." A son of General and Mrs. Blake Knocker.

Knocker, Miss. "The Wheel of Time." The sister of General Blake Knocker; she cares for the Knocker children in Heidelberg.

Kremnitz, Countess. "The Two Faces." The mother of Valda, whose marriage to Lord Gwyther Mrs. May Grantham feels compelled to resent.

A. L. "A Light Man." A person remembered by Max Austin as a former girl-friend.

L—, Miss. "De Grey, A Romance." A girl whose engagement to Paul De Grey in Europe is broken; she then dies in Naples.

L—. "Travelling Companions." The American consul in Venice.

L—, Mrs. "Travelling Companions." The wife of the American consul in Venice.

Ladle. "In the Cage." The name of a furnished apartment.

Lambert, Nora. *Watch and Ward.* The ward of Roger Lawrence; she is perhaps loved by Rev. Mr. Hubert Lawrence; she is almost compromised by her cousin George Fenton; she is loved and won by Roger Lawrence.

Lambert. *Watch and Ward.* The father of Nora Lambert; he commits suicide when she is little.

Lambert, Mrs. *Watch and Ward.* The poverty-stricken mother of Nora Lambert; deceased.

Lambeth, Lord. "An International Episode." The son of the Duke and Duchess of Bayswater; he loves Bessie Alden, but prejudice prevents their marrying.

Langrish, Lady Aurora. *The Princess Casamassima.* An aristocratic liberal; she is friendly with Hyacinth Robinson, Paul and Rosy Muniment, and the Princess Casamassima.

Lansing. "Pandora." A man sent by D. F. Bellamy, Pandora Day's fiance, to help the Day family through the New York customs.

Lappington, Lady. *The Outcry.* A British aristocrat who sells Breckenridge Bender a painting by Longhi.

Latimer, Miss. "Osborne's Revenge." An amateur actress who is overshadowed by Henrietta Congreve in a private theatrical.

Latouche. "Four Meetings." The traveling companion of the narrator; they visit Latouche's mother in New England; he laters dies in the Levant.

Latouche, Mrs. "Four Meetings." The mother of the narrator's traveling companion; at her home the narrator first meets Caroline Spencer.

Latrobe. "The Impressions of a Cousin." A guest at a dinner party given by Eunice, the painter-narrator Catherine Condit's cousin.

Lavinia. "Maud-Evelyn." The daughter of a former governess of Lady Emma; she rejected Marmaduke.

Lawrence, Rev. Mr. Hubert. *Watch and Ward.* Roger Lawrence's cousin and an egocentric parson; he temporarily attracts Nora Lambert.

Lawrence, Roger. *Watch and Ward.* A young man who after being rejected by Isabel Morton adopts Nora Lambert to rear her for his wife.

Lawrence, Mrs. *Watch and Ward.* The mother of Roger Lawrence; she died while Roger Lawrence had scarlet fever at college.

Leary, Josephine. "A Landscape Painter." A young woman who jilts Locksley, the rich painter-diarist, at the outset.

Leavenworth. *Roderick Hudson.* The pretentious, rich patron in Rome of Roderick Hudson, who insults him; he takes up with Augusta Blanchard.

Leblond, Abbe. *Watch and Ward.* Mrs. Isabel Morton Keith's confessor in Rome.

Lechmere. "Owen Wingrave." The obedient young fellow-pupil with Owen Wingrave under the military coach Spencer Coyle.

Ledoux. *The American.* A second, with M. de Grosjoyeux, at Valentin de Bellegarde's duel with Stanislas Kapp.

Lefevre, Lucretia. "De Grey, A Romance." A woman loved and hence destroyed by Paul De Grey, an ancestor of the present Paul De Grey, in accordance with the De Grey family curse.

Lejaune, Gustave. "The Point of View." A member of the French Academy and a critic of things American in a letter to

Adolphe Bouche; he is admired by Aurora Church.

Lemon, Lady Barbarina Clement. "Lady Barbarina." A daughter of Lord Philip Canterville; she marries Dr. Jackson Lemon but cannot abide New York City and therefore returns to London.

Lemon, Dr. Jackson. "Lady Barbarina." A wealthy New York physician who marries Lady Barbarina Clement and ultimately is obliged to live in London.

Lemon, Mrs. Mary. "Lady Barbarina." The mother of Dr. Jackson Lemon.

Lemon, Miss. "Lady Barbarina." The infant daughter of Dr. Jackson Lemon and his wife Lady Barbarina Clement Lemon.

Lendon, Mrs. Urania. *The Tragic Muse.* Charles Carteret's sister.

Lennox, John. "The Story of a Masterpiece." The fiance of Marian Everett; he slashes her portrait, painted by Stephen Baxter, but then marries her.

Letitia. "The Impressions of a Cousin." The mother of Eunice, the painter-narrator Catherine Condit's cousin.

Leverett, Louis. "A Bundle of Letters." A fatuous young American in Paris, who comments in a letter to Harvard Tremont in Boston about Aurora Church and her mother, Miranda Hope, Evelyn Vane, and things French. "The Point of View." From Boston he writes Harvard Tremont, now in Paris, about the dullness of life in America; he likes Aurora Church even more now.

Light, Christina. *Roderick Hudson, The Princess Casamassima.* See Casamassima, Princess.

Light. *Roderick Hudson.* A former American consul at an Italian port city on the Adriatic coast; he was the husband of Christina Light's mother; deceased.

Light, Mrs. (nee Savage). *Roderick Hudson.* The wife of an American consul in Italy; she is the ambitious, unprincipled mother of Christina Light, whose father is Cavaliere Giuseppe "Giuseppino" Giacosa.

Lilienthal, Miss. *Watch and Ward.* A German piano duetist with Nora Lambert.

Limbert, Ralph "Ray." "The Next Time." An unpopular but superb novelist; he is the brother-in-law of popular novelist Mrs. Jane Highmore.

Limbert, Mrs. Ray (Maud Stannace). "The Next Time." The pretty wife of the unpopular novelist Ray Limbert; she is the sister of the popular novelist Mrs. Jane Highmore.

Lindeck, Mary. "Julia Bride." The fiancee of Murray Brush, who was formerly attentive to Julia Bride.

Lisle, Theodore. "A Light Man." The companion of rich, dying Frederick Sloane, who comes to prefer Lisle's friend Max Austin.

Lisle. "A Light Man." The deceased father of Theodore Lisle; he was a former friend of rich Frederick Sloane.

Littledale, Captain. "An International Episode." A Britisher whom J. L. Westgate of New York treated hospitably at one time.

Littlefield. "The Story of a Year." A Leatherborough gentleman in whose home Lizzie Crowe visits; while there, she meets Robert Bruce.

Littlefield, Mrs. "The Story of a Year." The wife of Littlefield, in whose Leatherborough home Lizzie Crowe visits and meets Robert Bruce.

Littlemore, George. "The Siege of London." A rich American widower and the detached observer of Mrs. Nancy Grenville Beck Headway's siege of Sir Arthur Demesne; he is Mrs. Agnes Dolphin's brother and a friend of American legation official Rupert Waterville.

Littlemore, Miss. "The Siege of London." The infant daughter of George Littlemore.

Lloyd, Arthur. "The Romance of Certain Old Clothes." The British husband in America of Perdita Willoughby, at whose death he marries her sister Viola Willoughby.

Lloyd, Mrs. Arthur (Perdita Willoughby). "The Romance of Certain Old Clothes." The sister of Viola Willoughby; she is the first wife of Arthur Lloyd and dies in childbirth.

Lloyd, Mrs. Arthur (Viola Willoughby). "The Romance of Certain Old Clothes." The sister of Perdita Willoughby, at whose death she marries Perdita's husband; she is fatally jealous of her dead but ghostly sister's wedding clothes.

Lloyd, Miss. "The Romance of Certain Old Clothes." The infant daughter of Arthur Lloyd and Perdita Willoughby Lloyd.

Locket. "Sir Dominick Ferrand." The editor of *The Promiscuous Review* for whom Peter Baron refuses to write an essay based on Sir Dominick Ferrand's private papers.

Locksley. "A Landscape Painter." The rich painter-diarist; he is jilted by Josephine Leary and later marries Miriam Quarterman.

Loder. "Nona Vincent." Dramatist Allan Wayworth's manager.

Long, Mrs. "The Modern Warning." A New York society friend of Agatha Grice, Lady Chasemore.

Long, Gilbert. *The Sacred Fount.* The extremely handsome, markedly now suave friend of the narrator; he is perhaps the tapper of Mrs. May Server's "sacred fount."

Longdon. *The Awkward Age.* The well-to-do, aging observer of the effete social circle of Mrs. Brookenham; he was a friend of her lovely and now deceased mother Lady Julia; he wants to adopt Mrs. Brookenham's daughter Nanda.

Longmore. "Madame de Mauves." The American admirer of Mme. Euphemia Cleve de Mauves.

Longstaff, Reginald. "Longstaff's Marriage." The man who when supposedly dying proposes to Diana Belfield, whose refusal is followed by his recovery.

Longstraw, Lady Agnes Clement. "Lady Barbarina." See Clement, Lady Agnes.

Longstraw, Herman. "Lady Barbarina." A cowboy who wooes and wins Lady Agnes Clement, a younger sister of Lady Barbarina Clement Lemon; he then sponges off his brother-in-law wealthy Dr. Jackson Lemon.

Longueville, Bernard. *Confidence.* The friend of fellow-American Gordon Wright, who asks him to pass judgment on Angela

Vivian; he criticizes her to Wright but ultimately marries her himself.

Lottie. "A Round of Visits." Newton Winch's sister-in-law whom Mark Monteith meets.

Lovelock, Captain Augustus. *Confidence.* The British escort of Blanche Evers both before and after her marriage to Gordon Wright.

Lovick, Edmund. *The Tragic Muse.* A colleague of the diplomat Peter Sherringham; he is Basil Dashwood's brother-in-law.

Lovick, Mrs. Edmund. *The Tragic Muse.* The wife of a colleague of diplomat Peter Sherringham; she is the sister of Basil Dashwood, who marries Miriam Rooth.

Lowder, Mrs. Maud Manningham. *The Wings of the Dove.* Kate Croy's aunt and an old-time friend of Mrs. Susan Shepherd Stringham, through whom she meets Milly Theale and becomes her London hostess.

Luard, Sir Baldwin. "Greville Fane." The husband of Lady Ethel Stormer Luard, the useless daughter of novelist Greville Fane.

Luard, Lady Ethel Stormer. "Greville Fane." The useless daughter of the novelist Greville Fane, the brother of Leolin Stormer, and Sir Baldwin Luard's wife.

Luce. *The Portrait of a Lady.* The husband of a friend in Paris of Lydia Touchett, Isabel Archer's aunt.

Luce, Mrs. *The Portrait of a Lady.* A friend in Paris of Lydia Touchett, Isabel Archer's aunt.

Ludlow, Edmund. *The Portrait of a Lady.* The husband of Isabel Archer's sister Lilian.

Ludlow, Mrs. Edmund (Lilian Archer). *The Portrait of a Lady.* One of Isabel Archer's sisters.

Ludlow, John. *Washington Square.* An unsuccessful suitor of Catherine Sloper.

Ludlow, Thomas "Tom." "A Day of Days." A New York scientist who comes to see Herbert Moore but talks briefly with his sister Adela Moore instead.

Luke. "The Turn of the Screw." A friend or servant of Miles.

Lumley, Laura. *The Tragic Muse.* A woman who rents a house in London to Mrs. Rooth and her daughter Miriam Rooth.

Luna, Mrs. Adelina Chancellor. *The Bostonians.* The widowed sister of Olive Chancellor; she is much attracted to Basil Ransom.

Luna, Newton. *The Bostonians.* The young son of the widowed Mrs. Adelina Luna.

Lusignan, Duchesse de. *The American.* A hostess whom Mme. Claire de Bellegarde de Cintre does not visit.

Lutch, Dotty. *The Golden Bowl.* The sister of Kitty Lutch; they are parasites on Adam Verver until Charlotte Stant drives them out of Fawns.

Lutch, Kitty. *The Golden Bowl.* The sister of Dotty Lutch; they are parasites on Adam Verver until Charlotte Stant drives them out of Fawns.

Lutley, Lady John. *The Sacred Fount.* The wife of Lord John Lutley; the narrator decides that she is not Gilbert Long's "sacred fount."

Lutley, Lord John. *The Sacred Fount.* A guest who is to arrive at Newmarch later, with Mrs. Froome.

Luttrel, Major Robert. "Poor Richard." A dishonest suitor of Gertrude Whittaker who is foiled when Richard Maule tells Gertrude the truth that both men lied to Captain Edmund Severn; he becomes General Luttrel in the Civil War and later marries Miss Van Winkel.

Lyon, Oliver. "The Liar." The admirer of Mrs. Everina Brant Capadose; he paints a portrait of her husband Colonel Clement Capadose, liar.

Macalister. *Washington Square.* An unsuccessful suitor of Catherine Sloper.

Macgeorge. *The Tragic Muse.* A politician mentioned by Mrs. Julia Sherringham Dallow; he bores Nick Dormer.

Mackenzie, George. "The Story of a Year." A man facetiously mentioned to Lieutenant John Ford by Lizzie Crowe as one with whom she might be in love.

Mackern, Philip "Phil." "The Given Case." A young man who loves Margaret Hamer; her awareness of Barton Reeve's love for Mrs. Kate Despard makes her responsive to Phil Mackern.

Mackintosh, Dr. "The Author of Beltraffio." The physician who attends Dolcino Ambient but is soon dismissed by the dying boy's mother.

Mackintosh. *The Outcry*. An art dealer with whom Lord Theign places his Mantovano painting.

Maclane, Ella. *Confidence*. A mutual friend from Baltimore of Bernard Longueville and Blanche Evers; she wants to visit Baden-Baden while traveling in Europe.

Maclane. *Confidence*. The father of Ella Maclane, who is traveling in Europe.

Maclane, Mrs. *Confidence*. The mother of Ella Maclane, who is traveling in Europe.

Macpherson, Lady Muriel. *The Tragic Muse*. The young woman who captures rich Goodwood Grindon, in whom Biddy Dormer is not interested.

Maddalena. *Roderick Hudson*. Mrs. Sarah Hudson's maid in Florence.

Maddock, Lord George. "The Coxon Fund." See Gravener, George.

Maddock, Lady. "The Coxon Fund." George Gravener's sister-in-law.

Maddock, Lord. "The Coxon Fund." George Gravener's brother; his death and that of his son enable George Gravener to become Lord Maddock.

Maddock, Lord. "The Coxon Fund." The son of Lord Maddock, George Gravener's brother; the death of the son of Lord Maddock enables George Gravener to become Lord Maddock.

Maddock, Miss. *The Golden Bowl*. An Irish neighbor of Adam Verver living near his estate of Fawns.

Magaw, Mattie. "Fordham Castle." The daughter of Mrs. Magaw; she uses the pseudonym of Miss Vanderplank to help her catch Lord Dunderton.

Magaw. "Fordham Castle." The husband of Mrs. Magaw mentioned by her in conversation with Abel F. Taker in such a way as to suggest that he is dead.

Magaw, Mrs. "Fordham Castle." A woman forced by her daughter Mattie Magaw to leave England and receive mail under the pseudonym of Mrs. Vanderplank so that the daughter can score a social success in England.

Magawisca. "A Problem." An Indian woman who predicts that David and Emma will have a daughter who will die.

Maisonrouge, Mme. de. "A Bundle of Letters." The proprietress in Paris of the Pension Maisonrouge, which caters to American and British clients; she is Leon Verdier's cousin.

Major, Mrs. *The Princess Casamassima.* The London landlady of Paul and Rosy Muniment.

Mallet, Jonas. *Roderick Hudson.* The deceased father of Rowland Mallet; he was an austere, Puritannical businessman.

Mallet, Mrs. Jonas. *Roderick Hudson.* The deceased mother of Rowland Mallet; she was the daughter of Captain Rowland, a retired sea-captain.

Mallet, Rowland. *Roderick Hudson.* The wealthy sponsor of the sculptor Roderick Hudson in Rome; he secretly admires Mary Garland, Roderick Hudson's fiancee.

Mallow, Lancelot "Lance." "The Tree of Knowledge." The son of the sculptor Morgan Mallow; he paints briefly and not well; he discovers through study in Paris that his father is untalented and pretentious.

Mallow, Morgan. "The Tree of Knowledge." The inoffensively pretentious and untalented sculptor of Carrara Lodge near London; he is the father of Lance Mallow, who discovers his father's lack of ability.

Mallow, Mrs. Morgan. "The Tree of Knowledge." The loyal wife of the untalented sculptor Morgan Mallow; she unsinfully loves Peter Brench.

Manger, Algie. *The Awkward Age.* A friend of Harold Brookenham; he is evidently the brother of Booby Manger; he is the tutor of rich Baron Schack (or Schmack).

Manger, Booby. *The Awkward Age.* A friend of Harold Brookenham; he is evidently the brother of Algie Manger; he is engaged to a rich American girl.

Manger. *The Awkward Age.* A friend of Harold Brookenham; evidently Algie and Booby Manger are his sons.

Manger, Mrs. *The Awkward Age.* A friend of Harold Brookenham; evidently Algie and Booby Manger are her sons.

Mangler, Bessie. "The Chaperon." A daughter of Lady Maresfield and a sister of Guy Mangler.

Mangler, Fanny. "The Chaperon." A daughter of Lady Maresfield and a sister of Guy Mangler.

Mangler, Guy. "The Chaperon." The son of Lady Maresfield; Rose Tramore will not encourage him because he will not support her ostracized mother socially.

Mangler, Maggie. "The Chaperon." A daughter of Lady Maresfield and a sister of Guy Mangler.

Manning, Miss. *The Other House.* Mrs. Bream's business-like maid.

Mantovano. *The Outcry.* The painter of a work Lord Theign owns and Breckenridge Bender wants to buy.

Marchant, Lady. *The Princess Casamassima.* A neighbor at nearby Broome of the Princess Casamassima at Medley, where she visits with her three daughters.

Marchant, Miss. *The Princess Casamassima.* A daughter of Lady Marchant of Broome.

Marchant, Miss. *The Princess Casamassima.* A daughter of Lady Marchant of Broome.

Marchant, Miss. *The Princess Casamassima.* A daughter of Lady Marchant of Broome.

Marcher, John. "The Beast in the Jungle." A friend of May Bartram; he is the one man in all the world to whom nothing happens.

Marden, Charlotte "Chartie." "Sir Edmund Orme." The attractive daughter of the widowed Mrs. Marden; her acceptance of the narrator's hand exorcises the ghost of Sir Edmund Orme, who in life was rejected by Charlotte's mother.

Marden, Major. "Sir Edmund Orme." The deceased husband of Mrs. Marden, whose acceptance of him caused Sir Edmund Orme to commit suicide; he is the father of Charlotte Marden.

Marden, Mrs. "Sir Edmund Orme." The mother of Charlotte Marden; her acceptance of Major Marden instead of Sir Edmund Orme caused the latter to commit suicide and later to haunt Mrs. Marden.

Maresfield, Lady. "The Chaperon." The sister of rich Mrs. Bray; she is the mother of Mrs. Charlotte Mangler Vaughan-Vesey, Bessie Mangler, Maggie Mangler, young Fanny Mangler, and Guy Mangler, the last of whom she unsuccessfully urges Rose Tramore to accept.

Margaret, Lady. "The Siege of London." A fellow-guest with Mrs. Headway at the Demesne estate of Longlands.

Marguerite. "In the Cage." A name mentioned in one of Lady Bradeen's telegrams processed by the unnamed girl "in the cage."

Marignac, Mme. de. *The Reverberator.* A deceased friend of Gaston Probert's father; she is the mother of Mme. de Villepreux.

Mark, Lord. *The Wings of the Dove.* A friend of Mrs. Maud Manningham Lowder, who wants her niece Kate Croy to marry him; he loves Milly Theale and in frustration tells her of Kate Croy's liaison with Merton Densher, who professes to love Milly Theale.

Marmaduke. "Maud-Evelyn." A strange man rejected by Lavinia; with the help of Mr. and Mrs. Dedrick, he gradually comes to believe that he is their long-dead daughter Maud-Evelyn's bereaved husband.

Marmaduke, Sir Henry. "Lady Barbarina." The husband of the woman who introduces Dr. Jackson Lemon to Lady Beauchemin, the sister of Lady Barbarina Clement.

Marmaduke, Lady. "Lady Barbarina." The woman who introduces Dr. Jackson Lemon to Lady Beauchemin, the sister of Lady Barbarina Clement.

Marsh. *The Other House.* A guest of Mrs. Kate Beever.

Marsh, Mrs. *The Other House.* A guest of Mrs. Kate Beever.

Marshal, Mortimer. "The Papers." An inept playwright who likes the journalist Maud Blandy and seeks publicity through her fellow-journalist Howard Bight.

Martin, Mrs. "Poor Richard." Captain Edmund Severn's sister, whom Gertrude Whittaker thinks of visiting for news of Severn.

Martinet. "The Sweetheart of M. Briseux." The owner of the studio which Pierre Briseux invades to complete brilliantly Harold Staines's poor portrait of the narrator.

Martle, Jean. *The Other House.* A friend of Mrs. Kate Beever, who wants her son Paul Beever to marry her; she loves Tony Bream.

Martle. *The Other House.* The father of Jean Martle and the second cousin of Mrs. Kate Beever; he is an invalid at Brighton.

Mary. "In the Cage." The recipient of a telegram from Captain Count Philip Everard.

Masham, Lord. "The Lesson of the Master." A fellow-guest who sits next to Marian Fancourt during the luncheon at the St. Georges.

Mason, Augustus. "A Most Extraordinary Case." The presumably deceased husband of Maria Mason; he was the uncle of Colonel Ferdinand Mason.

Mason, Mrs. Augustus (Maria). "A Most Extraordinary Case." The kind wife of convalescent Colonel Ferdinand Mason's presumably deceased uncle; she tries unsuccessfully to nurse Colonel Mason back to health.

Mason, Colonel Ferdinand. "A Most Extraordinary Case." The convalescent Civil War veteran who grows worse and dies upon learning that Caroline Hofmann is to marry Dr. Horace Knight; he is unsuccessfully nursed by Mrs. Maria Mason.

Mason. "In the Cage." A name mentioned in one of Lady Bradeen's telegrams processed by the unnamed girl "in the cage."

Massin, Mme. "Fordham Castle." The proprietress of a Swiss pension to which the wife of Abel F. Taker has sent him.

Masters, Miss. "A Most Extraordinary Case." A guest at a dance given at the Stapleton home, which convalescent Colonel Ferdinand Mason rashly attends.

Maule, Mrs. George. "Julia Bride." A woman mentioned by Julia Bride in conversation with Pitman as hating her and her mother; she wants any one of her four daughters to marry Basil French.

Maule, Miss. "Julia Bride." A daughter of Mrs. George Maule.

Maule, Miss. "Julia Bride." A daughter of Mrs. George Maule.

Maule, Miss. "Julia Bride." A daughter of Mrs. George Maule.

Maule, Miss. "Julia Bride." A daughter of Mrs. George Maule.

Mauves, Countess Euphemia Cleve de. "Madame de Mauves." The American wife of Count Richard de Mauves and the object of Longmore's affections.

Mauves, Marie. "Madame de Mauves." See Clairin, Mme. Marie de Mauves.

Mauves, Count Richard de. "Madame de Mauves." The philandering husband of Euphemia Cleve de Mauves and the brother of Mme. Marie de Mauves Clairin; he commits suicide.

Mauves, Mme. de. "Madame de Mauves." The grandmother of Richard and Marie de Mauves who is puzzled by Euphemia Cleve, later Richard de Mauves's wife.

Mavis, Grace "Gracie." "The Patagonia." The fiancee of Porterfield; she is the subject of much gossip aboard the *Patagonia* because Jasper Nettlepoint flirts selfishly with her; she commits suicide by jumping overboard.

Mavis. "The Patagonia." The sick father of Grace Mavis.

Mavis, Mrs. "The Patagonia." The mother of Grace Mavis and a friend of Mrs. Nettlepoint.

Max. "The Siege of London." Mrs. Nancy Grenville Beck Headway's courier.

Meadows, Minnie. "The Next Time." A lady humorist whose popular works contrast with Ray Limbert's serious writing; the magazine-owner Bousefield prefers her writing.

Medwin, Mrs. "Mrs. Medwin." An ambitious woman who pays Mamie Cutter to get her introduced into British social circles.

Meldrum, Mrs. "Glasses." A bespectacled friend who introduces the painter-narrator to Flora Saunt.

Mellifont, Lady. "The Private Life." Windy Lord Mellifont's wife, who seems to know her husband's secret.

Mellifont, Lord. "The Private Life." An affable, fluent man who without an audience is literally nothing.

Meredith, Miss. "A Light Man." The niece of rich Frederick

Sloane who in the absence of any will by him receives his money at his death.

Merle, Mme. Geraldine. *The Portrait of a Lady.* The original name in the magazine publication for Mme. Serena Merle, which see.

Merle, Mme. Serena. *The Portrait of a Lady.* The widow of a Swiss merchant and the former mistress of Gilbert Osmond, by whom she had Pansy Osmond; she is the friend of Lydia Touchett and the victimizer of Isabel Archer.

Merriman, Arthur. "A New England Winter." The husband of Joanna Daintry Merriman, Florimond Daintry's sister; he is the father of six children.

Merriman, Mrs. Arthur (Joanna Daintry). "A New England Winter." The sister of Florimond Daintry; she and her husband have six children.

Merriman, Miss. *The Awkward Age.* The governess of Agnesina.

Mesh, Donald. "A New England Winter." The husband of Pauline Mesh, who is a friend of Lucretia Daintry; he is related to Rachel Torrance.

Mesh, Mrs. Donald (Pauline). "A New England Winter." A friend of Lucretia Daintry; when Florimond Daintry appears to be falling for Mrs. Mesh, his mother urges him to return to Paris.

Meyrau, Vicomte Louis de. "A Tragedy of Error." Mme. Hortense Bernier's lover who is murdered by mistake instead of her husband Charles Bernier.

Michael. "A Most Extraordinary Case." Colonel Ferdinand Mason's servant.

Middlemas, Dr. "A Most Extraordinary Case." Colonel Ferdinand Mason's New York physician.

Middlemas, Mrs. "A Most Extraordinary Case." The wife of Colonel Ferdinand Mason's New York physician; through her, Mrs. Maria Mason learned of Colonel Mason's sickness.

Middleton, Mrs. *Watch and Ward.* A would-be matchmaker who introduces Miss Sands to Roger Lawrence.

Midmore, Molly. *The Sense of the Past.* The fiancee of the

eighteenth-century Ralph Pendrel; the present Ralph Pendrel meets her but prefers her more modern sister Nan Midmore.

Midmore, Nancy "Nan." *The Sense of the Past.* The sister of Molly Midmore; Molly is the fiancee of the eighteenth-century Ralph Pendrel, but the present Ralph Pendrel prefers the more modern Nan.

Midmore, Peregrine "Perry." *The Sense of the Past.* The thick brother of Molly and Nan Midmore, in the eighteenth century.

Midmore, Mrs. *The Sense of the Past.* The London tenant of Ralph Pendrel; she is the mother of Molly, Nan, and Perry Midmore in the eighteenth century.

Miles. "The Turn of the Screw." The nephew of the governess's employer and the brother of Flora; he is perhaps victimized by the spirit of Peter Quint.

Miller, Annie P. "Daisy." "Daisy Miller." An innocent but socially gauche American girl in Switzerland and then Rome; she loves Frederick Forsyth Winterbourne; after she is escorted to the Colosseum by Giovanelli, she catches a fever and dies.

Miller, Ezra B. "Daisy Miller." The rich Schenectady businessman father of Daisy and Randolph Miller.

Miller, Mrs. Ezra B. "Daisy Miller." The inept mother of Daisy and Randolph Miller.

Miller, Randolph. "Daisy Miller." Daisy Miller's wild little brother.

Millington. *The Princess Casamassima.* A neighbor of the Princess Casamassima, of Broome.

Millington, Mrs. *The Princess Casamassima.* A neighbor of the Princess Casamassima, of Broome.

Millward. "The Marriages." The host where Colonel Chart and Mrs. Churchley have met.

Millward, Mrs. "The Marriages." The hostess where Colonel Chart and Mrs. Churchley have met.

Milsom, Mrs. "The Death of the Lion." Fanny Hurter's sister.

Minch, Lady Augusta. "The Death of the Lion." This lady and

Lord Dorimont lose Neil Paraday's priceless last manuscript between them.

Mirandola. *The Bostonians.* A refugee once aided in Boston by Miss Birdseye.

Mitchell, Father. *The Golden Bowl.* Maggie Verver's priest at the estate of Fawns.

Mitchett "Mitchy." *The Awkward Age.* A rich member of Mrs. Brookenham's circle; he is declined by Nanda Brookenham and marries Agnesina.

Mitton. *The Tragic Muse.* Charles Carteret's lawyer who arranges Carteret's will to exclude Nick Dormer.

Mixter. "Four Meetings." The dull pupil of the supposed countess, who gives French lessons while sponging off Caroline Spencer.

Moddle. *What Maisie Knew.* The nurse for Maisie Farange hired by her father Beale Farange.

Molesley, Lady. "The Marriages." Once a friend of Adela Chart's deceased mother.

Molyneux, Miss Mildred. *The Portrait of a Lady.* The young sister of Lord Warburton; she likes Isabel Archer.

Molyneux, Miss. *The Portrait of a Lady.* The sister of Lord Warburton; she likes Isabel Archer.

Monarch, Major. "The Real Thing." A model for the painter-narrator who proves ineffectual because he is too real and inflexible.

Monarch, Mrs. "The Real Thing." The wife of Major Monarch; a model for the painter-narrator who proves ineffectual because she is too real and inflexible.

Montaut, Guy de. "The Solution." A French attache in Rome; he and the narrator in jest persuade callow Henry Wilmerding that he has compromised Veronica Goldie.

Montbron, M. de. *The Ambassadors.* The suitable young man selected to be the husband of Jeanne de Vionnet by her mother Mme. Marie de Vionnet and by Chad Newsome.

Monteith, Mark P. "A Round of Visits." A victim of embezzler Phil Bloodgood; he visits Mrs. Florence Ash and Newton Winch.

Montenero. "In the Cage." A name mentioned in one of Lady

Bradeen's telegrams processed by the unnamed girl "in the cage."

Montgomery, Mrs. *Washington Square.* The sister of Morris Townsend; she is the widowed mother of five children; Dr. Austin Sloper forces her to criticize her brother.

Montravers, Malcolm. "Mora Montravers." The deceased father of Mora Montravers.

Montravers, Mrs. Malcolm. "Mora Montravers." The deceased mother of Mora Montravers; she was the half-sister of Mrs. Jane Traffle, Mora Montravers's foster-mother.

Montravers, Mora. "Mora Montravers." The daughter of the half-sister of Mrs. Jane Traffle, the foster-mother of Mora Montravers; she marries Walter Puddick to gain Jane Traffle's money for him; then she divorces him for Sir Bruce Bagley.

Moore, Adela. "A Day of Days." The sister of Herbert Moore, who is visited by the scientist Tom Ludlow; she and Ludlow poignantly attract one another briefly.

Moore, Herbert. "A Day of Days." Adela Moore's scientist brother, whom Tom Ludlow comes to visit briefly.

Moreen, Adolphe. "The Pupil." The original name in the magazine publication for Ulick Moreen, which see.

Moreen, Amy. "The Pupil." A sister of Morgan Moreen who cannot attract a suitor.

Moreen, Morgan. "The Pupil." Pemberton's precocious pupil; he adversely judges his parents; later he dies of a heart attack.

Moreen, Paula. "The Pupil." A sister of Morgan Moreen who cannot attract a suitor.

Moreen, Ulick. "The Pupil." The older, toadying brother of Morgan Moreen; he gambles; later he takes Morgan's death like a man of the world.

Moreen. "The Pupil." The father of Ulick, Amy, Paula, and Morgan Moreen; he takes Morgan's death like a man of the world.

Moreen, Mrs. "The Pupil." The mother of Ulick, Amy, Paula, and Morgan Moreen; she thinks that Pemberton is stealing Morgan's affections from the family.

Morgan, Mrs. *The Europeans.* A bold woman whom William Wentworth thinks of when he hears of Baroness Eugenia Munster's morganatic marriage.

Morrish. "Sir Dominick Ferrand." A music publisher who purchases the song which Mrs. Ryves and Peter Baron write.

Morrow. "The Death of the Lion." The representative of a syndicate of thirty-seven journals; his articles provide the novelist Neil Paraday fatal publicity.

Morton, Isabel. *Watch and Ward.* See Keith, Mrs. Isabel Morton.

Morton. *Watch and Ward.* The brother of Isabel Morton; at his home, Roger Lawrence visits her.

Morton, Mrs. *Watch and Ward.* The wife of Isabel Morton's brother; Roger Lawrence visits Miss Morton at her brother's home.

Morton, Miss. *Watch and Ward.* The little daughter of the brother and sister-in-law of Isabel Morton.

Moseley, Eliza P. *The Bostonians.* A feminist known by several women in the Boston feminist movement.

Mostyn, Mrs. "Nona Vincent." A casual, ignorant friend of Mrs. Alsager.

Motcomb. "A London Life." A man who has seen Mrs. Selina Berrington with the notorious Lady Ringrose in Paris, according to Lionel Berrington.

Moyle, Pat. "The Next Time." A political correspondent whose works compete with Ray Limbert's literary works in a journal.

Mudge. "In the Cage." The fiance of the unnamed girl "in the cage."

Muldoon, Mrs. "The Jolly Corner." The Irish cleaning woman at "the jolly corner" property owned by Spencer Brydon.

Mullet, Lady. "The Great Good Place." A woman who wants to meet the busy novelist George Dane.

Mulliner. "The Lesson of the Master." An editor who sits next to Marian Fancourt at the luncheon of the St. Georges.

Mulville, Kent. "The Coxon Fund." A man who aids and is basely treated by Frank Saltram.

Mulville, Mrs. Kent (Adelaide). "The Coxon Fund." A woman who aids and is basely treated by Frank Saltram.

Mumby, Miss. *The Ivory Tower.* This woman, Miss Goodenough, and Miss Ruddle are Frank B. Betterman's nurses.

Munden, Mrs. "The Beldonald Holbein." A friend of the painter-narrator and the sister-in-law of the widowed Lady Beldonald.

Muniment, Paul. *The Princess Casamassima.* The brother of Rosy Muniment; he is a tough-minded anarchist, a friend of Hyacinth Robinson and the Princess Casamassima.

Muniment, Rosy. *The Princess Casamassima.* The invalid sister of Paul Muniment; she is a friend of Lady Aurora Langrish, Hyacinth Robinson, and the Princess Casamassima.

Muniment. *The Princess Casamassima.* A deceased coal-miner and inventor; he was the father of Rosy and Paul Muniment.

Muniment, Mrs. *The Princess Casamassima.* The deceased washwoman mother of Rosy and Paul Muniment.

Munson. "Travelling Companions." The friend of Mark Evans whose sickness in Milan obliges Evans to leave his daughter Charlotte Evans and the narrator Brooke alone in Venice.

Munster, Baroness Eugenia-Camilla-Delores Young. *The Europeans.* The daughter of the half-sister of William Wentworth, the sister of Felix Young, and the morganatic wife of Prince Adolf of Silberstadt-Schreckenstein; she somewhat charms but does not win Robert Acton near Boston.

Munster. *The Reverberator.* Whitney Dosson's former partner.

Munster. *The Ambassadors.* A friend of Maria Gostrey, who was with Mr. and Mrs. Munster at Liverpool.

Munster, Mrs. *The Ambassadors.* A friend of Maria Gostrey, who was with Mr. and Mrs. Munster at Liverpool.

Murray, Miss. *Watch and Ward.* Nora Lambert's piano teacher.

Musgrave, Edgar. "Guest's Confession." The narrator David's step-brother whom John Guest swindled.

Nash, Gabriel. *The Tragic Muse.* The idle, aesthetic, loquacious friend of Nick Dormer and Miriam Rooth.

Nettlepoint, Jasper. "The Patagonia." The Bostonian whose flirtation aboard the *Patagonia* with Grace Mavis is partially responsible for her suicide; their mothers are friends.

Nettlepoint, Mrs. "The Patagonia." The mother of Jasper Nettlepoint and the friend of Mrs. Mavis, whose daughter commits suicide after a flirtation with Jasper Nettlepoint aboard the *Patagonia*.

Newman, Christopher. *The American.* The rich American whose attempt in Paris to marry Claire de Bellegarde de Cintre is thwarted by her mother Mme. de Bellegarde and her brother Urbain de Bellegarde.

Newsome, Abel. *The Ambassadors.* The deceased husband of Mrs. Newsome and the father of Chad Newsome and Mrs. Sarah Newsome Pocock.

Newsome, Mrs. Abel. *The Ambassadors.* The awesome, never-seen widowed mother of Chad Newsome and Mrs. Sarah Newsome Pocock; she will marry Lambert Strether only if he succeeds as her ambassador to rescue Chad from a Parisian entanglement.

Newsome, Chadwick "Chad." *The Ambassadors.* The son of Mr. and Mrs. Abel Newsome; he is the lover of Mme. Marie de Vionnet and the nominal fiance of Mamie Pocock.

Niblett. "Crawford's Consistency." An old patient who gossips with the physician-narrator about the ill fortune of Crawford.

Niedermeyer. "Eugene Pickering." A gossipy Austrian friend of the narrator; he tells the narrator about Mme. Anastasia Blumenthal's background.

Ninetta. "Adina." Angelo Beati's former girl-friend.

Nioche, Noemie. *The American.* A copyist whom Christopher Newman meets at the Louvre; Valentin de Bellegarde dies in a duel with Stanislas Kapp over her.

Nioche. *The American.* Noemie Nioche's father, who gives Christopher Newman lessons in French.

Noble, Mrs. *The Golden Bowl.* The nurse of the infant son Principino of Maggie Verver and her husband Prince Amerigo.

Northmore, Lord John. "The Abasement of the Northmores."
The supposedly illustrious deceased statesman whose
family Mrs. Warren Hope declines to abase; his published
letters are fatuous.

Northmore, Lady. "The Abasement of the Northmores." The
widow of Lord John Northmore; Mrs. Warren Hope
declines to abase her.

Northover. *The Ivory Tower.* A deceased Britisher, the second
husband of Graham Fielder's mother.

Northover, Mrs. Fielder. *The Ivory Tower.* The half-sister of
Frank B. Betterman and the mother of Graham Fielder.

Nutkins. "The Marriages." The gardener at Brinton, the country estate of the Chart family; Adela Chart's now deceased mother taught him.

Obert, Ford. *The Sacred Fount.* A painter who is tolerant of
his friend the narrator.

Offord, Oliver. "Brooksmith." The recently deceased master of
the now unemployed servant Brooksmith.

Olimpia. "The Aspern Papers." Juliana Bordereau's maid.

Orme, Sir Edmund. "Sir Edmund Orme." The rejected suitor
of the woman who became Mrs. Marden; after his suicide
by poison his ghost haunts her daughter Charlotte Marden until she accepts the narrator.

Orme, Lady Agnes. "In the Cage." A name mentioned in one
of Lady Bradeen's telegrams processed by the unnamed
girl "in the cage."

Oronte. "The Real Thing." The Italian model-valet of the
painter-narrator.

Orville, Lady. "The Given Case." The hostess at Pickenham who
is embarrassed because Mrs. Kate Despard did not bring
her lover Barton Reeve.

Osborne, Philip. "Osborne's Revenge." The friend of Robert
Graham, for whose suicide Osborne wrongly blames
Henrietta Congreve.

Osmond, Gilbert. *The Portrait of a Lady.* The cruelly refined
father of Pansy Osmond and the brother of Countess

Amy Gemini; he is the former lover of Mme. Serena Merle, Pansy's mother; at Mme. Merle's suggestion, he marries Isabel Archer.

Osmond, Mrs. Gilbert (Isabel Archer). *The Portrait of a Lady.* See Archer, Isabel.

Osmond, Pansy. *The Portrait of a Lady.* The convent-flower illegitimate daughter of Gilbert Osmond and Mme. Serena Merle; she adores her step-mother Mrs. Isabel Archer Osmond; she falls in love with Ned Rosier.

Osmond, Mrs. *The Portrait of a Lady.* The deceased mother of Gilbert Osmond and Countess Amy Osmond Gemini; she was a pretentious writer — "The American Corinne."

Ottavio, Don. *The Golden Bowl.* Prince Amerigo's Roman cousin.

Outreau, Paul. "The Beldonald Holbein." The painter-narrator's French painter friend who sees elements of Holbein in Lady Beldonald's companion Mrs. Louisa Brash.

d'Outreville, Duchess. *The American.* A woman whom Christopher Newman meets at the Bellegarde party; he later decides against telling her of the Bellegarde murder.

d'Outreville, Mme. *The Reverberator.* A friend of Suzanne de Brecourt, Gaston Probert's sister.

Overmore, Miss. *What Maisie Knew.* An attractive woman who, after Beale and Ida Farange's divorce, is hired by Beale Farange as a nurse for Maisie Farange; he then marries her; she then becomes the mistress of Sir Claude, Ida Farange's next husband.

Overt, Paul. "The Lesson of the Master." A serious young novelist who takes the master-novelist Henry St. George's advice, does not propose marriage to Marian Fancourt, but instead writes; later he is puzzled when St. George, who has become a widower, marries Miss Fancourt.

Overt, Mrs. "The Lesson of the Master." The recently deceased invalid mother of the novelist Paul Overt.

Packard, General. *The American.* An unimportant American mentioned by Christopher Newman as one of his friends in Paris.

Pallant, Henry. "Louisa Pallant." The deceased husband of Louisa Pallant and the father of cold Linda Pallant.

Pallant, Mrs. Henry (Louisa). "Louisa Pallant." The mother of cold Linda Pallant; she warns Archie Parker about her ambitious daughter since her own conscience troubles her for having jilted Parker's uncle, the narrator.

Pallant, Linda. "Louisa Pallant." The daughter of Henry and Louisa Pallant; her selfish ambition to marry Archie Parker is thwarted by her conscience-stricken mother; she later marries Gimingham.

Pappendick. *The Outcry.* The Brussels art critic, less able than Bardi of Milan.

Paraday, Neil. "The Death of the Lion." The distinguished novelist whose sudden lionizing indirectly causes his death.

Paraday, Mrs. Neil. "The Death of the Lion." The estranged wife of the novelist.

Pardon, Matthias. *The Bostonians.* The journalist admirer of Verena Tarrant.

Parker, Archie. "Louisa Pallant." The narrator's nephew and the temporary object of predatory Linda Pallant, whose mother frustrates Linda's plan.

Parker, Mrs. Charlotte. "Louisa Pallant." The mother of Archie Parker and the sister of the narrator.

Parker. "The Pension Beaurepas." A man mentioned by Mrs. Ruck as having stayed at the Pension Beaurepas.

Parker, Mrs. "The Pension Beaurepas." A woman mentioned by Mrs. Ruck as having stayed at the Pension Beaurepas.

Parker, Mrs. "A Light Man." Theodore Lisle's sister.

Parker, Miss. "A Light Man." The infant daughter of Theodore Lisle's sister.

Parker, Miss. "Louisa Pallant." The delicate little sister of Archie Parker, the narrator's nephew.

Parminter. "Mrs. Temperly." A friend of Mrs. Temperly in Paris.

Parminter, Mrs. "Mrs. Temperly." A friend of Mrs. Temperly in Paris.

Parminter, Miss. "Mrs. Temperly." The pianist daughter of Mr. and Mrs. Parminter, friends of Mrs. Temperly in Paris.

Pasquale. "The Aspern Papers." The critic-narrator's Venetian gondolier.

Pasquale. *The Wings of the Dove.* Milly Theale's Venetian gondolier.

Patten, Rev. Mr. "The Third Person." The vicar of Marr, where Susan and Amy Frush inherit a house and now live.

Patti, Adelina. *The American.* The real-life coloratura soprano, heard in Paris. "Eugene Pickering." Heard in Homburg. "The Chaperon." Heard in London.

Paul, Mrs. *Watch and Ward.* Nora Lambert's New York hostess-captor, in league with George Fenton.

Pearson, Harriet. "The Liar." The real name, according to Colonel Clement Capadose, liar, of the tipsy model who calls herself at Oliver Lyon's studio Miss Geraldine, which see.

Peck, Mrs. "The Patagonia." The leading gossip aboard the *Patagonia* and the mother of four uncontrollable children; she is the friend of Mrs. Gotch and Mrs. Jarvie, and they all contribute to Grace Mavis's misery.

Pegg, Hall. "Covering End." The object of the affections of Cora Prodmore, whose father objects.

Pemberton. "The Pupil." The tutor and friend of Morgan Moreen.

Pemble. "The Beast in the Jungle." A casual friend of John Marcher but not of May Bartram.

Pemble, Mrs. "The Beast in the Jungle." A casual friend of John Marcher but not of May Bartram.

Pendexter, Miss. "Poor Richard." A relative of Gertrude Whittaker's recently deceased father; she is now Miss Whittaker's house companion.

Pendrel, Philip Augustus. *The Sense of the Past.* The deceased cousin of Ralph Pendrel; he wills Ralph a house in London.

Pendrel, Ralph. *The Sense of the Past.* A New York historian who is refused by the widowed Mrs. Aurora Coyne and who goes to London to his inherited property, where he meets in fantasy Molly Midmore, the fiancee of his eighteenth-century ancestor Ralph Pendrel, and also meets her mother Mrs. Midmore, brother Perry Midmore, and sister Nan Midmore.

Pendrel. *The Sense of the Past.* Ralph Pendrel's recently deceased father.

Penniman, Rev. Mr. *Washington Square.* The deceased husband of Lavinia Sloper Penniman, Catherine Sloper's aunt.

Penniman, Mrs. Lavinia Sloper. *Washington Square.* The sister of Dr. Austin Sloper and Mrs. Jefferson Almond; she is the ineffectual aunt of Catherine Sloper and the would-be aid of Morris Townsend, Miss Sloper's suitor.

Penniman. *The Outcry.* An unimportant society person.

Penniman, Mrs. *The Outcry.* An unimportant society person.

Pensil, Lady. *The Portrait of a Lady.* Bob Bantling's sister, to whose estate Henrietta Stackpole finally obtains an invitation.

Percival. *The American.* An art-loving friend of Rev. Mr. Benjamin Babcock, who is Christopher Newman's temporary traveling companion.

Percy. *The Tragic Muse.* Nick Dormer's uncle; he is probably Percy Dormer.

Perriam. *What Maisie Knew.* One of Ida Farange's many lovers.

Petherton, Lord. *The Awkward Age.* A parasite on Mitchett; he is the lover of Duchess Jane of Naples.

Pickering, Eugene. "Eugene Pickering." The somewhat ingenuous friend of the narrator; he thinks that he is in love with Mme. Anastasia Blumenthal but later really falls in love with Isabel Vernor, whom his now deceased father recommended.

Pickering. "Eugene Pickering." The deceased father of ingenuous Eugene Pickering; he recommended Isabel Vernor to his son as a charming young girl.

Pigeonneau. "The Pension Beaurepas." An admirer of Aurora Church in Geneva.

Pimlico, Countess of. "An International Episode." The daughter of the Duke and Duchess of Bayswater, and the sister of Lord Lambeth, who loves Bessie Alden.

Pinhorn. "The Death of the Lion." The critic-narrator's editor.

Pinks. *The Tragic Muse.* A deceased politician discussed by members of the Dormer family.

Pinthorpe, Mary. *The Awkward Age.* A casual friend of the Brookenhams.

Pitman. "Julia Bride." One of Julia Bride's step-fathers; he loves the widow Mrs. David E. Drack.

Pitman, Mrs. "Julia Bride." See Connery, Mrs. Bride Pitman.

Platt, Henry. "Georgina's Reasons." An uncle of Agnes Theory, the sister-in-law of Mildred and Kate Theory.

Platt, William. "A Bundle of Letters." The stay-at-home boyfriend of Miranda Hope, whose letters to her mother back in Bangor, Maine, mention him.

Plummeridge. "The Point of View." The man servant of Edward Antrobus.

Pochintesta. "The Aspern Papers." The Venetian lawyer friend of Juliana and Tina Bordereau.

Pocock, Jim. *The Ambassadors.* The rather coarse husband of Mrs. Abel Newsome's daughter Sarah Newsome Pocock; he is the brother of Mamie Pocock, the nominal fiancee of Mrs. Newsome's son Chad Newsome.

Pocock, Mrs. Jim (Sarah Newsome). *The Ambassadors.* The daughter of Mrs. Abel Newsome, Lambert Strether's fiancee; she is the wife of Jim Pocock, whose sister Mamie Pocock is the nominal fiancee of Sarah's brother Chad Newsome.

Pocock, Mamie. *The Ambassadors.* The charming sister of Jim Pocock and the nominal fiancee of Chad Newsome, the brother of her sister-in-law Mrs. Sarah Newsome Pocock.

Porterfield, David. "The Patagonia." An architecture student in Paris, the fiance of Grace Mavis; going to him from Boston to Liverpool, she commits suicide by jumping overboard from the *Patagonia.*

Portico, Mrs. "Georgina's Reasons." The reluctant companion of pregnant Mrs. Georgina Gressie Benyon on a trip to Italy, where Georgina abandons her baby son; Mrs. Portico writes Raymond Benyon, the father, and then later dies.

Pouncer, Mrs. "Mrs. Medwin." A lady of fashion who, according to Mamie Cutter, has approved of Mrs. Medwin.

Poupin, Eustace. *The Princess Casamassima.* A French bookbinder socialist in London; he is a friend of Anastasius Vetch and later of Hyacinth Robinson.

Poupin, Mme. Eustace. *The Princess Casamassima.* The fat common-law wife of Eustace Poupin.

Poyle, Miss. "The Figure in the Carpet." The woman to whom Hugh Vereker says that the critic-narrator's article on him is twaddle; the narrator overhears.

Prance, Dr. Mary J. *The Bostonians.* A woman physician in Boston; she is the friend of several feminists; she attends Miss Birdseye during her final sickness.

Prendergast. "A Landscape Painter." A local lawyer unsuccessfully interested in Miriam Quarterman.

Prest, Mrs. "The Aspern Papers." The woman in Venice who helps the critic-narrator get started in his plan to obtain "the Aspern papers."

Prime, Arthur. "Paste." Charlotte Prime's cousin; he seemingly refuses to believe that his deceased step-mother's pearl necklace can be genuine and not paste.

Prime, Charlotte. "Paste." Arthur Prime's cousin; she accepts his deceased step-mother's pearl necklace as a gift and then discovers it to be genuine and not paste.

Prime, Rev. Mr. "Paste." Arthur Prime's deceased father, the husband of the actress-owner of the pearl necklace.

Prime, Mrs. "Paste." The former actress Miss Bradshaw, owner of the pearl necklace; she is now deceased.

Principino. *The Golden Bowl.* The infant son of Prince Amerigo and his wife Princess Maggie Verver.

Probert, Alphonse. *The Reverberator.* The deceased brother of Gaston Probert.

Probert, Gaston. *The Reverberator.* The brother of Suzanne (Susan) de Brecourt, Marguerite (Margaret) de Cliche, and Jeanne (Jane) de Douves; he is the fiance of Francie Dosson.

Probert. *The Reverberator.* The deceased grandfather of Gaston Probert.

Probert. *The Reverberator.* The father of Gaston Probert; he is aghast at Francie Dosson, the fiancee of his son, for gossiping to the American journalist George Flack.

Probert, Mme. *The Reverberator.* The deceased mother of Gaston Probert.

Prodmore, Cora. "Covering End." The daughter of the mortgage-holder of Captain Clement Yule's estate Covering End; she loves Hall Pegg and is befriended by Mrs. Gracedew.

Prodmore. "Covering End." The mortgage-holder of Captain Clement Yule's estate Covering End; he is bought off by Mrs. Gracedew.

Puddick, Walter. "Mora Montravers." The painter whom Mora Montravers marries to gain her foster-mother Mrs. Jane Traffle's money for him; he is then divorced.

Pudney. "The Coxon Fund." A host of Frank Saltram until Saltram is offensive.

Pudney, Mrs. "The Coxon Fund." A hostess of Frank Saltram until he is offensive.

Purvis, Lord Frederick. *The Princess Casamassima.* The deceased natural father of Hyacinth Robinson by Florentine Vivier, who murdered him.

Putchin, Miss. "The Birthplace." The retiring guide of The Birthplace; she brashly answers Morris Gedge's preliminary questions.

Pynsent, Amanda "Pinnie." *The Princess Casamassima.* The devoted seamstress guardian of Hyacinth Robinson; she is a friend of Anastasius Vetch; when she dies, she leaves a small sum to Hyacinth.

Pynsent, Rev. Mr. Weatherby. "A Day of Days." A friend of Herbert and Adela Moore.

Quarterman, Miriam. "A Landscape Painter." The young lady who marries the rich painter-diarist Locksley when he is on the rebound.

Quarterman, Captain. "A Landscape Painter." The father of Miriam Quarterman; he is a retired sea-captain.

Quint, Peter. "The Turn of the Screw." The male ghost seen by the governess-narrator and perhaps by Miles.

Raddle. "Lord Beaupre." The deceased glue-manufacturing father of young Raddle.

Raddle. "Lord Beaupre." A rich young man who does not marry Maud Ashbury, to her mother's distress.

Raddle, Mrs. "Lord Beaupre." The rather old wife of rich young Raddle.

Ramage, Dr. Robert. *The Other House.* A friend of the Beever and Bream families; he hushes up the murder of Effie Bream by Rose Armiger.

Ramage, Mrs. Robert. *The Other House.* The wife of Dr. Ramage.

Ramsey, Rutland. "The Real Thing." A volume by the tardily famous Philip Vincent which the painter-narrator is commissioned to illustrate.

Rance. *The Golden Bowl.* The absent husband of Mrs. Rance, who is a parasite on Adam Verver until Charlotte Stant drives her away from Fawns.

Rance, Mrs. *The Golden Bowl.* A parasite on Adam Verver until Charlotte Stant drives her away from Fawns.

Randage. *The Awkward Age.* The deceased possessor of dirty books; he is discussed by Mrs. Brookenham and Mitchett.

Ransom, Basil. *The Bostonians.* A Confederate Army veteran, lawyer, and writer; he loves Verena Tarrant and wins her away from the feminist movement in Boston.

Rasch, Cornelia. "Crapy Cornelia." A friend of White-Mason during their youth, years ago; they happily renew their acquaintance.

Rawson. "A Passionate Pilgrim." The fallen English gentleman whom Clement Searle and the narrator meet in Oxford.

Ray, Violet. "A Bundle of Letters." A well-to-do New York businessman's daughter who is staying with her mother in Paris; she writes superciliously to Agnes Rich about Miranda Hope, her fellow-guest at Mme. Maisonrouge's pension.

Ray. "A Bundle of Letters." A well-to-do New York businessman called home from Paris.

Ray, Mrs. "A Bundle of Letters." A well-to-do New York businessman's wife; she stays in Paris with her daughter Violet Ray.

Redwood, Mrs. "The Modern Warning." A New York society friend of Agatha Grice, Lady Chasemore.

Reeve, Barton. "The Given Case." A lawyer; he is the lover of Mrs. Kate Despard and appeals to Margaret Hamer for help.

Reeves, Mrs. Sherrington. "Fordham Castle." The pseudonym of Mrs. Abel F. Taker, which see.

Rich, Agnes. "A Bundle of Letters." The recipient of a letter from Violet Ray.

Rimmle, Jane. "Europe." The sister of Maria and Becky Rimmle; in spite of her mother's selfishness, she goes to Europe.

Rimmle, Maria. "Europe." The sister of Jane and Becky Rimmle; because of her mother's selfishness, she does not go to Europe but instead supports Jane's journey there.

Rimmle, Rebecca "Becky." "Europe." The sister of Jane and Maria Rimmle; because of her mother's selfishness, she does not go to Europe; she later dies.

Rimmle. "Europe." The well-traveled, windy, now deceased father of Jane, Maria, and Becky Rimmle.

Rimmle, Mrs. "Europe." The selfish, immemorially old, widowed mother of Jane, Maria, and Becky Rimmle who feigns sickness to prevent their trip to Europe.

Ringrose, Lady. "A London Life." A promiscuous lady with whom Mrs. Selina Berrington has gone to Paris, according to Lionel Berrington, Selina's husband.

Ringrose, Lady. "The Private Life." A society lady gossiped about by the author Clare Vawdrey.

Ripley, Mrs. "The Modern Warning." A New York society friend of Agatha Grice, Lady Chasemore.

Rivet, Claude. "The Real Thing." A colleague who recommends Major and Mrs. Monarch as models for the painter-narrator.

Robert. "A Light Man." Rich, dying Frederick Sloane's servant.

Robertson. "The Story of a Year." A partner in the firm of Bruce and Robertson.

Robineau, Mme. *The American.* A hostess to be visited by Mme. Claire de Bellegarde de Cintre.

Robinson, Hyacinth. *The Princess Casamassima.* The illegitimate son of Lord Frederick Purvis and Florentine Vivier; he lives with Amanda Pynsent; he likes Millicent Henning, Paul Muniment, and the Princess Casamassima; he works in Crookenden's bookbindery, joins the anarchistic movement, and commits suicide.

Rochambeau, Marquis de. "Gabrielle de Bergerac." A nobleman who is mentioned as having provided troops to aid the American revolutionary insurgents.

Rochefidele, Count de. *The American.* A nobleman whom Christopher Newman meets at a party given by Mme. de Bellegarde.

Rochefidele, Countess de. *The American.* A noble lady whom Christopher Newman meets at a party given by Mme. de Bellegarde.

Roker. *The Princess Casamassima.* A fellow-bookbinder with Hyacinth Robinson in Crookenden's shop.

Root, Dr. *The Ivory Tower.* Frank B. Betterman's physician, with Dr. Hatch.

Rooth, Miriam. *The Tragic Muse.* A talented Jewish actress, trained by Mme. Honorine Carre, loved vainly by diplomat Peter Sherringham, painted by Nick Dormer, and married by Basil Dashwood.

Rooth, Mrs. Rudolph. *The Tragic Muse.* The aggressive mother of the Jewish actress Miriam Rooth; she is the wife of Rudolph Roth.

Roper, Captain. "The Bench of Desolation." A suitor of Kate Cookham, who snubs him to prove her loyalty to Herbert Dodd.

Rosalie. "A New England Winter." Mrs. Donald Mesh's sister.

Rose-Agathe. "Rose-Agathe." The hairdresser dummy mistaken by the narrator for the wife of the hairdresser; it is obtained by Sanguinetti, a Paris collector of dummies.

Rosenheim, Cora. *The Reverberator.* A name appearing on a banker's record in Paris.

Rosenheim, D. S. *The Reverberator.* A name appearing on a banker's record in Paris.

Rosenheim, Mrs. D. S. *The Reverberator.* A name appearing on a banker's record in Paris.

Rosenheim, Samuel. *The Reverberator.* A name appearing on a banker's record in Paris.

Rosier, Edward "Ned." *The Portrait of a Lady.* A friend from Isabel Archer's childhood who falls in love with Pansy Osmond, sells his collection of bibelots to impress her father, Gilbert Osmond, and then is not encouraged.

Rossiter. *The Portrait of a Lady.* A man who owns a New York house mentioned as suitable for Isabel Archer to rent.

Rossiter, Mrs. *The Portrait of a Lady.* The wife of a man who owns a New York house mentioned as suitable for Isabel Archer to rent.

Roth, Rudolph. *The Tragic Muse.* The deceased father of the Jewish actress Miriam Rooth.

Roth, Mrs. Rudolph. *The Tragic Muse.* See Rooth, Mrs. Rudolph.

Roulet. *The Ivory Tower.* A traveling friend of Graham Fielder and Horton Vint in Neuchatel years ago.

Rover, Fanny. *The Tragic Muse.* A London actress whom Miriam Rooth likes.

Rowland, Captain. *Roderick Hudson.* The father of Rowland Mallet's mother; now deceased, he was a retired sea-captain.

Roy, Agnes. "Georgina's Reasons." See Theory, Mrs. Percival.

Roy, Cora. "Georgina's Reasons." Mrs. Percival Theory's deceased sister; she was William Roy's first wife.

Roy, William. "Georgina's Reasons." The second husband of bigamous Georgina Gressie Benyon Roy.

Roy, Mrs. William (Georgina Gressie Benyon). "Georgina's Reasons." The bigamous wife of William Roy; earlier she married Raymond Benyon; later she abandoned in Italy her son by Benyon.

Roy. "Georgina's Reasons." The son of William Roy and his bigamous wife Georgina Gressie Benyon Roy.

Ruck, Sophy. "The Pension Beaurepas." A spendthrift daughter traveling with her parents in Europe; they stop in Geneva;

she is a casual friend of Aurora Church. "The Point of View." Her father is mentioned as now bankrupt in a letter from Aurora Church to Miss Whiteside.

Ruck. "The Pension Beaurepas." A man who though worried travels in Europe with his extravagant wife and daughter Sophy; they stop in Geneva. "The Point of View." He is mentioned as now bankrupt in a letter from Aurora Church to Miss Whiteside.

Ruck, Mrs. "The Pension Beaurepas." A woman who, though her husband is financially worried, travels in Europe shopping extravagantly with her daughter Sophy; they stop in Geneva. "The Point of View." Her husband is mentioned as now bankrupt in a letter from Aurora Church to Miss Whiteside.

Ruddle, Miss. *The Ivory Tower.* This woman, Miss Goodenough, and Miss Mumby are Frank B. Betterman's nurses.

Ruffler, Mrs. *The Princess Casamassima.* An actress performing in *The Pearl of Paraguay,* which is attended by Hyacinth Robinson and Millicent Henning.

Ruggieri. *The Tragic Muse.* A friend of Miriam Rooth who, exceptionally, could tell the actress something.

Rumble. "The Death of the Lion." A painter who is popular in society.

Runkle, Mrs. "Pandora." The sister-in-law from Natchez of the President of the United States.

Rushbrook. "The Solution." The deceased naval officer husband of the narrator's fiancee.

Rushbrook, Mrs. "The Solution." The fiancee of the narrator, who appeals to her to aid Henry Wilmerding; she extricates Wilmerding from his forced engagement with Veronica Goldie by marrying him herself.

Rushbrook, Miss. "The Solution." The young daughter of widowed Mrs. Rushbrook, the narrator's fiancee.

Rye, Lord. "In the Cage." A client of Mrs. Jordan, a flower-arranger.

Ryves, Sidney. "Sir Dominick Ferrand." The young son of the widowed Mrs. Ryves, the song-writer friend of Peter Baron; he is the grandson of the deceased Sir Dominick Ferrand.

Ryves, Mrs. "Sir Dominick Ferrand." The widowed illegitimate daughter of Sir Dominick Ferrand; she is a song-writer who collaborates with Peter Baron.

Saintonge, Mlle. de. *The Reverberator.* A friend of Suzanne de Brecourt, Gaston Probert's sister.

Saltram, Frank. "The Coxon Fund." A fluent but irresponsible genius, the guest of the Mulvilles and the Pudneys; he is awarded money from the Coxon Fund through the generosity and honesty of Ruth Anvoy; he fails thereafter to produce.

Saltram, Mrs. Frank. "The Coxon Fund." The wife of the brilliant but irresponsible genius Frank Saltram; she is the mother of his four children.

Salvi, Count. "The Diary of a Man of Fifty." The husband of Countess Bianca Salvi and the father of Countess Bianca Scarabelli; he was killed by Count Camerino in a duel.

Salvi, Countess Bianca. "The Diary of a Man of Fifty." The widow of Count Salvi; she was loved but distrusted by the diarist-narrator; she has a daughter who is loved by Edmund Stanmer; after the death of her first husband, Countess Salvi married Count Camerino, who killed Count Salvi in a duel.

Salvi-Scarabelli, Countess Bianca. "The Diary of a Man of Fifty." The widowed daughter of Countess Bianca Salvi; she marries Edmund Stanmer, to the consternation of the diarist-narrator.

Sanders, Mrs. "Daisy Miller." A woman who is mentioned as a possible teacher in America for Randolph Miller, Daisy's brother.

Sandgate, Lady Amy. *The Outcry.* A close friend of Lord Theign; her painting, by Sir Thomas Lawrence, Breckenridge Bender wants but fails to buy.

Sands, Miss. *Watch and Ward.* A young New York lady introduced to Roger Lawrence by would-be matchmaker Mrs. Middleton.

Sanguinetti. "Rose-Agathe." A Paris collector of hairdresser dummies; he obtains Rose-Agathe.

Sarah. "The Story of a Masterpiece." The beautiful fiancee of Stephen Baxter, who paints Marian Everett's portrait.

Saulges, M. de. "A Tragedy of Error." A friend of Vicomte Louis de Meyrau.

Saunt, Flora Louise. "Glasses." The beautiful girl whose approaching blindness causes Lord Iffield to decline marriage with her and enables Geoffrey Dawling to win her hand.

Savage. *Roderick Hudson.* Mrs. Light's mild consular father, long deceased.

Savoy. "In the Cage." A name mentioned in one of Lady Bradeen's telegrams processed by the unnamed girl "in the cage."

Scarabelli, Count. "The Diary of a Man of Fifty." The deceased husband of Countess Bianca Salvi-Scarabelli, the daughter of Countess Bianca Salvi.

Scarabelli, Countess Bianca. "The Diary of a Man of Fifty." See Salvi-Scarabelli, Countess Bianca.

Scarabelli, Signorina. "The Diary of a Man of Fifty." The little daughter of Countess Bianca Scarabelli.

Schack (or Schmack), Baron. *The Awkward Age.* The rich pupil of Algie Manger, a friend of Harold Brookenham.

Schafgans. *Roderick Hudson.* A German painter in Rome known long ago by Mme. Grandoni.

Schinkel. *The Princess Casamassima.* A cabinet-maker and an anarchist; he is a friend of Paul Muniment, Eustace Poupin, and Hyacinth Robinson.

Scholastica. "Benvolio." The learned object of part of the affections of allegorical Benvolio, who also loves society (the Countess).

Schooling, Fanny. "A London Life." A friend of Wendover; the sister of Katie Schooling.

Schooling, Katie. "A London Life." A friend of Wendover; the sister of Fanny Schooling.

Scrope, Magdalen. "De Grey, A Romance." A woman loved and hence destroyed by Paul De Grey, an ancestor of the present Paul De Grey, in accordance with the De Grey family curse.

Scrope, Sam. "Adina." The scientist whose greed for the
Tiberian topaz owned by Angelo Beati causes him to
lose his fiancee Adina Waddington to Beati.

Scudamore, R. P. *The Reverberator.* A name on luggage in a
Paris hotel.

Searle, Clement. "A Passionate Pilgrim." An Oxford ancestor
of the present-day Searles.

Searle, Clement. "A Passionate Pilgrim." An American who
returns as "a passionate pilgrim" to England and tries
unsuccessfully to claim Lackley, the estate there of his
distant cousin Richard Searle; he later dies and is buried
in England.

Searle, Cynthia. "A Passionate Pilgrim." An ancestor of the
present-day Searles; she had a younger sister, Margaret
Searle, who eloped to Paris.

Searle, Margaret. "A Passionate Pilgrim." An ancestor of the
present-day Searles; she was the younger sister of Cynthia
Searle and eloped to Paris with an impoverished violinist.

Searle, Richard. "A Passionate Pilgrim." A British estate-holder
at Lackley and a distant relative of Clement Searle, the
American "passionate pilgrim" to England who tries
to claim Richard Searle's estate.

Searle, Miss. "A Passionate Pilgrim." The sister of Richard
Searle, whose British estate Clement Searle tries unsuccessfully to claim.

Serafina. "The Madonna of the Future." The aging model of
the unproductive painter Theobald.

Server, Mrs. May. *The Sacred Fount.* The woman who is perhaps "the sacred fount" of Gilbert Long.

Severn, Captain Edmund. "Poor Richard." The Union Army
officer during the Civil War who loves but does not
propose marriage to Gertrude Whittaker because of her
wealth; he is killed in the War.

Sherringham, Peter. *The Tragic Muse.* Mrs. Julia Sherringham
Dallow's diplomat brother; he loves but fails to win the
talented Jewish actress Miriam Rooth; he is loved by
Biddy Dormer, the sister of the painter Nick Dormer.

Sholto, Captain Godfrey Gerald. *The Princess Casamassima.*

The attendant of the Princess Casamassima, to whom he introduces Hyacinth Robinson.

Silberstadt-Schreckenstein, Prince Adolph of. *The Europeans.* See Adolph of Silberstadt-Schreckenstein, Prince.

Silberstadt-Schreckenstein, Grand Duke of. "The Liar." The nobleman who took Oliver Lyon's portrait of Mrs. Everina Brant Capadose, according to her husband Colonel Clement Capadose, liar.

Simmons, Abijah. "A Passionate Pilgrim." Clement Searle's lawyer.

Simpkin. "In the Cage." The name of a furnished apartment.

Simpson. "The Story of a Year." A guest of Mr. and Mrs. Littlefield at a party attended by Lizzie Crowe.

Singleton, Sam. *Roderick Hudson.* The American painter friend of Roderick Hudson and Rowland Mallet in Rome.

Slater, Tim. "A Round of Visits." A business friend of Newton Winch.

Sloane, Frederick. "A Light Man." A dying man whose wealth both Theodore Lisle and Max Austin want but fail to get.

Sloper, Dr. Austin. *Washington Square.* The autocratic father of Catherine Sloper who disapproves of her friend Morris Townsend; he is the brother of Lavinia Penniman and Elizabeth Almond.

Sloper, Mrs. Austin (Catherine Harrington). *Washington Square.* The deceased wife of Dr. Austin Sloper and the mother of Catherine Sloper.

Sloper, Catherine. *Washington Square.* The plain but firm-minded daughter of Dr. Austin Sloper; she refuses to abide by his wishes concerning the object of her affections, Morris Townsend; however, they do not marry.

Sloper. *Washington Square.* The son of Dr. Austin Sloper who died at the age of three.

Sorbieres, M. de. "Gabrielle de Bergerac." Gaston de Treuil's wealthy, dying uncle.

Spencer, Caroline. "Four Meetings." A gullible New England schoolteacher who gives her cousin money in Le Havre and thus deprives herself of a European tour.

Spencer, Henrietta. "De Grey, A Romance." A woman loved

and hence destroyed by John De Grey in accordance with the De Grey family curse.

Spooner. *Roderick Hudson.* The Northampton law partner of Barnaby Striker, Roderick Hudson's former employer.

St. Dunstans, Lady. *The Tragic Muse.* The aged godmother of Nick Dormer's deceased father.

Saint Dunstans, Lord Earl of. *The American.* The deceased father of Mme. Emmeline de Bellegarde.

St. George, Henry. "The Lesson of the Master." The master novelist whose wife has weakened his work; at her death, he marries Marian Fancourt, whom Paul Overt, the young novelist, admires.

St. George, Mrs. Henry. "The Lesson of the Master." The wife who weakens the work of her husband, the master novelist Henry St. George.

St. George, Mrs. Henry. "The Lesson of the Master." See Fancourt, Marian.

Stackpole, Henrietta. *The Portrait of a Lady.* A friend of Isabel Archer; she writes travel letters for American newspapers; she is to marry Bob Bantling.

Staines, Harold. "The Sweetheart of M. Briseux." A mediocre painter whose fiancee, the narrator, gives him up to let Pierre Briseux use her as a model and paint over Staines's poor portrait of her.

Staines. "The Sweetheart of M. Briseux." The husband of Lucretia Staines who died of overwork at .the age of thirty-five.

Staines, Mrs. Lucretia. "The Sweetheart of M. Briseux." The widowed mother of the mediocre painter Harold Staines; she is the informal guardian of his fiancee, the narrator.

Stamm, Lisa. *Watch and Ward.* The sister of Mlle. Stamm, who is a German friend of Nora Lambert; she is in a convent in Rome.

Stamm, Mlle. *Watch and Ward.* A German friend of Nora Lambert.

Stanmer, Edmund. "The Diary of a Man of Fifty." The young man who loves and marries the widowed Countess Bianca Salvi-Scarabelli, to the consternation of the diarist-narrator, who years ago loved her mother, the widowed

Countess Bianca Salvi under similarly disturbing circumstances.

Stannace. "The Next Time." A pallid writer, the father of Mrs. Stannace's husband.

Stannace. "The Next Time." The husband of Mrs. Stannace; he published the pallid writing of his father.

Stannace, Mrs. "The Next Time." The mother of Maud Stannace Limbert, the wife of the unpopular novelist Ray Limbert, and the mother of Jane Stannace Highmore, the popular but superficial novelist.

Stant, Charlotte. *The Golden Bowl.* The friend of Maggie Verver, the mistress of Maggie Verver's husband Prince Amerigo, and then the second wife of Maggie Verver's father Adam Verver.

Stapleton, Edith. "A Most Extraordinary Case." A young woman who admires the convalescent Colonel Ferdinand Mason without his knowing it; after going to a party at her home, he suffers a relapse and dies.

Stapleton, George. "A Most Extraordinary Case." The second son in the family which includes Edith Stapleton.

Stapleton. "A Most Extraordinary Case." The first son in the family which includes Edith Stapleton.

Staub, Dr. Rudolph. "A Bundle of Letters." The militantly pro-German visitor at Mme. Maisonrouge's pension; he writes a scientific colleague, Dr. Julius Hirsch, his criticisms of Frenchmen, Englishmen, and Americans there.

Staverton, Alice. "The Jolly Corner." A New Yorker who loves Spencer Brydon when he returns to "the jolly corner" and seeks out his alter ego.

Steet, Miss. "A London Life." The governess of Scratch and Parson Berrington, the sons of Lionel and Selina Berrington.

Steuben, Commodore. "Pandora." The deceased Southern husband of Mrs. Steuben, who wears his portrait around her neck.

Steuben, Mrs. "Pandora." The Southern widow of Commodore Steuben, whose portrait she wears around her neck; she talks in Washington with Count Otto Vogelstein about her protegee Pandora Day.

Stevens. "Guest's Confession." A business associate of Edgar Musgrave, who mentions him in conversation with the swindler John Guest.

Stirling, Isabel. "De Grey, A Romance." A woman loved and hence destroyed by Stephen De Grey in accordance with the De Grey family curse.

Stock-Stock, Mrs. "The Aspern Papers." A supposedly high-society former friend of the Bordereaus.

Stoddard. "Guest's Confession." The lawyer of Edgar Musgrave; he is a partner in Stoddard and Hale.

Stokes, Mrs. Short. "Mrs. Medwin." A woman mentioned by Mamie Cutter to Lady Wantridge as a person whom Mamie Cutter got into society.

Stone, Rev. Mr. "Osborne's Revenge." A serious young minister who is a casual friend of Henrietta Congreve.

Stormer, Leolin. "Greville Fane." The pretentious writer son of the novelist Greville Fane; he is the brother of the useless Lady Ethel Stormer Luard.

Stormer, Mrs. Leolin. "Greville Fane." An old woman whom Leolin Stormer marries.

Stormer, Mrs. "Greville Fane." See Fane, Greville.

Straith, Stuart. "Broken Wings." An unsuccessful painter friend of the unsuccessful writer Mrs. Harvey.

Stransom, George. "The Altar of the Dead." The altar-keeping friend of the dead Mary Antrim; he reluctantly forgives the wrong-doing of the recently deceased Acton Hague.

Strether, Lewis Lambert. *The Ambassadors.* The widowed Mrs. Abel Newsome's fiance and first ambassador to Paris to rescue her son Chad Newsome; he becomes the friend of Maria Gostrey and Mme. Marie de Vionnet.

Strether, Mrs. Lewis Lambert. *The Ambassadors.* The long-deceased wife of Strether.

Strether. *The Ambassadors.* The son of Lambert Strether who died at the age of ten.

Strett, Sir Luke. *The Wings of the Dove.* Milly Theale's impressive London physician.

Striker, Barnaby. *Roderick Hudson.* The Northampton lawyer of the firm of Striker and Spooner who disapproves of his former employee Roderick Hudson's plan to study sculpture in Rome.

Striker, Miss. *Roderick Hudson.* The daughter of Roderick Hudson's former employer Barnaby Striker.

Stringham, Mrs. Susan Shepherd. *The Wings of the Dove.* A Vermont-born writer; she is the companion in Europe of Milly Theale and an old-time friend of Mrs. Maud Manningham Lowder, to whom she introduces Milly in London.

Sturch, Remson. "The Special Type." An unpleasant man who marries Mrs. Brivet when she divorces her husband Frank Brivet.

Sturdy, Miss. "The Point of View." The sister of the Newport host of Edward Antrobus; she writes Mrs. Draper at Ouchy.

Sturtevant, Miss. *Washington Square.* The young lady who marries John Ludlow when he is rejected by Catherine Sloper.

Sutton, Shirley. "The Two Faces." The passive man who observes the hard face of Mrs. May Grantham and the frightened but pretty face of Lady Valda Gwyther, her victim.

Synge, Bertie Hammond. "Glasses." The son of Mr. and Mrs. Hammond Synge, who chaperon and bilk Flora Saunt.

Synge, Hammond. "Glasses." The ostensible chaperon of Flora Saunt, who in reality is bilked by him.

Synge, Mrs. Hammond. "Glasses." The mercenary chaperon of Flora Saunt.

Tacchini, Dr. *The Wings of the Dove.* A Venetian physician consulted by Milly Theale.

Taker, Abel F. "Fordham Castle." A man whose wife has forced him to take the name of C. P. Addard and stay in Geneva while she, as Mrs. Sherrington Reeves, makes her way in English society; he meets Mrs. Magaw, posing as Mrs. Vanderplank, whose daughter his wife meets in England.

Taker, Mrs. Abel F. (Sue). "Fordham Castle." The wife of Abel F. Taker, whom she has forced to take the name of C. P. Addard and stay in Geneva while she, as Mrs. Sherrington Reeves, makes her way in English society.

Tarrant, Dr. Selah. *The Bostonians.* The mesmeric healer father of the feminist orator Verena Tarrant; Olive Chancellor bribes him into releasing Verena to her.

Tarrant, Mrs. Selah. *The Bostonians.* The daughter of Mr. and Mrs. Abraham Greenstreet; she is the mother of the feminist orator Verena Tarrant.

Tarrant, Verena. *The Bostonians.* The daughter of Dr. and Mrs. Selah Tarrant; she is the feminist orator protegee of Mrs. Amariah Farrinder and the friend of Olive Chancellor; she leaves the feminist movement for love of Basil Ransom.

Tatton. *The Awkward Age.* The butler of the Brookenham family.

Teagle, Miss. "Sir Dominick Ferrand." The governess of Sidney Ryves, the small son of the widowed Mrs. Ryves.

Temperly, Dora. "Mrs. Temperly." The oldest daughter of Mrs. Maria Temperly; she and her mother's cousin Raymond Bestwick are frustratedly in love; she is the sister of Effie and Tishy Temperly.

Temperly, Effie. "Mrs. Temperly." The second daughter of Mrs. Maria Temperly; she is the sister of Dora and Tishy Temperly.

Temperly, Mrs. Maria. "Mrs. Temperly." The socially ambitious widowed mother of uncooperative Dora Temperly, who loves her mother's cousin Raymond Bestwick, and of Effie and Tishy Temperly.

Temperly, Tishy. "Mrs. Temperly." Mrs. Maria Temperly's third daughter, who remains diminutive; she is the sister of Dora and Effie Temperly.

Temple, Edith. *The Tragic Muse.* A stage name of Miriam Rooth at one time.

Teresa "Teresita." *Watch and Ward.* A Peruvian beauty with whom Roger Lawrence falls very briefly in love until Nora Lambert's letter arrives.

Tester, Ambrose. "The Path of Duty." The lover of married Lady Margaret Vandeleur; he becomes engaged to Joscelind Bernardstone to please his father Sir Edmund Tester; then Lord Vandeleur dies.

Tester, Sir Edmund. "The Path of Duty." The father of Ambrose Tester; he wants his son to marry.

Tester, Francis "Frank." "The Path of Duty." The older brother of Ambrose Tester; he drinks, gambles, and dies.

Tester. "The Path of Duty." The son of Ambrose Tester and his wife Joscelind Bernardstone Tester.

Tester, Miss. "The Path of Duty." The daughter of Ambrose Tester and his wife Joscelind Bernardstone Tester.

Theale, Milly. *The Wings of the Dove.* The wealthy, mortally sick companion of Mrs. Susan Shepherd Stringham, the guest of Mrs. Maud Manningham Lowder, the victim of Kate Croy, and the redeemer of Merton Densher.

Theign, Lord. *The Outcry.* The widowed father of Lady Kitty Imber and Lady Grace, the close friend of Lady Amy Sandgate, and the owner of the disputed Mantovano painting which Hugh Crimble reveres and Breckenridge Bender wants to buy.

Theobald. "The Madonna of the Future." The loquacious but unproductive painter in Florence whose madonna, to be modeled by the aging Serafina, remains "of the future."

Theolinde. "Rose-Agathe." The original name in the magazine publication for Rose-Agathe, which see.

Theory, Kate. "Georgina's Reasons." The younger sister of Percival and Mildred Theory; Raymond Benyon wishes to divorce Georgina Gressie Benyon (Roy) to marry Kate Theory.

Theory, Mildred. "Georgina's Reasons." The sick sister of Percival and Kate Theory.

Theory, Percival. "Georgina's Reasons." The brother of Mildred and Kate Theory; he is the husband of Agnes Roy Theory.

Theory, Mrs. Percival (Agnes Roy). "Georgina's Reasons." William Roy's sister and the sister-in-law of Mildred and Kate Theory.

Thompson, Angelica. "Osborne's Revenge." The fictitious name which Philip Osborne assigns to a person whose photograph he has purchased to deceive Henrietta Congreve.

Thompson. "The Abasement of the Northmores." A person asked by Lady Northmore for letters from Lord John Northmore.

Thrupp. "In the Cage." The name of a furnished apartment.

Tiblaud, Abbe. "Gabrielle de Bergerac." A friend of the Baroness de Bergerac, the mother of the narrator; he is disliked by the narrator's father.

Tischbein. *What Maisie Knew.* One of Ida Farange's many lovers.

Toovey, Mrs. Blanche Bertha Nancy Vanderbank. *The Awkward Age.* Gustavus Vanderbank's sister Nancy.

Topping, Florine (Dorine?). *The Reverberator.* A lady journalist who aids George Flack.

Torrance, Rachel. "A New England Winter." A woman invited by Mrs. Donald Mesh to Boston at the indirect request of Mrs. Susan Daintry, to brighten the vacation of her son Florimond Daintry; Miss Torrance correctly judges him to be shallow.

Torrance, Mrs. "A New England Winter." Rachel Torrance's sick mother.

Tottenham. "A Passionate Pilgrim." Richard Searle's butler at Lackley.

Touchett, Daniel Tracy. *The Portrait of a Lady.* A rich, retired, American-born British banker; he is the husband of Lydia Touchett, Isabel Archer's aunt, and the father of Ralph Touchett; he bequeathes Isabel Archer a large sum of money.

Touchett, Mrs. Daniel Tracy (Lydia). *The Portrait of a Lady.* The independent, semi-estranged wife of the rich banker Daniel Tracy Touchett; she is the mother of Ralph Touchett, the aunt of Isabel Archer, and the friend of Mme. Serena Merle.

Touchett, Ralph. *The Portrait of a Lady.* The invalid son of Daniel Tracy Touchett and Lydia Touchett; he is the devoted cousin of Isabel Archer, to whom he persuades his dying father to leave a large sum of money.

Townsend, Arthur. *Washington Square.* Morris Townsend's cousin who is to marry Marian Almond, Dr. Austin Sloper's niece.

Townsend, Morris. *Washington Square.* Catherine Sloper's self-centered suitor, of whom Dr. Austin Sloper, her father, rightly but callously disapproves.

Townsend, Mrs. Morris. *Washington Square.* Morris Townsend's unhappy wife; she dies.

Traffle, Sidney. "Mora Montravers." The husband of the foster-mother of Mora Montravers, whose bohemianism he wistfully admires.

Traffle, Mrs. Sidney (Jane). "Mora Montravers." The foster-mother of Mora Montravers; she gives Walter Puddick a large sum of money to marry Mora.

Tramore, Mrs. Charles. "The Chaperon." The socially ostra-cized mother of Rose Tramore, whose determination wins her mother a position again in society.

Tramore, Edith. "The Chaperon." Rose Tramore's selfish younger sister.

Tramore, Eric. "The Chaperon." Rose Tramore's polo-playing older brother.

Tramore, Julia. "The Chaperon." Rose Tramore's aunt, the sister of Rose Tramore's deceased father; she intends to will her money to Edith Tramore rather than to Rose.

Tramore, Rose. "The Chaperon." The daughter of the widowed and socially ostracized Mrs. Charles Tramore; through her determination she wins her mother a position again in society; she spurns Guy Mangler and marries Captain Bertram Jay.

Tramore, Mrs. "The Chaperon." The grandmother of Rose Tramore, who disregards the old woman's wishes and pres-sure.

Trantum, Lady. *The Reverberator.* A friend of Suzanne de Bre-court, Gaston Probert's sister.

Trantum, Lord. *The Reverberator.* A friend of Suzanne de Bre-court, Gaston Probert's sister.

Tredick, Mary Juliana. "The Tone of Time." The artist whom Mrs. Bridgenorth commissions to paint a supposedly imaginary portrait, which turns out to be that of a mutual friend of the two women.

Tregent, Arthur. "The Wheel of Time." Mrs. Fanny Knocker Tragent's handsome son, who cannot become interested in plain little Vera Glanvil.

Tregent, Fanny Knocker. "The Wheel of Time." A woman who when young was so plain that she repelled Maurice Glanvil; twenty years later her son Arthur Tregent fails to like Vera, Maurice Glanvil's plain little daughter.

Tremayne, Roland. "The Path of Duty." The hero of an imaginary novel entitled *A Lawless Love;* the narrator says Ambrose Tester resembles him.

Tremont, Harvard. "A Bundle of Letters." The Boston recipient of a letter from Louis Leverett, a fatuous young American in Paris. "The Point of View." In Paris he receives another letter from Louis Leverett, now discontentedly back home in Boston.

Tressilian, Florence "Florry." *The Tragic Muse.* A London friend of Biddy Dormer.

Treuil, Vicomte Gaston de. "Gabrielle de Bergerac." The aristocrat whom her brother wishes Gabrielle de Bergerac to marry; she elopes instead with Pierre Coquelin.

Tristram, Tom. *The American.* A light, likable American friend of Christopher Newman in Paris.

Tristram, Mrs. Tom (Lizzie). *The American.* The American wife of Christopher Newman's friend of Paris; she arranges the meeting of Christopher Newman and Mme. Claire de Bellegarde de Cintre.

Tripp. *The Princess Casamassima.* A neighbor of the Princess Casamassima, of Broome.

Tripp, Mrs. *The Princess Casamassima.* A neighbor of the Princess Casamassima, of Broome.

Trumpington. "Lady Barbarina." The host at a party in London attended by Dr. Jackson Lemon and Lady Barbarina Clement.

Trumpington, Mrs. "Lady Barbarina." The hostess at a party in London attended by Dr. Jackson Lemon and Lady Barbarina Clement.

Tucker, Mrs. *What Maisie Knew.* The real name of the woman whom Beale Farange introduces to his daughter Maisie Farange as "the countess."

Turnover, Miss. "A Bundle of Letters." The new governess of the Vane family mentioned in a letter from Evelyn Vane to Lady Augusta Fleming.

Undle, Mrs. Minnie. *The Ivory Tower.* A friend of Rosanna Gaw.

Upjohn, Kitty. *The American.* An unimportant American mentioned by Christopher Newman as one of his friends
in Paris.

Valentine. "A Tragedy of Error." Mme. Hortense Bernier's
cook.

Valerio, Count Marco. "The Last of the Valerii." An Italian
nobleman who neglects his American wife Martha Valerio
through temporary love of an exhumed statue of Juno.

Valerio, Countess Martha. "The Last of the Valerii." The
American wife of Count Marco Valerio, who neglects
her through temporary love of an exhumed statue of
Juno until she buries it again.

Van Winkle, Miss. "Poor Richard." A rich Philadelphia girl
whom General Robert Luttrel marries.

Vandeleur, Lady Margaret. "The Path of Duty." The married
object of the affections of Ambrose Tester, who, however,
becomes engaged to Joscelind Bernardstone to please his
father; then Lord Vandeleur dies.

Vandeleur, Lord. "The Path of Duty." The husband of Ambrose Tester's mistress; he dies after Ambrose Tester becomes engaged to Joscelind Bernardstone.

Vanderbank, Gustavus "Van." *The Awkward Age.* A friend
of Longdon; he loves but does not marry Nanda Brookenham; he is a government employee.

Vanderbank, Mary. *The Awkward Age.* The deceased sister of
Gustavus Vanderbank.

Vanderbank, Miles. *The Awkward Age.* The deceased brother
of Gustavus Vanderbank.

Vanderdecken. "Georgina's Reasons." A name seen by Mrs.
Percival Theory in a hotel book in Rome.

Vanderdecken, Mrs. "Georgina's Reasons." A name seen by
Mrs. Percival Theory in a hotel book in Rome.

Vanderdecker, Mrs. "Lady Barbarina." A woman who attends
Lady Barbarina Clement Lemon's New York salon.

Vanderplank, Mrs. "Fordham Castle." The pseudonym of Mrs.
Magaw, which see.

Vane, Adelaide. "A Bundle of Letters." The girl mentioned as the sister of Evelyn Vane in her letter to Lady Augusta Fleming.

Vane, Evelyn. "A Bundle of Letters." A supercilious British girl traveling on the Continent; she writes Lady Augusta Fleming of Brighton in criticism of persons staying at Mme. Maisonrouge's pension in Paris.

Vane, Fred. "A Bundle of Letters." The young man mentioned as the brother of Evelyn Vane in her letter to Lady Augusta Fleming.

Vane, Georgina. "A Bundle of Letters." The girl mentioned as the consumptive sister of Evelyn Vane in her letter to Lady Augusta Fleming.

Vane, Gladys. *The Tragic Muse.* A stage name of Miriam Rooth at one time.

Vane, Gus. "A Bundle of Letters." The young man mentioned as the brother of Evelyn Vane in her letter to Lady Augusta Fleming.

Vane, Harold. "A Bundle of Letters." The young man mentioned as the brother of Evelyn Vane in her letter to Lady Augusta Fleming; he has come to Paris to study French.

Vane, Mary. "A Bundle of Letters." The girl mentioned as the sister of Evelyn Vane in her letter to Lady Augusta Fleming.

Vane. "A Bundle of Letters." The man mentioned as the father of Evelyn Vane in her letter to Lady Augusta Fleming.

Vane, Mrs. "A Bundle of Letters." The woman mentioned as the mother of Evelyn Vane in her letter to Lady Augusta Fleming.

Varian, Mrs. *The Portrait of a Lady.* Isabel Archer's paternal aunt.

Vaughan-Vesey, Bob. "The Chaperon." The husband of Charlotte Mangler Vaughan-Vesey, one of Lady Maresfield's four daughters.

Vaughan-Vesey, Mrs. Bob (Charlotte Mangler). "The Chaperon." One of Lady Maresfield's four daughters; she is the sister of Bessie, Maggie, young Fanny, and Guy Mangler.

Vavasour, Maud. *The Tragic Muse.* A stage name of Miriam Rooth at one time.

Vawdrey, Clarence "Clare." "The Private Life." A brilliant writer who is inept in society; he is admired by the actress Blanche Adney.

Vendemer, Felix. "Collaboration." The French poet friend of and collaborator on an opera with Herman Heidenmauer; he is the estranged fiance of Paule de Brindes.

Ventnor, Lady. "In the Cage." A client of Mrs. Jordan, a flower-arranger.

Verdier, Leon. "A Bundle of Letters." The cousin of Mme. Maisonrouge of the Pension Maisonrouge in Paris; he writes his friend Prosper Gobain about teaching French to Miranda Hope.

Vereker, Hugh. "The Figure in the Carpet." The novelist whose "figure in the carpet" of his works challenges the critic-narrator and his critic-friend George Corvick; he dies of fever in Rome.

Vereker, Mrs. Hugh. "The Figure in the Carpet." The wife of the novelist; she dies shortly after the death of her husband of fever in Rome.

Vernham, Miss. "The Middle Years." The companion of an opulent, sick countess; she upbraids the dying novelist Dencombe for distracting her friend Dr. Hugh from the countess, his patient.

Vernor, Isabel. "Eugene Pickering." The object of the affections of Eugene Pickering, whose father recommended her.

Vernor. "Eugene Pickering." Isabel Vernor's father, who was the beneficiary of a kindness of Eugene Pickering's now deceased father.

Verschoyle, Lord. "The Pupil." The son of Lord and Lady Dorrington; he does not propose to Amy or Paula Moreen.

Verver, Adam. *The Golden Bowl.* A rich American art collector, the widowed father of Maggie Verver, Prince Amerigo's wife; he becomes the husband of Charlotte Stant, Prince Amerigo's mistress.

Verver, Mrs. Adam (Charlotte Stant). *The Golden Bowl.* See Stant, Charlotte.

Verver, Princess Maggie. *The Golden Bowl.* The daughter of the rich American art collector Adam Verver, the wife of

Prince Amerigo, and the friend of Charlotte Stant and Mrs. Fanny Assingham.

Vesey, Bob. "The Chaperon." See Vaughan-Vesey, Bob.

Vesey, Mrs. Bob (Charlotte Mangler). "The Chaperon." See Vaughan-Vesey, Mrs. Bob.

Vetch, Anastasius. *The Princess Casamassima.* A neighborhood friend of Amanda Pynsent and of her ward Hyacinth Robinson.

Vetch, Fleda. *The Spoils of Poynton.* A friend of Mrs. Adela Gereth, the mother of Owen Gereth, whom Fleda Vetch loves; she urges him to be honorable toward his unpleasant fiancee Mona Brigstock.

Vetch, Maggie. *The Spoils of Poynton.* The sister of Fleda Vetch; she marries a parson.

Vetch. *The Spoils of Poynton.* The unprepossessing father of Fleda and Maggie Vetch.

Vidal, Denis. *The Other House.* The commercial, hard, reliable lover of Rose Armiger; he takes her away after she drowns Effie Bream.

Villepreux, Mme. Leonie de. *The Reverberator.* The daughter of Mme. de Marignac; Marquis Maxime de Cliche, Gaston Probert's brother-in-law, takes tea with her, according to gossip.

Vincent, Nona. "Nona Vincent." The titular heroine of Allan Wayworth's play; she appears to him in a dream.

Vincent, Philip. "The Real Thing." The imaginary author whose belated de luxe edition the painter-narrator hopes to illustrate; he is the author of *Rutland Ramsey.*

Vint, Horton "Haughty." *The Ivory Tower.* A friend of Graham Fielder, who asks Vint to manage his financial affairs.

Vionnet, Jeanne de. *The Ambassadors.* The charming young daughter of Mme. Marie de Vionnet; she is to marry M. de Montbron.

Vionnet, Comte de. *The Ambassadors.* The absent husband of Mme. Marie de Vionnet, Chad Newsome's mistress.

Vionnet, Comtesse Marie de. *The Ambassadors.* The charming mistress of Chad Newsome, the mother of Jeanne de Vionnet, and the admirer of Lambert Strether.

Vivian, Angela. *Confidence.* The object of Gordon Wright's affections; his friend Bernard Longueville adversely judges her and then marries her himself.

Vivian, Mrs. *Confidence.* The mother of Angela Vivian, who is the object of Gordon Wright's affections and later Bernard Longueville's wife.

Vivier, Florentine. *The Princess Casamassima.* The French mistress and then the murderess of Lord Frederick Purvis; they are the parents of the illegitimate Hyacinth Robinson, who visits Mlle. Vivier in prison.

Vivier, Hyacinth. *The Princess Casamassima.* Florentine Vivier's father, now deceased.

Vogelstein, Count Otto. "Pandora." The German legation secretary in Washington; he admires but is puzzled by the self-made American girl Pandora Day.

Voisin, Mlle. *The Tragic Muse.* A Theatre Francais actress admired by Miriam Rooth and Peter Sherringham.

Vose. *Watch and Ward.* A butcher, mentioned in conversation between Nora Lambert and Roger Lawrence.

Voyt, Colonel. "The Story in It." The admirer of Mrs. Dyott; he is secretly admired by widowed Mrs. Maud Blessingbourne, who is Mrs. Dyott's guest.

Voyt, Mrs. "The Story in It." The wife of Colonel Voyt, who admires Mrs. Dyott.

Waddington, Adina. "Adina." The fiancee of Sam Scrope, who because of greed for the Tiberian topaz owned by Angelo Beati loses her to him.

Waddington, Mrs. "Adina." The mother of Adina Waddington, who deserts her fiance Sam Scrope to marry Angelo Beati.

Walker, Mrs. "Daisy Miller." A prominent American lady in Rome who criticizes and then snubs Daisy Miller.

Walker. *The Other House.* Tony Bream's servant.

Walsingham, Guy. "The Death of the Lion." The pen-name of Miss Collop, a popular authoress.

Wantridge, Lady. "Mrs. Medwin." A prominent British lady who is intrigued by Mamie Cutter's half-brother Scott Homer; she approves of Mrs. Medwin.

Warburton, Lord. *The Portrait of a Lady.* A prominent British aristocrat whose proposal Isabel Archer refuses; later he almost proposes to Pansy Osmond, Isabel Archer Osmond's step-daughter; he is a friend of Ralph Touchett.

Warden, Amy. "The Given Case." John Grove-Stewart's sister, mentioned in conversation between Mrs. Kate Despard and Phil Mackern.

Warmington, Lady Eva. *The Princess Casamassima.* Lady Aurora Langrish's sister.

Warmington, Lord. *The Princess Casamassima.* Lady Aurora Langrish's brother-in-law.

Waterbridge, Duchess of. *The Outcry.* An ancestor of Lord Theign and the subject of a valuable painting by Sir Joshua Reynolds which Theign owns.

Waterlow, Charles. *The Reverberator.* An American impressionistic painter at whose studio his friend Gaston Probert meets Francie Dosson.

Watermouth, Lady. "A London Life." Mrs. Selina Berrington's sick friend.

Watermouth, Lady. "The Lesson of the Master." The hostess at Summersoft where the young novelist Paul Overt meets the master novelist Henry St. George.

Watermouth, Lord. "The Lesson of the Master." The host at Summersoft where the young novelist Paul Overt meets the master novelist Henry St. George.

Waterville, Rupert. "The Siege of London." An American legation official in London; he is a friend of George Littlemore, who refuses to gossip about Mrs. Nancy Grenville Beck Headway.

Waymarsh. *The Ambassadors.* Lambert Strether's sour friend; he comes to like Mrs. Sarah Newsome Pocock.

Waymarsh, Mrs. *The Ambassadors.* The estranged wife of Lambert Strether's sour friend Waymarsh.

Wayworth, Allan. "Nona Vincent." A young playwright, the author of *Nona Vincent;* he is advised by Mrs. Alsager and later marries the actress Violet Grey.

Wayworth. "Nona Vincent." The father of playwright Allan Wayworth.

Wayworth, Mrs. "Nona Vincent." The mother of playwright Allan Wayworth.

Wayworth, Miss. "Nona Vincent." The sister of playwright Allan Wayworth.

Wayworth, Miss. "Nona Vincent." The sister of playwright Allan Wayworth.

Webster. "Madame de Mauves." The friend whom Longmore, for love of Mme. Euphemia Cleve de Mauves, does not join for a tour through the Low Countries.

Wells, Lady. *The Wings of the Dove.* A guest of Milly Theale in Venice.

Wendover. "A London Life." The serious young American whom Laura Wing meets through her sister Mrs. Selina Berrington; he loves but is puzzled by Laura Wing.

Wenham, Adelaide. "Flickerbridge." The odd, charming owner of the estate of Flickerbridge; Frank Granger admires her; she is distantly related to Addie Wenham, Granger's fiancee.

Wenham, Adelaide "Addie." "Flickerbridge." A short-story and article writer; she is the fiancee of the painter Frank Granger and a distant relative of Adelaide Wenham of Flickerbridge.

Wenham, Dr. "Flickerbridge." Adelaide Wenham's father.

Wenham, Mrs. "Flickerbridge." Addie Wenham's deceased mother.

Wenham, Mrs. "Flickerbridge." Addie Wenham's step-mother.

Wentworth, Charlotte. *The Europeans.* The daughter of William Wentworth and the sister of Gertrude and Clifford Wentworth; she will marry the Rev. Mr. Brand.

Wentworth, Clifford. *The Europeans.* The son of William Wentworth and the young brother of Gertrude and Charlotte Wentworth; he drinks.

Wentworth, Gertrude. *The Europeans.* The daughter of William Wentworth and the sister of Charlotte and Clifford Wentworth; her father wants her to marry the Rev. Mr. Brand, but she falls in love with and is won by Felix Young.

Wentworth, William. *The Europeans.* The rigidly honorable

New England father of Gertrude, Charlotte, and Clifford Wentworth; he was the half-brother of the mother of Baroness Eugenia Munster and Felix Young.

Westgate, J. L. "An International Episode." The husband of Kitty Westgate, the sister of Bessie Alden; he is a rich New York businessman who befriends Lord Lambeth and Percy Beaumont when they visit America.

Westgate, Mrs. J. L. (Kitty Alden). "An International Episode." The wife of the rich New York businessman and the sister of Bessie Alden, who loves Lord Lambeth.

Whitefoot, Rev. Mr. *Roderick Hudson.* A young New England minister who goes on the picnic attended by Roderick Hudson, Rowland Mallet, Mary Garland, and others.

White-Mason. "Crapy Cornelia." The middle-aged traveling American whose affection for Mrs. Worthingham dims when he renews acquaintance with Cornelia Rasch.

Whiteroy, Lady Bessie. "Lord Beaupre." A clever woman who evidently likes Guy Firminger, Lord Beaupre, and therefore sponsors Mary Gosselin for him; her plan fails.

Whiteroy, Lord. "Lord Beaupre." The sociable husband of Lady Bessie Whiteroy.

Whiteroy, Lord. *The Princess Casamassima.* The brother of Lord Frederick Purvis, the murdered father of illegitimate Hyacinth Robinson.

Whiteroy, Lord. "The Chaperon." A nobleman who loans his yacht to Bob Vaughan-Vesey.

Whiteside, Mrs. Catherine. *The Europeans.* The aunt of William Wentworth and the grandmother of Baroness Eugenia Munster and Felix Young.

Whiteside, Louisa. "The Point of View." The recipient of a letter from Aurora Church, the American girl traveling frugally with her mother.

Whittaker, Gertrude. "Poor Richard." The rich rural neighbor of Richard Maule, who ineffectually loves her; Captain Edmund Severn also loves her to no avail; Maule prevents Major Robert Luttrel from winning her.

Wilkes, Mrs. Anna. "Osborne's Revenge." Henrietta Congreve's invalid sister.

Wilkes, Tom. "Osborne's Revenge." Henrietta Congreve's little
nephew; Philip Osborne rescues him from possible drown-
ing and thus meets Miss Congreve.

Willoughby, Bernard. "The Romance of Certain Old Clothes."
The son of the widowed Mrs. Bernard Willoughby and
the brother of Viola and Perdita Willoughby; his friend
Arthur Lloyd marries Perdita and later Viola.

Willoughby, Mrs. Bernard. "The Romance of Certain Old
Clothes." The widowed mother of Bernard, Viola, and
Perdita Willoughby.

Willoughby, Mrs. Bernard. "The Romance of Certain Old
Clothes." The wife of Bernard Willoughby, the son of
the widowed Mrs. Bernard Willoughby.

Willoughby, Perdita. "The Romance of Certain Old Clothes."
The sister of Bernard, Viola, and Perdita Willoughby;
she dies in infancy.

Willoughby, Perdita. "The Romance of Certain Old Clothes."
See Lloyd, Mrs. Arthur (Perdita Willoughby).

Willoughby, Viola. "The Romance of Certain Old Clothes."
See Lloyd, Mrs. Arthur (Viola Willoughby).

Wilmerding, Henry. "The Solution." The American secretary
of legation in Rome; he is persuaded to believe that he
has compromised Veronica Goldie by walking with her
unchaperoned in a secluded grove; he is saved by the
widowed Mrs. Rushbrook, who marries him herself.

Wimbush, Weeks. "The Death of the Lion." The rich brewer
whose wife lionizes the novelist Neil Paraday to death;
he owns the estate of Prestidge.

Wimbush, Mrs. Weeks. "The Death of the Lion." The rich
society woman who at her estate of Prestidge lionizes
the novelist Neil Paraday to death.

Winch, Newton. "A Round of Visits." A larcenist; Mark
Monteith visits him and so sympathizes with the probable
feelings of Phil Bloodgood, who has swindled Monteith,
that Winch commits suicide.

Winch, Mrs. Newton. "A Round of Visits." The recently deceased
wife of Newton Winch, the larcenist; she was the sister
of Lottie, whom Mark Monteith meets.

Windon. "John Delavoy." A poor dramatist whose play the critic-narrator and Miss Delavoy attend.

Windrush, Lady. *The Tragic Muse.* The mother of Peter Sherringham and Mrs. Julia Sherringham Dallow.

Wing, Laura. "A London Life." The nervous unmarried sister of corrupt Mrs. Selina Berrington; she is befriended by Lady Davenant and loves Wendover.

Wingrave, Bernard. "The Romance of Certain Old Clothes." The original name in the magazine publication for Bernard Willoughby, which see.

Wingrave, Mrs. Bernard. "The Romance of Certain Old Clothes." The original name in the magazine publication for Mrs. Bernard Willoughby, which see.

Wingrave, Jane. "Owen Wingrave." Owen Wingrave's militant aunt.

Wingrave, Owen. "Owen Wingrave." Owen Wingrave's father, killed in an Afghan raid.

Wingrave, Mrs. Owen. "Owen Wingrave." The mother of Philip and Owen Wingrave; she died in childbirth in India.

Wingrave, Owen. "Owen Wingrave." A sensitive young man who in spite of terrible family pressure gives up his plan to study under Spencer Coyl for a military school and a military career; because of Kate Julian's taunts, he spends a night in a haunted room and dies.

Wingrave, Perdita. "The Romance of Certain Old Clothes." The original name in the magazine publication for Perdita Willoughby, which see.

Wingrave, Sir Philip. "Owen Wingrave." Owen Wingrave's militant grandfather.

Wingrave, Philip. "Owen Wingrave." Owen Wingrave's imbecile older brother.

Wingrave, Rosalind. "The Romance of Certain Old Clothes." The original name in the magazine publication for Viola Willoughby, which see.

Wingrave, Colonel. "Owen Wingrave." Owen Wingrave's ancestor who in anger struck and killed his own child; next morning he was found dead in the room which since then has been regarded as haunted.

Wingrave. "Owen Wingrave." The son of Owen Wingrave's ancestor Colonel Wingrave, who in anger struck and killed him.

Winkworth, Miss. *The Bostonians.* The young lady to whom Henry Burrage, Jr., is rumored to have been engaged.

Winkle, Susan. "Mrs. Temperly." Mrs. Maria Temperly's maid in New York.

Winterbourne, Frederick Forsyth. "Daisy Miller." The Europeanized American whom Daisy Miller loves; his timidity in the face of her social gaucherie indirectly causes her death.

Wispers, Lady. "The Papers." A hostess of Sir A. B. C. Beadel-Muffet.

Wispers, Lord. "The Papers." A host of Sir A. B. C. Beadel-Muffet.

Withermore, George. "The Real Right Thing." The young man who tries to write the biography of the deceased author Ashton Doyne, until Doyne's ghost convinces him that he should desist.

Withers. *The Princess Casamassima.* A servant of the Princess Casamassima at Medley.

Wix, Clara Matilda. *What Maisie Knew.* The deceased little daughter of Mrs. Wix, Maisie Farange's moral governess.

Wix. *What Maisie Knew.* The mysterious, long-deceased husband of Mrs. Wix, Maisie Farange's moral governess.

Wix, Mrs. *What Maisie Knew.* Maisie Farange's dowdy, righteous governess.

Woodley, Willie. "An International Episode." An American in London who escorts Mrs. Kitty Westgate and Bessie Alden; he finds Lord Lambeth in Hyde Park. "The Impressions of a Cousin." He is a guest at a dinner party given by Eunice, the painter-narrator Catherine Condit's cousin.

Worthingham, Mrs. "Crapy Cornelia." The rich, flashy woman for whom White-Mason cares less and less as he renews acquaintance with Cornelia Rasch.

Wright, Gordon. *Confidence.* The young American who asks his friend Bernard Longueville to pass judgment on

Angela Vivian, whom Longueville then criticizes; Wright marries Blanche Evers.

Yarracome, Lord. "John Delavoy." A member of the theater audience during Windon's play, which is also attended by the critic-narrator and Miss Delavoy.

Young, Adolphus. *The Europeans.* The American father, born in Sicily, of Baroness Eugenia Munster and Felix Young; he is now deceased.

Young, Mrs. Adolphus (Catherine). *The Europeans.* The half-sister of William Wentworth; she is the headstrong mother of Baroness Eugenia Munster and Felix Young; she is now deceased.

Young, Felix. *The Europeans.* The son of the half-sister of William Wentworth and the brother of Baroness Eugenia Munster; he loves and wins William Wentworth's daughter Gertrude.

Young, Frederic. "The Story of a Masterpiece." An admirer in Europe of Marian Everett; he is mentioned in conversation between Mrs. Denbigh and Stephen Baxter.

Young, Mrs. "The Story of a Masterpiece." The handsome old mother of Frederic Young, who admired Marian Everett when they were in Europe.

Yule, Captain Marmaduke Clement . . . "Covering End." The owner of the estate of Covering End, which is heavily mortgaged to Prodmore; he is rescued by the money and sympathy of the American widow Mrs. Gracedew.

Yule, Dame Dorothy. "Covering End." An ancestor of Captain Clement Yule.

Yule, John Anthony. "Covering End." An ancestor of Captain Clement Yule.

Zenobie. "The Pupil." Morgan Moreen's former governess; she was evidently cheated by his parents.